MOUNTAIN BIKE!
The Midwest
Ohio, Indiana, and Illinois

MOUNTAIN BIKE!
The Midwest Ohio, Indiana, and Illinois

A GUIDE TO THE CLASSIC TRAILS

RICHARD RIES
AND DAVE SHEPHERD

Menasha Ridge Press

Library of Congress Cataloging-in-Publication Data
is available from the Library of Congress.

Photos by the authors unless otherwise credited
Maps by Bryan Steven Jones and Jeff Goodwin
Cover photo by Dennis Coello
Cover and text design by Suzanne Holt

Menasha Ridge Press
700 28th Street South
Suite 206
Birmingham, Alabama 35233
www.menasharidge.com

All trails described in this book are legal for mountain bikes. But rules can change—especially for off-road bicycles, the new kid on the outdoor recreation block. Land-access issues and conflicts between cyclists, hikers, equestrians, and other users can cause the rewriting of recreation regulations on public lands, sometimes resulting in a ban of mountain bike use on specific trails. That's why it's the responsibility of each rider to check and make sure that he or she rides only on trails where mountain biking is permitted.

CAUTION

Outdoor recreational activities are by their very nature potentially hazardous. All participants in such activities must assume the responsibility for their own actions and safety. The information contained in this guidebook cannot replace sound judgment and good decision-making skills, which help reduce risk exposure, nor does the scope of this book allow for disclosure of all the potential hazards and risks involved in such activities.

Learn as much as possible about the outdoor recreational activities in which you participate, prepare for the unexpected, and be cautious. The reward will be a safer and more enjoyable experience.

CONTENTS

AMERICA BY MOUNTAIN BIKE! · Map Legend

Ride trailhead

Primary bike trail

Direction of travel

Optional bike trail and trailhead

Other trail

Hiking-only trail

Interstate highways (64)

US routes (51)

State routes (82)

Other paved roads (251B)

Unpaved roads (may be 4WD only)

---

0 1/2 1
MILES
Scale

N True north

County roads (200E)

Forest Service roads (726)

State border

STATE PARK
Public lands*

Richmond ⊙ Hinsdale ⊙
Cities and towns

Lake) Dam
River or stream

✈ Airport

♥ Archeological or historical site

Boat ramp

▲ Campground (CG)

≡ Cattle guard

† Cemetery or gravesite

♠ Church

🚲 Drinking water

Knob or hill

Power Station

Fire tower or lookout

Falls or rapids

🅕 Food

Gate

House or cabin

Lodging

Mountain pass

△ Mountain summit
3312 (elevation in feet)

✕ Mine or quarry

Gas well

Ⓟ Parking

Park office or ranger station

⊼ Picnic area

Power line or pipeline

Rest rooms

Spring

Stable, corral, or ranch

Swimming Area

Transmission towers

Tunnel or bridge

Farm or barn

Cliff, Bluff or Outcropping

---

* Remember; Private property exists in and around our national forests.

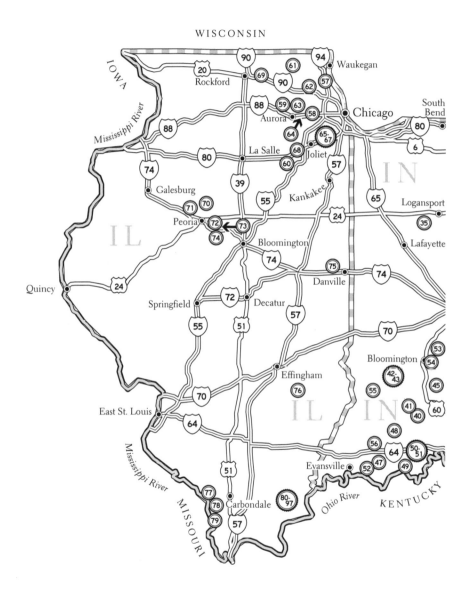

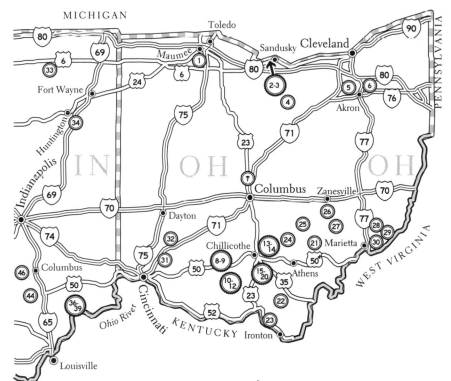

LIST OF MAPS

ACKNOWLEDGMENTS

Thanks to all the people who offered advice, encouragement, or other help. This includes people at the bike shops I've mentioned. And it includes Scott Irons at Indy Cycle Specialists, who doesn't get mentioned but deserves thanks for helping me select a replacement bike when my old Hard Rock finally died. Thanks to Jeff Jones and the other members of the Shawnee Mountain Bike Association for their dedication to the Shawnee, their encyclopedic knowledge of the trails there, and their willingness to spend hours around a table or on the phone with me. Thanks to Molly Burns and everyone at Menasha Ridge, and to Dennis Coello. Thanks to my wife, Julie, for her patience and support. And special thanks to riding buddy, Joe Ernst, who showed me how I could ride if only I were younger, stronger, lighter, and braver.

—*Richard Ries*

FOREWORD

Welcome to *Mountain Bike!*, a series designed to provide all-terrain bikers with the information they need to find and ride the very best trails around. Whether you're new to the sport and don't know where to pedal, or an experienced mountain biker who wants to learn the classic trails in another region, this series is for you. Drop a few bucks for the book, spend an hour with the detailed maps and route descriptions, and you're prepared for the finest in off-road cycling.

My role as editor of this series was simple: First, find a mountain biker who knows the area and loves to ride. Second, ask that person to spend a year researching the most popular and very best rides around. And third, have that rider describe each trail in terms of difficulty, scenery, condition, elevation change, and all other categories of information that are important to trail riders. "Pretend you've just completed a ride and met up with fellow mountain bikers at the trailhead," I told each author. "Imagine their questions, be clear in your answers."

As I said, the *editorial* process—that of sending out riders and reading the submitted chapters—is a snap. But the work involved in finding, riding, and writing about each trail is enormous. In some instances our authors' tasks are made easier by the information contributed by local bike shops or cycling clubs, or even by the writers of local "where-to" guides. Credit for these contributions is provided, when appropriate, in each chapter, and our sincere thanks goes to all who have helped.

But the overwhelming majority of trails are discovered and pedaled by our authors themselves, then compared with dozens of other routes to determine if they qualify as "classic"—that area's best in scenery and cycling fun. If you've ever had the experience of pioneering a route from outdated topographic maps or entering a bike shop to request information from local riders who would much prefer to keep their favorite trails secret, or if you know how it is to double- and triple-check data to be positive your trail info is correct, then you have an idea of how each of our authors has labored to bring about these books. You and I, and all the mountain bikers of America, are the richer for their efforts.

You'll get more out of this book if you take a moment to read the Introduction, which explains how to read the trail listings. The Topographic Maps section will help you understand how useful topos will be on a ride, and will also tell you where to get them. And though this is a "where-to," not a "how-to" guide, those of you who have not traveled the backcountry might find Hitting the Trail of particular value.

In addition to the material above, newcomers to mountain biking might want to spend a minute with the glossary, page 341, so that terms like *hardpack, singletrack,* and *waterbars* won't throw you when you come across them in the text.

Finally, the tips in the Afterword on mountain biking etiquette and the land-use controversy might help us all enjoy the trails a little more.

All the best.

Dennis Coello
St. Louis

PREFACE

I've lived a lot of places. I've ridden a lot of places. In many ways, I like the Midwest the best. I like the small towns and farms. I like the lakes and streams and woods. I like the affordability. I like the lack of crowds.

Is there typical Midwestern riding? Not really. There's too much variety. Most of the rides I did for this book, though, were in the southern parts of the three states. It's still not typical, but patterns emerge. The trails tend to be tight and technical. Hills tend to be short, steep, and frequent.

The riding season is all year. Spring is full of wildflowers and rushing water. Summer is hot, humid and lush. Fall is dry; it can still be hot, but the humidity has generally abated. Winter is a great time to ride, with pleasantly mild weather much of the time and great sight distances through the leafless trees.

Each season has its own hazards. In spring, water crossings can be dangerously deep and fast. In summer, ticks and other insects can be a problem. (Ticks roam anytime the leaves are green, but peak in June.) Hunters take to the woods from October through May and are especially active during the fall deer season. In winter, shallow, slick mud can make trails impassable.

Now some more specific tips:

Let's start with trail conditions and the riding season. First, always assume there's mud. Here's the deal: soils in these areas drain poorly. There are often springs, streams, and other sources of water in these woods. Many trails have erosion resulting from poor design or gullies caused by soil compaction and other forces. Many trails have had surface soil and leaf litter removed by all-terrain vehicle (ATV) riders, whether they're on the site legally (as in Ohio) or illegally (as in Indiana and Illinois).

The net result is that you can expect to see mud on these trails. It's worse following rain or during snowmelt, but the only time the trail will be mostly dry is after extended periods without precipitation. That's usually, but not always, from mid-July to the end of September.

Riding in mud requires certain skills, but this since this isn't a primer on how to ride, we'll skip that lecture. For equipment, consult a shop near where you'll be riding and see what they recommend. Sometimes a wide tire works better, because it floats atop the mud. Other times a narrow tire is the ticket, because it penetrates the mud and hooks up with the firmer surface below. Widely spaced knobs shed mud better than denser patterns. Mud clearance between the tires and the stays—especially the chainstays—is important. More important is clearance at the fork. Many times my riding buddies' front wheels have loaded up and stopped turning.

The trickiest mud occurs in winter, when the nights get below freezing and the days get above freezing. The surface soil warms and turns from frozen crust to snotty mud. But the soil an inch or two down stays frozen, slick, and hard. Traction is at a premium then, and some trail sections are unrideable. How will you know? Call a local shop. Check the forecast. Other than that, it's a crapshoot.

What about the environmental consequences of riding in mud? Since mud's present in this part of the country in all but the driest of times, it's impractical to stay off the trails whenever mud may be present. Besides, these soils are pretty resilient and will stand up to some use in sloppy conditions. There are times when it's best to stay off the trails for a few days after a heavy rain. If in doubt, call the property manager for the site you intend to ride.

While we're on the subject, there are other ways to be environmentally responsible. Don't ride around water bars, standing water, fallen logs, and other obstacles. Doing so only lenses out the trail (makes it wider), which is bad aesthetics and can cause erosion. Don't ride off the trail; no bushwhacking or cutting of switchbacks. Don't skid.

What about snow? Here's the deal on snow: in our part of the world, there's no real pattern. We can get 5 inches of snow in a whole winter, or 18 inches in a single snowfall. Sometimes the snow hits the ground overnight and is melted by noon. Other times it falls on Monday and is still there two weeks later.

We ride in an area prone to weather extremes. We get cold, dry blasts from Canada followed by warm, wet fronts from the Gulf of Mexico. Makes life interesting, but it also makes it darn tough to plan ahead for a ride on Saturday. All that being said, there's no need to shy away from these trails. Except for the worst conditions, our trails stay mostly accessible, most of the time.

Unlike other parts of the country where weather is maddeningly reliable, our world requires you do a little homework. Mid-day highs can be 75 degrees in January and July. It can rain in December and snow in May.

The most predictable time of year is late summer. Rain is rare then. The only bad news is that it's typically hot. And the humidity slaps you like a wet towel in a junior high locker room. Don't pooh-pooh this effect. Riders come here from other areas that are supposedly hotter and suffer badly in our unique combination of heat and humidity.

Drinking water helps, but it only hydrates you—it doesn't keep you cool. Perspiration doesn't evaporate well in 95% humidity, so your body's core temperature can get dangerously high. Excessive heat can make you sick and can even be fatal. Learn the signs of heat exhaustion and heat stroke. Learn prevention and treatment. The Red Cross and your local hospital are good sources for this information.

Other hazards? Don't drink the water. According to the Indiana Department of Environmental Management, two-thirds of this state's surface water is unfit for fishing or swimming, let alone drinking. Pesticides, herbicides, and runoff from unregulated septic tanks and livestock operations can flow underground for miles, then pop up in that lovely little spring deep in the woods. Illinois and Ohio have similar problems.

Rabies is on the upswing among woodland critters. Skunks are particularly common carriers, although other animals are only slightly less likely to offer infected fangs. Rule of thumb: if an animal approaches you, get away! (While you're at the Red Cross, grab some rabies info, too.)

And finally, a word about creepy crawlies. Black widows and brown recluse spiders are fairly common and cause really nasty reactions in some people. Poisonous snakes are rare, but water moccasins and rattlesnakes do exist out there. Deer ticks share the gift of Lyme disease, which is essentially a lifetime of flu symptoms unless you get early, aggressive treatment.

Your best course of action is to stay on the trails. These critters generally avoid human activity and view trails as too rich with humans to be attractive. But none will hesitate to latch on if you suddenly stick a body part in front of them. Go back one more time to that Red Cross office or local hospital for more information. You need to know how to avoid these things, how to recognize their bites, and how to provide emergency treatment until the victim can get to a doctor.

Oh, and let's add bees to that list. They're a minor nuisance all summer, then go berserk just before fall. That's when they're in full sugar-seeking mode. They love to invade open soda cans, sandwiches, and any other food source. At those times everyone should be careful; those with hypersensitivity must carry their bee kit with them. How do you know if you're hypersensitive? Two ways to find out. Go to a doctor and get tested. Or get stung on the trail and lapse into anaphylactic shock.

Hope this doesn't scare you away. In all the years I've been riding in the Midwest, I've never had a life-threatening situation arise, nor have any of my buddies. A few bee stings, ticks by the bagful, but nothing that had us praying for the paramedics.

Maybe the biggest risk is from adjacent property owners. They've been known to run off straying riders at gunpoint. Many of the backwoods dwellers around here have a Daniel Boone complex; they've carved out their little piece of dirt and are ready to defend it against all comers. The solution, again, is to stay on the marked trails. That can be a challenge since many trails are poorly marked, and a lot of landowners build their own access trails into the woods. Use a map. Pay attention. If you're caught in someone's yard, just ask how to get back onto the legal trail. Most locals simmer down when they realize you're on their turf by mistake, not willfulness.

So is the Midwest a horrible place to ride? On the contrary, it's a blast. The trails are technical, scenic, and remote. Access is either cheap or free. There are some risks involved, but nothing extraordinary, nothing a little common sense and preparation can't handle.

Then is the Midwest the ideal mountain biking location? Probably not. But in terms of overall experience, it has to rate right up there. Come see for yourself.

And now a word about other information I've provided. Although you may not know it when you're out on the trails, the Midwest is fairly densely populated. That means there's usually civilization nearby. I'll try to make it clear whether a town has a gas-n-go, a greasy spoon, a five-star restaurant, or whatever. I'll also try to indicate where the nearest emergency medical care is offered. Keep in mind, though, that this type of information is known for changing quickly and constantly.

I thought it would be better to give a general sense of the level of services provided by a given pocket of humanity, but I was instructed by my editor to give much more detailed info. So I have. But don't send me hate mail if the Kwickee Mart I mention has since closed, or if you drove 20 miles east to a restaurant when there was a new one 3 miles west. And by all means don't you—or your attorney—come looking for me if the medical care information has become dated.

Understand, too, that bike shops are like mushrooms on the forest floor. They pop up all over when the conditions are right, then implode when things dry up. Unless I specifically mention a bike shop in a town, there's not one there. I will note every bike shop I know of near these trails; if I don't say there's a shop somewhere, there isn't. Or at least there wasn't when I did my research. Of course, if all you need is a tube or a water bottle cage bolt, you can always stop into Wal-Mart or True Value. I don't know where those are, and I make no attempt to list them.

I also need to add some clarification about maps. Apparently, there are folks who have the luxury of riding in places where there are multiple maps from which to choose. 'Taint so here. Generally, there is one and only one map covering a particular trail. Where exceptions exist, they will be duly noted.

This all seems unnecessarily complicated to me. Maybe it's because this is my home turf. Maybe it's because this really is too complicated. I rode all the way across the country—over 3,000 miles—with much less information than you have here. Maybe it's just a difference in philosophy. I think a guide book should offer insights and insider information that make an intelligent visitor's trip more rewarding. Others believe a guide should be dumbed down so that any idiot with a bike and a book can get into and out of the woods safely.

Whatever category you fall into, I hope you enjoy riding our patch of Earth. Bring your bike, this book, your senses of adventure and humor, maybe a couple of friends, and see what happens in America's heartland.

We like it here, and think you will, too.

Beginners and Families

8 Paint Creek State Park, North Loop
9 Paint Creek State Park, South Loop
19 Scioto Trail State Forest, Trail "C"
20 Scioto Trail State Forest, Trail "D"
40 Lick Creek
44 Ogala

47 Tipsaw Lake
55 Crane/Lake Greenwood
80 Camp Cadiz
81 Williams Hill, Option 1
97 Eagle Mountain

Intermediate

11 Pike State Forest APV Area, Middle Loop "B"
12 Pike State Forest APV Area, Short Loop "C"
17 Scioto Trail State Forest, Trail "A"
18 Scioto Trail State Forest, Trail "B"
21 Hocking Technical College
36 Bloody Run Ramble
37 Double Drop With a Comley-Fagg Option
38 Amish Amble
39 Freefall
41 Young's Creek
43 Shirley Creek Trail, West Loop
45 Hickory Ridge
46 Nebo Ridge

48 Birdseye Trail
49 Mogan Ridge West
50 Oriole Trail West
51 Oriole Trail East
52 German Ridge Trail
55 Crane/Lake Greenwood
82 Williams Hill, Option 2
83 Williams Hill, Option 3
84 Millstone, Option 1
86 Palestine Church, Option 1
89 Palestine Church, Option 4
90 War Bluff, Option 1
92 Camp Ondessonk
94 High Knob, Option 2
95 High Knob, Option 3
96 One Horse Gap

Advanced

10 Pike State Forest APV Area, Outer Loop "A"
13 Great Seal State Park, South Loop
14 Great Seal State Park, North Loop
17 Scioto Trail State Forest, Trail "A"
41 Young's Creek

42 Shirley Creek Trail, East Loop
85 Millstone, Option 2
87 Palestine Church, Option 2
88 Palestine Church, Option 3
91 War Bluff, Option 2
93 High Knob, Option 1

Training

10 Pike State Forest APV Area, Outer Loop "A"
11 Pike State Forest APV Area, Middle Loop "B"
12 Pike State Forest APV Area, Short Loop "C"
41 Young's Creek

46 Nebo Ridge
50 Oriole Trail West
52 German Ridge Trail
91 War Bluff, Option 2
96 One Horse Gap
97 Eagle Mountain

Technical

13 Great Seal State Park, South Loop
14 Great Seal State Park, North Loop
17 Scioto Trail State Forest, Trail "A"
43 Shirley Creek Trail, West Loop
51 Oriole Trail East
55 Crane/Lake Greenwood

84 Millstone, Option 1
85 Millstone, Option 2
88 Palestine Church, Option 3
93 High Knob, Option 1
96 One Horse Gap

Best Scenery

13 Great Seal State Park, South Loop
14 Great Seal State Park, North Loop
36 Bloody Run Ramble
37 Double Drop With a Comley-Fagg
      Option
38 Amish Amble
39 Freefall
48 Birdseye

85 Millstone, Option 2
87 Palestine Church, Option 2
90 War Bluff, Option 1
91 War Bluff, Option 2
92 Camp Ondessonk
93 High Knob, Option 1
94 High Knob, Option 2
96 One Horse Gap

Best Side Trips/Area Attractions

 8 Paint Creek State Park, North Loops
 9 Paint Creek State Park, South Loops
Paint Creek State Park has excellent
      camping, as well as hiking and a
      lake.
36 Bloody Run Ramble
37 Double Drop With a Comley-Fagg
      Option
38 Amish Amble
39 Freefall
All the above rides are near Madison,
      Indiana. Madison offers antiques,
      museums, art galleries, restaurants,
      tours of historic homes and gardens,
      community festivals, and much
      more. Nearby Clifty Falls State Park
      has camping and hiking but alas, no
      mountain biking as of this writing.
44 Ogala Trail
The public is welcome to attend the
      annual Indian purification cere-
      mony, with some restrictions.

46 Nebo Ridge
This trail's proximity to Nashville is a
      bonus. Nashville is an artists' com-
      munity, with galleries and shops in
      every available building. There are
      also restaurants and lodging in
      town. Just outside of town is Brown
      County State Park, one of the most
      popular in the state with great hik-
      ing and the Abe Martin Lodge.
47 Tipsaw Lake
Here you'll find a lake with an excellent
      beach and picnic facilities. There's
      also camping, including group
      camping.
77 through 97 Shawnee National Forest
This area has plenty of camping, hiking,
      and such, but the real appeal is the
      geology. Hiking and climbing are
      two ways to enjoy the endless rock.
      Take time to visit the Garden of the
      Gods; the rock formations there are
      among the best in the eastern U.S.

INTRODUCTION

TRAIL DESCRIPTION OUTLINE

Each trail in this book begins with key information that includes length, configuration, aerobic and technical difficulty, trail conditions, scenery, and special comments. Additional description is contained in 11 individual categories. The following will help you to understand all of the information provided.

Trail name: Trail names are as designated on United States Geological Survey (USGS) or Forest Service or other maps, and/or by local custom.

At a Glance Information

Length/configuration: The overall length of a trail is described in miles, unless stated otherwise. The configuration is a description of the shape of each trail — whether the trail is a loop, out-and-back (that is, along the same route), figure eight, trapezoid, isosceles triangle, decahedron . . . (just kidding), or if it connects with another trail described in the book. See the Glossary for definitions of *point-to-point* and *combination*.

Aerobic difficulty: This provides a description of the degree of physical exertion required to complete the ride.

Technical difficulty: This provides a description of the technical skill required to pedal a ride. Trails are often described here in terms of being paved, unpaved, sandy, hard-packed, washboarded, two- or four-wheel-drive, single-track or double-track. All terms that might be unfamiliar to the first-time mountain biker are defined in the Glossary.

Note: For both the aerobic and technical difficulty categories, authors were asked to keep in mind the fact that all riders are not equal, and thus to gauge the trail in terms of how the middle-of-the-road rider — someone between the newcomer and Ned Overend—could handle the route. Comments about the trail's length, condition, and elevation change will also assist you in determining the difficulty of any trail relative to your own abilities.

Scenery: Here you will find a general description of the natural surroundings during the seasons most riders pedal the trail and a suggestion of what is to be found at special times (like great fall foliage or cactus in bloom).

Special comments: Unique elements of the ride are mentioned.

Category Information

General location: This category describes where the trail is located in reference to a nearby town or other landmark.

Elevation change: Unless stated otherwise, the figure provided is the total gain and loss of elevation along the trail. In regions where the elevation variation is not extreme, the route is simply described as flat, rolling, or possessing short steep climbs or descents.

Season: This is the best time of year to pedal the route, taking into account trail conditions (for example, when it will not be muddy), riding comfort (when the weather is too hot, cold, or wet), and local hunting seasons.

Note: Because the opening and closing dates of deer, elk, moose, and antelope seasons often change from year to year, riders should check with the local Fish and Wildlife Department or call a sporting goods store (or any place that sells hunting licenses) in a nearby town before heading out. Wear bright clothes in the fall, and don't wear suede jackets while in the saddle. Hunter's-orange tape on the helmet is also a good idea.

Services: This category is of primary importance in guides for paved-road tourers and is far less crucial to most mountain bike trail descriptions because there are usually no services whatsoever to be found. Authors have noted when water is available on desert or long mountain routes and have listed the availability of food, lodging, campgrounds, and bike shops. If all these services are present, you will find only the words, "All services available in . . ."

Hazards: Special hazards like steep cliffs, great amounts of deadfall, or barbed-wire fences very close to the trail are noted here.

Rescue index: Determining how far one is from help on a particular trail can be difficult due to the backcountry nature of most mountain bike rides. Authors therefore state the proximity of homes or Forest Service outposts, nearby roads where one might hitch a ride, or the likelihood of other bikers being encountered on the trail. Phone numbers of local sheriff departments or hospitals have not been provided because phones are almost never available. If you are able to reach a phone, the local operator will connect you with emergency services.

Land status: This category provides information regarding whether the trail crosses land operated by the Forest Service, the Bureau of Land Management, or a city, state, or national park; whether it crosses private land whose owner (at the time the author did the research) has allowed mountain bikers right of passage; and so on.

Note: Authors have been extremely careful to offer only those routes that are open to bikers and are legal to ride. However, because land ownership changes over time, and because the land-use controversy created by mountain bikes still has not completely subsided, it is the duty of each cyclist to look for and heed signs warning against trail use. Don't expect this book to get you off the hook when you're facing some small-town judge for pedaling past a "Biking Prohibited" sign erected the day before you arrived. Look for these signs, read them, and heed the advice. And remember, there's always another trail.

Maps: The maps in this book have been produced with great care and, in conjunction with the trail-following suggestions, will help you stay on course. But as every experienced mountain biker knows, things can get tricky in the backcountry. It is therefore strongly suggested that you avail yourself of the detailed information found in the USGS (United States Geological Survey) 7.5 minute series topographic maps. In some cases, authors have found that specific Forest Service or other maps may be more useful than the USGS quads, and they tell how to obtain them.

Finding the trail: Detailed information on how to reach the trailhead and where to park your car is provided here.

Sources of additional information: Here you will find the address and/or phone number of a bike shop, governmental agency, or other source from which trail information can be obtained.

Notes on the trail: This is where you are guided carefully through any portions of the trail that are particularly difficult to follow. The author also may add information about the route that does not fit easily in the other categories. This category will not be present for those rides where the route is easy to follow.

ABBREVIATIONS

The following road-designation abbreviations are used in the *Mountain Bike!* series:

CR	County Road	I-	Interstate
FR	Farm Route	IR	Indian Route
FS	Forest Service road	US	United States highway

State highways are designated with the appropriate two-letter state abbreviation, followed by the road number. Example: IN 417 = Indiana State Highway 417.

Postal Service two-letter state codes:

AL	Alabama	AZ	Arizona
AK	Alaska	AR	Arkansas
CA	California	NV	Nevada
CO	Colorado	NH	New Hampshire
CT	Connecticut	NJ	New Jersey
DE	Delaware	NM	New Mexico
DC	District of Columbia	NY	New York
FL	Florida	NC	North Carolina
GA	Georgia	ND	North Dakota
HI	Hawaii	OH	Ohio
ID	Idaho	OK	Oklahoma
IL	Illinois	OR	Oregon
IN	Indiana	PA	Pennsylvania
IA	Iowa	RI	Rhode Island
KS	Kansas	SC	South Carolina
KY	Kentucky	SD	South Dakota
LA	Louisiana	TN	Tennessee
ME	Maine	TX	Texas
MD	Maryland	UT	Utah
MA	Massachusetts	VT	Vermont
MI	Michigan	VA	Virginia
MN	Minnesota	WA	Washington
MS	Mississippi	WV	West Virginia
MO	Missouri	WI	Wisconsin
MT	Montana	WY	Wyoming
NE	Nebraska		

RIDE CONFIGURATIONS

Combination: This type of route may combine two or more configurations. For example, a point-to-point route may integrate a scenic loop or an out-and-back spur midway through the ride. Likewise, an out-and-back may have a loop at its farthest point (this configuration looks like a cherry with a stem attached; the stem is the out-and-back, the fruit is the terminus loop). Or a loop route may have multiple out-and-back spurs and/or loops to the side. Mileage for a combination route is for the total distance to complete the ride.

Loop: This route configuration is characterized by riding from the designated trailhead to a distant point, then returning to the trailhead via a different route (or simply continuing on the same in a circle route) without doubling back. You always move forward across new terrain but return to the starting point when finished. Mileage is for the entire loop from the trailhead back to trailhead.

Out-and-back: A ride where you will return on the same trail you pedaled out. While this might sound far more boring than a loop route, many trails look very different when pedaled in the opposite direction.

Point-to-point: A vehicle shuttle (or similar assistance) is required for this type of route, which is ridden from the designated trailhead to a distant location, or endpoint, where the route ends. Total mileage is for the one-way trip from the trailhead to endpoint.

Spur: A road or trail that intersects the main trail you're following.

Ride Configurations contributed by Gregg Bromka

TOPOGRAPHIC MAPS

The maps in this book, when used in conjunction with the route directions present in each chapter, will in most instances be sufficient to get you to the trail and keep you on it. However, you will find superior detail and valuable information in the USGS 7.5 minute series topographic maps. Recognizing how indispensable these are to bikers and hikers alike, many bike shops and sporting goods stores now carry topos of the local area.

If you're brand new to mountain biking you might be wondering, "What's a topographic map?" In short, these differ from standard "flat" maps in that they indicate not only linear distance but elevation as well. One glance at a topo will show you the difference, for contour lines are spread across the map like dozens of intricate spider webs. Each contour line represents a particular elevation, and at the base of each topo a particular contour interval designation is given. Yes, it sounds confusing if you're new to the lingo, but it truly is a simple and wonderfully helpful system. Keep reading.

Let's assume that the 7.5 minute series topo before us says "Contour Interval 40 feet," that the short trail we'll be pedaling is two inches in length on the map, and that it crosses five contour lines from its beginning to end. What do we know? Well, because the linear scale of this series is 2,000 feet to the inch (roughly $2^3/_4$ inches representing 1 mile), we know our trail is approximately $^4/_5$ of a mile long (2 inches × 2,000 feet). But we also know we'll be climbing or descending 200 vertical feet (5 contour lines × 40 feet each) over that distance. And the elevation designations written on occasional contour lines will tell us if we're heading up or down.

The authors of this series warn their readers of upcoming terrain, but only a detailed topo gives you the information you need to pinpoint your position on a map, steer yourself toward optional trails and roads nearby, and to see at a glance if you'll be pedaling hard to take them. It's a lot of information for a very low cost. In fact, the only drawback with topos is their size—several feet square. I've tried rolling them into tubes, folding them carefully, even cutting them into blocks and photocopying the pieces. Any of these systems is a pain, but no matter how you pack the maps you'll be happy they're along. And you'll be even happier if you pack a compass as well.

In addition to local bike shops and sporting goods stores, you'll find topos at major universities and some public libraries, where you might try photocopying the ones you need to avoid the cost of buying them. But if you want your own and can't find them locally, contact:

USGS Map Sales
Box 25286
Denver, CO 80225
(800) HELP MAP (435-7627)

VISA and MasterCard are accepted. Ask for an index while you're at it, plus a price list and a copy of the booklet *Topographic Maps*. In minutes you'll be reading them like a pro.

A second excellent series of maps available to mountain bikers is that put out by the United States Forest Service. If your trail runs through an area designated as a national forest, look in the phone book (white pages) under the United States Government listings, find the Department of Agriculture heading, and run your finger down that section until you find the Forest Service. Give them a call, and they'll provide the address of the regional Forest Service office, from which you can obtain the appropriate map.

TRAIL ETIQUETTE

Pick up almost any mountain bike magazine these days and you'll find articles and letters to the editor about trail conflict. For example, you'll find hikers' tales of being blindsided by speeding mountain bikers, complaints from mountain bikers about being blamed for trail damage that was really caused by horse or cattle traffic, and cries from bikers about those "kamikaze" riders who through their antics threaten to close even more trails to all of us.

The authors of this series have been very careful to guide you to only those trails that are open to mountain biking (or at least were open at the time of their research), and without exception have warned of the damage done to our sport through injudicious riding. We can all benefit from glancing over the following International Mountain Bicycling Association (IMBA) Rules of the Trail before saddling up.

1. *Ride on open trails only.* Respect trail and road closures (ask if not sure), avoid possible trespass on private land, obtain permits and authorization as may be required. Federal and state wilderness areas are closed to cycling.

2. *Leave no trace.* Be sensitive to the dirt beneath you. Even on open trails, you should not ride under conditions where you will leave evidence of your passing, such as on certain soils shortly after rain. Observe the different types of soils and trail construction; practice low-impact cycling. This also means staying on the trail and not creating any new ones. Be sure to pack out at least as much as you pack in.

3. *Control your bicycle!* Inattention for even a second can cause disaster. Excessive speed can maim and threaten people; there is no excuse for it!

4. *Always yield the trail.* Make known your approach well in advance. A friendly greeting (or a bell) is considerate and works well; startling someone may cause loss of trail access. Show your respect when passing others by slowing to a walk or even stopping. Anticipate that other trail users may be around corners or in blind spots.

5. *Never spook animals.* All animals are startled by an unannounced approach, a sudden movement, or a loud noise. This can be dangerous for you, for others, and for the animals. Give animals extra room and time to adjust to you. In passing, use special care and follow the directions of horseback riders (ask if uncertain). Running cattle and disturbing wild animals is a serious offense. Leave gates as you found them or as marked.

6. *Plan ahead.* Know your equipment, your ability, and the area in which you are riding—and prepare accordingly. Be self-sufficient at all times. Wear a helmet, keep your machine in good condition, and carry necessary supplies for changes in weather or other conditions. A well-executed trip is a satisfaction to you and not a burden or offense to others.

For more information, contact IMBA, P.O. Box 7578, Boulder, CO 80306, (303) 545-9011.

HITTING THE TRAIL

Once again, because this is a "where-to," not a "how-to" guide, the following will be brief. If you're a veteran trail rider, these suggestions might serve to remind you of something you've forgotten to pack. If you're a newcomer, they might convince you to think twice before hitting the backcountry unprepared.

Water: I've heard the questions dozens of times. "How much is enough? One bottle? Two? Three?! But think of all that extra weight!" Well, one simple physiological fact should convince you to err on the side of excess when it comes to deciding how much water to pack: A human working hard in 90-degree temperature needs approximately ten quarts of fluids every day. Ten quarts. That's two and a half gallons—12 large water bottles or 16 small ones. And, with water weighing in at approximately 8 pounds per gallon, a one-day supply comes to a whopping 20 pounds.

In other words, pack along two or three bottles even for short rides. And make sure you can purify the water found along the trail on longer routes. When writing of those routes where this could be of critical importance, each author has provided information on where water can be found near the trail — if it can be found at all. But drink it untreated and you run the risk of disease. (See *giardia* in the Glossary.)

One sure way to kill the protozoans, bacteria, and viruses in water is to boil it. Right. That's just how you want to spend your time on a bike ride. Besides, who wants to carry a stove or denude the countryside stoking bonfires to boil water?

Luckily, there is a better way. Many riders pack along the inexpensive and only slightly distasteful tetraglycine hydroperiodide tablets (sold under the names Potable Aqua, Globaline, and Coughlan's, among others). Some invest in portable, lightweight purifiers that filter out the crud. Unfortunately, both iodine *and* filtering are now required to be absolutely sure you've killed all the nasties you can't see. Tablets or iodine drops by themselves will knock off the well-known *giardia*, once called "beaver fever" for its transmission to the water through the feces of infected beavers. One to four weeks after ingestion, giardia will have you bloated, vomiting, shivering with chills, and living in the bathroom. (Though you won't care while you're suffering, beavers are getting a bum rap, for other animals are carriers also.)

But now there's another parasite we must worry about—*cryptosporidium*. "Crypto" brings on symptoms very similar to giardia, but unlike that fellow protozoan it's equipped with a shell sufficiently strong to protect it against the chemical killers that stop giardia cold. This means we're either back to boiling or on to using a water filter to screen out both giardia and crypto, plus the iodine to knock off viruses. All of which sounds like a time-consuming pain, but really isn't. Some water filters come equipped with an iodine chamber to guarantee full protection. Or you can simply add a pill or drops to the water you've just filtered (if you aren't allergic to iodine, of course). The pleasures of backcountry biking—and the displeasure of getting sick—make this relatively minor effort worth every one of the few minutes involved.

Tools: Ever since my first cross-country tour in 1965 I've been kidded about the number of tools I pack on the trail. And so I will exit entirely from this discussion by providing a list compiled by two mechanic (and mountain biker) friends of mine. After all, since they make their livings fixing bikes, and get their kicks by riding them, who could be a better source?

These two suggest the following as an absolute minimum:

tire levers
spare tube and patch kit

air pump
Allen wrenches (3, 4, 5, and 6 mm)
six-inch crescent (adjustable-end) wrench
small flat-blade screwdriver
chain rivet tool
spoke wrench

But, while they're on the trail, their personal tool pouches contain these additional items:

channel locks (small)
air gauge
tire valve cap (the metal kind, with a valve-stem remover)
baling wire (ten or so inches, for temporary repairs)
duct tape (small roll for temporary repairs or tire boot)
boot material (small piece of old tire or a large tube patch)
spare chain link
rear derailleur pulley
spare nuts and bolts
paper towel and tube of waterless hand cleaner

First-Aid kit: My personal kit contains the following, sealed inside double Ziploc bags.

sunscreen
aspirin
butterfly-closure bandages
Band-Aids
gauze compress pads (a half-dozen 4" × 4")
gauze (one roll)
ace bandages or Spenco joint wraps
Benadryl (an antihistamine, in case of allergic reactions)
water purification tablets/water filter (on long rides)
Moleskin/Spenco "Second Skin"
hydrogen peroxide, iodine, or Mercurochrome (some kind of antiseptic)
snakebite kit

Final considerations: The authors of this series have done a good job suggesting that specific items be packed for certain trails—rain gear in particular seasons, a hat and gloves for mountain passes, or shades for desert jaunts. Heed their warnings, and think ahead. Good luck.

Dennis Coello

AND NOW, A WORD ABOUT CELLULAR PHONES...

Thinking of bringing the Flip-Fone along on your next off-road ride? Before you do, ask yourself the following questions:

- Do I know where I'm going? Do I have an adequate map? Can I use a compass effectively? Do I know the shortest way to civilization if I need to bail out early and find some help?

- If I'm on the trail for longer than planned, am I ready for it? Do I have adequate water? Have I packed something to eat? Will I be warm enough if I'm still out there after dark?

- Am I prepared for possible injuries? Do I have a first-aid kit? Do I know what to do in case of a cut, fracture, snakebite, or heat exhaustion?

- Is my tool kit adequate for likely mechanical problems? Can I fix a flat? Can I untangle a chain? Am I prepared to walk out if the bike is unrideable?

If you answered "yes" to *every* question above, you may pack the phone, but consider a good whistle instead. It's lighter, cheaper, and nearly as effective.

If you answered "no" to *any* of these questions, be aware that your cellular phone does little to reduce your risks in the wilderness. Sure, being able to dial 911 in the farthest corner of the White Mountains sounds like a great idea, but this ain't downtown, friend. If disaster strikes, and your call is routed to some emergency operator in Manchester or Bangor, and it takes awhile to figure out which ranger, sheriff, or search-and-rescue crew to connect you with, and you can't tell the authorities where you are because you're really not sure, and the closest they can come to pinpointing your location is a cellular tower that serves 60 square miles (160 square kilometres) of dense woods, and they start searching for you but dusk is only two hours away, and you have no signaling device and your throat is too dry to shout, and meanwhile you can't get the bleeding stopped, you are out of luck. I mean really out of luck.

And when the battery goes dead, you're on your own again. Enough said.

Jeff Faust
Author of Mountain Bike! New Hampshire

NORTHERN OHIO

When the Industrial Age swept the United States, it was Lake Erie that helped change Ohio's future from a rural agricultural state to a highly urbanized one. Nowhere is the industrial base more evident than along northern Ohio's lakefront. From Toledo in the west, where mills and factories emerged along the Maumee River, to Cleveland in the east, where steel production is renowned, northern Ohio is an icon of American industry. Even so, you can find places to mountain bike, and interestingly enough, some of the more popular places to ride are there not in spite of the industry but because of it.

Take the Miami and Erie Canal Towpath Trail along the Maumee River, for instance. Beginning in the 1800s, the canal was a vital part of the transportation system that helped industrialize this area. The Castalia Quarry opened for business near Sandusky in the 1870s and supplied limestone to the region on and off until 1965. Now it serves as a reserve area and is a popular riding place for the Sandusky Bicycle Club. Finally, the Ohio and Erie Canal helped make Akron and Cleveland the cities they are today. The towpath trail in the heart of the Cuyahoga Valley National Recreation Area gives mountain bikers a quiet, comfortable place to ride.

Northern Ohio is also home to the Resthaven Wildlife Area outside of Sandusky, which was known as the "Castalia prairie" before it was mined. The riding is easy here, but things can get a little more challenging as you head over to Hinckley Reservation and Findley State Park. Neither area presents insurmountable challenges, and you'll find that the riding is fun. Finally, the southernmost ride in this part of the state is at Alum Creek State Park just north of Columbus, where local mountain bikers have succeeded in getting a section of the park set aside for mountain bike use.

Another path referenced in the Findley State Park chapter and several of the other Ohio chapters is the Buckeye Trail. The Buckeye Trail does not officially appear in this guide, but it's worth mentioning. This trail connects the four corners of Ohio with over 1,200 miles of hiking trails and travels through more than 40 of the state's 88 counties. It follows everything from old canal towpaths and abandoned right-of-ways to farmlands, forests, parks, and urban areas. Though this is primarily a hiking trail, certain sections are open to mountain bikes—mostly, those sections that travel over public roads or through parks and forests already permitting bicycle use. For more information, write:

Buckeye Trail Association, Inc.
P.O. Box 254
Worthington, OH 43085

The trail descriptions that follow were written with the help of several people. Thanks to Tom Striggow for information about the Miami and Erie Canal Towpath Trail, Amy Grubbe for help with the Castalia Quarry Reserve and Resthaven Wildlife Area, Lou Vetter for input on Findley State Park and Hinckley Reservation, and Dan Negley for information about Alum Creek State Park.

RIDE 1 · Miami and Erie Canal Towpath Trail

AT A GLANCE

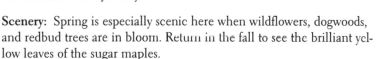

Length/configuration: 16-mile out-and-back (8 miles each way), dirt and stone double-track.

Aerobic difficulty: Easy

Technical difficulty: Easy

Scenery: Spring is especially scenic here when wildflowers, dogwoods, and redbud trees are in bloom. Return in the fall to see the brilliant yellow leaves of the sugar maples.

Special comments: Make sure you stop at Bend view for a panoramic sight of the Maumee River. Aside from the deer, red fox, and weasel, you might be lucky enough to see an osprey or a migratory bald eagle.

Riders of all ages and abilities will enjoy their ride down the remnants of the Miami and Erie Canal towpath from Providence Metropark to Farnsworth Metropark. Your impression of Toledo may be of industry, but this ride will change your mind. This dirt and stone double-track follows the Maumee River, affording many views of the waterway. A portion of the canal itself has been restored. A mule-drawn canal boat offers visitors a chance to experience what travel was like in the mid-1800s. Just east of the Providence trailhead is the Ludwig Mill. Built in 1864, the mill has an operating grain and sawmill complete with a working waterwheel. The structure also serves as an interpretative center with displays and demonstrations.

RIDE 1 · Miami and Erie Canal Towpath Trail

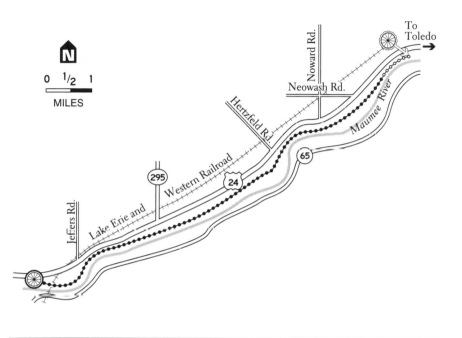

General location: The trail runs between Grand Rapids and Waterville.

Elevation change: The terrain is flat, and the riding is easy.

Season: The trail is off-limits to bikes from January through March because of soft soil conditions.

Services: Water and rest rooms are available at the trailheads and at Bend View Metropark. All services are available in Maumee and Toledo.

Hazards: Since the trail is popular, watch out for other trail users.

Rescue index: There are phones at both trailheads. You should find other users on the trail. Also, you're never far from US 24 if you need to flag someone down.

Land status: Toledo Metroparks

Maps: Write Toledo Metroparks at the address below for maps of Providence and Farnsworth Metroparks.

Finding the trail: Providence trailhead: From Interstate 80, take Exit 4, Reynolds Road. Go south on Reynolds Road, which becomes Conant Road, for about 4 miles. At the second light, turn right onto US 24 and in roughly 15 miles you will see the main entrance. To get to the trailhead, head toward the river. On the way to the Providence trailhead, you'll encounter Farnsworth Metropark about 1 mile after you pass OH 64.

Source of additional information:

Metropark District
Administrative Offices
5100 West Central Avenue
Toledo, OH 43615
(419) 535-3050

Notes on the trail: The trail is blazed in blue and easy to follow.

RIDE 2 · Castalia Quarry Reserve

AT A GLANCE

Length/configuration: Wide, 2-mile trail.

Aerobic difficulty: Moderate: you won't need a lot of stamina for this ride.

Technical difficulty: Moderate on the rim, more difficult in the quarry.

Scenery: Lake Erie; you may be able to see Perry's Victory and International Peace on Bass Island.

Special comments: Park regulations prohibit riding in the sand dunes in the quarry bed.

OH

This trail circles the Castalia Quarry Reserve, a quarry site active from the late 1870s to the 1960s. In fact, you can extend your trip by riding directly inside the quarry bed. Even though one spot on the trail is the point of highest elevation in Erie County, your lungs should remain safely in your chest. From that vantage point, you'll be able to look out onto Lake Erie and catch a glimpse of South Bass Island. You may also see the granite column of Perry's Victory and International Peace on the island. Bring a quarter for the viewer and check out all the sights. The trail is wide, and though you wouldn't want to take a short-cut into the quarry bed from the rim, you're still pretty safe from the edge. It's not fenced off, though, and you'll want to know how to ride a bike, or at least know where your brakes are.

RIDE 2 · Castalia Quarry Reserve

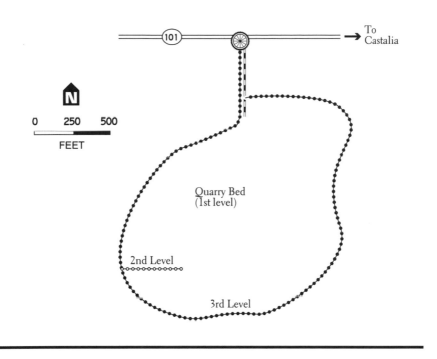

Riding in the quarry is a unique experience. Because it's more open, the quarry bed is windier than the rest of the area. So on days when it's normally cold and windy—well, don't open an umbrella. You'll need stronger technical skills because of the loose gravel and exposed limestone here. This is a great little trail to ride. If you're having fun on that family vacation out at Cedar Point Amusement Park in Sandusky, continue the fun at Castalia Quarry Reserve.

General location: One mile west of Castalia, off OH 101, about 6 miles southeast of Sandusky.

Elevation change: The climb along the quarry is gradual, and the overall elevation change is minor.

Season: All year. Winter can be windy down in the quarry bed. After a rain, the trail dries out quickly because of its limestone base; but if you ride when it's wet, it's like going through glue.

Services: Bring your own water. Castalia has a few food shops. Sandusky has all services.

Hazards: Don't ride too close to the edge—stay on the designated trail.

Amy pedals the trail around Castalia Quarry Reserve before heading into the quarry bed.

Rescue index: You're never far from OH 101, where you can flag down a motorist.

Land status: Erie Metroparks. In order to ride alone here, you will need to obtain a permit from Erie Metroparks. The permit process involves riding the trail with a Metroparks ranger who will point out the trails and areas of caution.

Maps: The map in this book may be as good as it gets, although you can look at the USGS 7.5 minute quad for Castalia.

Finding the trail: From I-80/90 Ohio Turnpike, take Exit 118, OH 250. Go north on OH 250 for 5.5 miles to OH 2. Take OH 2 west for 5.5 miles to OH 101 and go south for 4.5 miles, at which point you'll see a sign for Castalia Quarry Reserve. Park there on the right (north) side of the road. The trailhead entrance is on the other side of OH 101.

Source of additional information:

Erie Metroparks
3910 East Perkins Ave
Huron, OH 44839
(419) 625-7783

Notes on the trail: From the trailhead, ride up a short hill and curve to your right. If you go straight, you enter the quarry bed. There are three elevation levels. The first is the quarry bed itself. The second level is at the back of the quarry, accessible from the northwest edge of the main trail; you can ride to the dead end and glimpse the bed below and the upper rim above. The third level is the main trail itself that circles the outer rim of the quarry.

Resthaven Wildlife Area is on the other side of OH 101.

RIDE 3 · Resthaven Wildlife Area

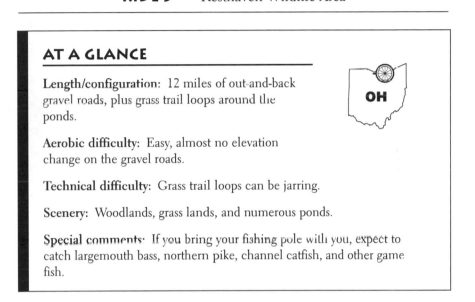

AT A GLANCE

Length/configuration: 12 miles of out-and-back gravel roads, plus grass trail loops around the ponds.

Aerobic difficulty: Easy, almost no elevation change on the gravel roads.

Technical difficulty: Grass trail loops can be jarring.

Scenery: Woodlands, grass lands, and numerous ponds.

Special comments· If you bring your fishing pole with you, expect to catch largemouth bass, northern pike, channel catfish, and other game fish.

OH

While Resthaven Wildlife Area's 2,272 acres are designated for hunting and fishing, folks in the Sandusky Bicycle Club like to come here to do a little off-road riding as well. Round trip, there are about 6 miles (12 miles total) of out-and-back gravel roads, but you can make this ride much longer by adding the grass trail loops that encircle many of the ponds. Traveling down the gravel roads is easy, and there is almost no elevation change. Taking the grass spurs is not too difficult, just a little jarring (this section is affectionately called Paris-Roubaix by members of the Sandusky Bicycle Club). Wildlife includes pheasant, raccoons, woodchucks, rail, woodcock, and gallinules. You'll also find prairie plants like big bluestem, little bluestem, Indian grass, and prairie dock. In short, the whole family will enjoy a pleasant ride, and the more adventurous can tackle "Paris-Roubaix."

General location: A mile west of Castalia, off OH 101, about 6 miles southeast of Sandusky

Elevation change: Negligible

Season: The grass trails can be overgrown in the summer. The interior access roads may be closed from the opening of hunting season in the fall until after the spring thaw, so you might want to check on availability with the wildlife manager at the address below.

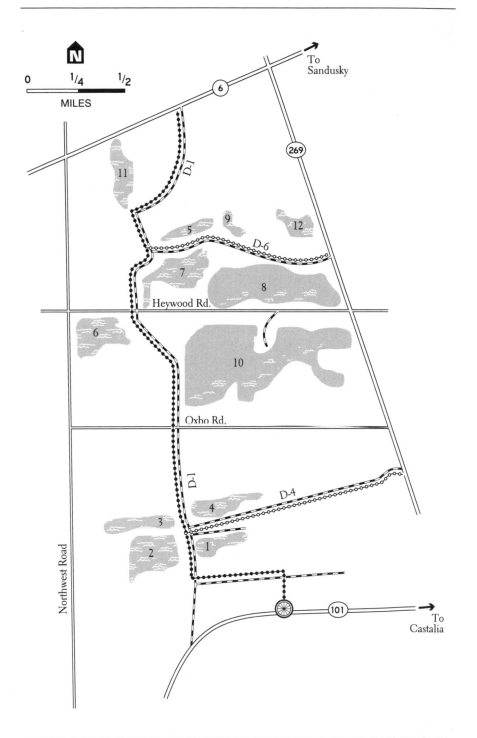

Amy tackles "Paris-Roubaix" around one of Resthaven's ponds.

Services: Bring your own water. Castalia has a few food shops. Sandusky has all services.

Hazards: Watch out for hunters and hikers. You may run into an occasional pothole on the gravel roads.

Rescue index: You can flag down traffic on OH 101 on the south side of Resthaven, OH 6 on the north side, and OH 269 on the east side. You may find less traffic on Northwest Road on the west side of Resthaven, and on Heywood Road and Oxbo Road, which cut through the center of the area.

Land status: Ohio Department of Natural Resources, Division of Wildlife.

Maps: You can get a map of Resthaven from the Ohio DNR. The USGS 7.5 minute quad for this area is Castalia.

Finding the trail: From I-80/90 Ohio Turnpike, take Exit 7, OH 250. Take OH 250 north 5.5 miles to OH 2. Take OH 2 west 5.5 miles to OH 101. Go south on OH 101 for 4.5 miles and you'll see a sign for Castalia Quarry Reserve. Park there on the right side of the road. You can begin your ride from the back of the parking lot.

Sources of additional information:

Resthaven Wildlife Area Manager
Box 155
Castalia, OH 44824
(419) 684-5049

Wildlife District Two Office
952 Lima Avenue
Box A
Findley, OH 45840
(419) 424-5000

Notes on the trail: From the rear of the parking lot, go straight back on a single-track trail that will swing slightly to the left. In a few yards, you'll come to a narrow, private gravel road. Go left on that road for half a mile until you run into Herr Road. Turn right on Herr, which will take you into Resthaven.

Your main out-and-back follows the gravel road, D-1. You might also explore other gravel roads such as D-4 and D-6, which are bordered by several ponds. Get out and explore the grass trails, too. Ponds 10 and 2 have nice grass trails circling them. In essence, if you see a grass trail that looks friendly, check it out!

Castalia Quarry Reserve is just on the other side of OH 101.

RIDE 4 · Findley State Park

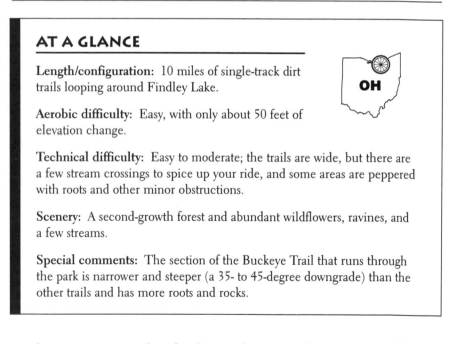

AT A GLANCE

Length/configuration: 10 miles of single-track dirt trails looping around Findley Lake.

Aerobic difficulty: Easy, with only about 50 feet of elevation change.

Technical difficulty: Easy to moderate; the trails are wide, but there are a few stream crossings to spice up your ride, and some areas are peppered with roots and other minor obstructions.

Scenery: A second-growth forest and abundant wildflowers, ravines, and a few streams.

Special comments: The section of the Buckeye Trail that runs through the park is narrower and steeper (a 35- to 45-degree downgrade) than the other trails and has more roots and rocks.

There are over ten miles of trails to explore at Findley State Park, which essentially forms a loop around Findley Lake. The dirt single-track trails are wide because they were originally used as logging roads when the area was a state forest. Most trails will be easy enough for everyday cyclists. You'll even find a couple of stream crossings, and you'll ride along several ravines on the Hickory Grove Trail. The wooded area along this trail is the most natural; many of the other trails have more recent growth.

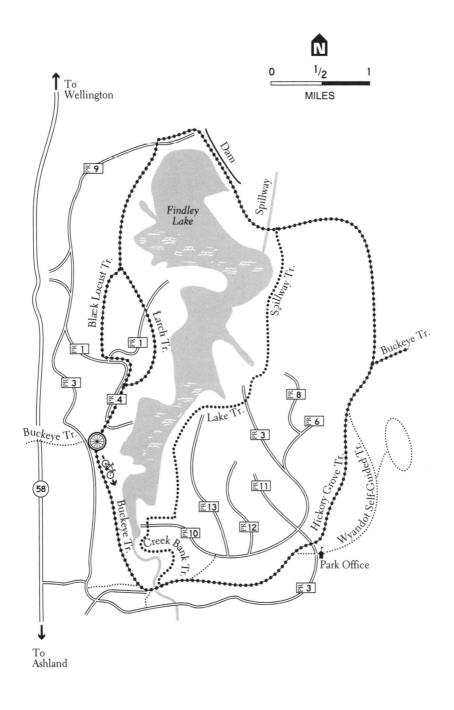

N

0   1/2   1

MILES

To
Wellington

PR 9

Dam

Spillway

Findley
Lake

Black Locust Tr.

Larch Tr.

Spillway Tr.

PR 1

PR 1

Buckeye Tr.

PR 1

PR 3

PR 4

PR 8

Lake Tr.

Buckeye Tr.

PR 6

PR 3

Hickory Grove Tr.

Wyandot Self-Guided Tr.

58

PR 11

Buckeye Tr.

PR 13

PR 12

PR 10

Creek Bank Tr.

Park Office

PR 3

To
Ashland

At Findley State Park, keep your eyes peeled for the Duke's skipper butterfly, but at this spot, keep your eye on the old wooden bridge.

At Findley State Park, you'll find red maple, white ash, wild black cherry, and red pine in this second growth forest, as well as wildflowers like spring beauties, Dutchman's breeches, trillium, and bloodroot. You'll likely see deer, red fox, and even migratory ospreys and hawks. And this park has a sanctuary for the Duke's skipper butterfly. If you're lucky, perhaps you'll spot one of these rare insects.

General location: Off OH 58, 2 miles south of Wellington

Elevation change: At 980 feet above sea level, the elevation change is only about 50 feet.

Season: Since this is a sensitive area and hikers get first priority, the winter is best; the cooler weather keeps down the number of hikers.

Services: Water and camping are available in the state park. Oberlin has all services.

Hazards: Since the area is popular, watch out for hikers.

Rescue index: There is usually someone available at the camp check-in station.

Land status: Ohio state park

Maps: The state park has a good map showing the trails. Pick one up at the check-in station or write to the park at the address below. The USGS 7.5 minute quad covering most of the area is Wellington. The southernmost section falls into Sullivan.

Finding the trail: From I-80/90, the Ohio Turnpike, take Exit 8, OH 57. Take OH 57 south for 0.5 miles to OH 113. Go west on OH 113 for 5.2 miles to OH 58. Then go south on OH 58 for 16 miles. The entrance to Findley State Park will be on your left. As you pull in, curve to the right and follow Park Road 3 to the Picnic Pines parking area.

Source of additional information:

Findley State Park
25381 State Route 58
Wellington, OH 44090-9208
(440) 647-4490

Notes on the trail: You can begin the ride on the Buckeye Trail (also called Hickory Grove Trail), which you'll see through the trees on the south side of the parking lot. If you ride instead through a clearing at the opposite end of the lot, you'll cross over a rickety bridge and out onto another parking lot. At the other end of that lot, you can pick up the Larch Trail and head that way. Or feel free to start your ride from any other parking area.

You can make a wide or narrow loop around the lake, depending on which trail you choose. The Spillway Trail is smooth and cuts closer to the lake. Farther out is the Hickory Grove Trail, where you'll find the ravines and stream crossings. Also, the Buckeye Trail, which runs parallel to the Creekbank Trail, is fairly steep. You may have to portage here.

Currently, Findley is not designating any of the trails specifically for bike use. All of the trails are now multi-use and are shared by all, including cyclists. The trails can get very wet at times, and state park officials ask that cyclists be very environmentally conscientious and only ride the trails when they are dry.

RIDE 5 · Hinckley Reservation

AT A GLANCE

Length/configuration: A paved, 3-mile loop around Hinckley Lake.

OH

Aerobic difficulty: Moderate

Technical difficulty: Paved trails make this a technically undemanding ride.

Scenery: Man-made Hinckley Lake, sections of pine and hardwoods.

Special comments: Though often crowded, the arrival of the buzzards each March is a sight.

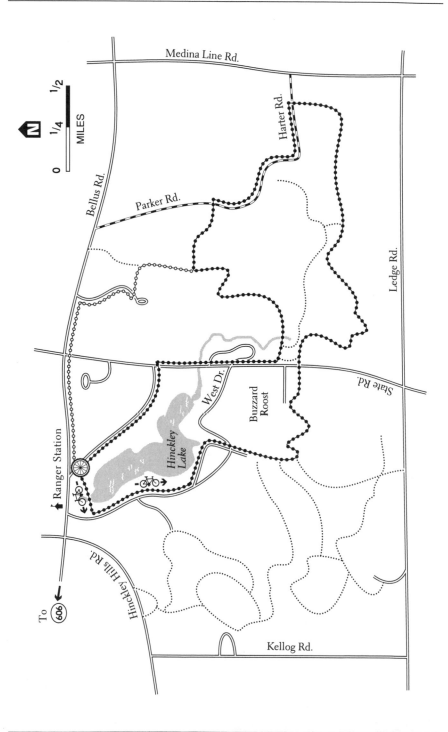

L et Capistrano keep its swallows. Hinckley Reservation has its buzzards. (More on that later.) Bicycling in Cleveland Metroparks is permitted only on the paved, all-purpose trails and is not permitted on the hiking or bridle trails.

Every March 15, the buzzards return to Hinckley Reservation, where they have been coming since before the turn of the century. As legend has it, back in the 1800s the local farmers wanted to get rid of all the wild animals in the area, so hunters formed a circle around the woods and walked to the center, killing everything in their path. They piled up the carcasses, which attracted the buzzards. Every year since, the birds have returned in search of another free meal. It may not be a pretty story, but it is compelling.

General location: About 20 miles south of Cleveland.

Elevation change: Although there isn't more than 50 feet of overall gain and the short climbs don't sound like a lot, you'll feel the elevation.

Season: Fall and summer riding is best. The weekend around March 15 gets quite busy as visitors come from miles around to see the buzzards return.

Services: Bring your own water. There is a concession stand open in the summer at the Hinckley Boathouse. Hinckley, Cleveland, and several of the surrounding suburbs have all services.

Hazards: Be careful riding along the top of the cliffs. There are no guardrails and you won't like the 90-degree drop of 20 to 30 feet. You don't have to ride up the cliffs, though; you can take a path around them.

Rescue index: You're never more than half a mile from civilization at any point on the trail.

Land status: Cleveland Metroparks.

Maps: The USGS 7.5 minute quad is West Richfield.

Finding the trail: From the Ohio Turnpike, take I-71 south for approximately 10 miles. Get off at OH 303 and take that east roughly 12 miles. Go through Hinckley and south on OH 606 for about 2 miles to Bellus Road. Turn left on Bellus and follow the signs. You'll see a small ranger station on your left and a dam on your right. Turn right on the first road before the dam. The entrance to the Boathouse area and parking are approximately 0.5 miles on the left.

Source of additional information:

Cleveland Metroparks
4101 Fulton Parkway
Cleveland, OH 44144-1923
(216) 351-6300

Notes on the trail: Hinckley Reservation is the pendant on what is referred to as the "Emerald Necklace," the system of reservations circling Cleveland. Several of the Park District facilities contain paved, all-purpose trails. Contact Cleveland Metroparks for more information.

RIDE 6 · Ohio and Erie Canal Towpath Trail

AT A GLANCE

Length/configuration: A 40-mile, gravel out-and-back (20 miles each way) along the remnants of the Ohio and Erie Canal.

OH

Aerobic difficulty: Easy

Technical difficulty: Easy

Scenery: Locks (some still functioning), woods, meadows, and marshes.

Special comments: If you have time the surrounding area is home to several interesting and historic attractions worth a visit.

The trail is limestone gravel and flat, making this a very easy ride for the entire family. There's much to see along the towpath route, including old houses, cornfields, meadows, marshes, and woods. You'll observe several locks and aqueducts, and even an operating old-time lock near Independence by the Canal Visitor Center. Your ride often parallels the Valley Railroad tracks and the Cuyahoga River. The canal is dry in spots, but contains more water north of Peninsula. You might want to get off your bike and visit Deep Lock Quarry, a former sandstone quarry and the site of the remains of the deepest lock on the canal. If you're more interested in natural construction projects, you'll find a beaver dam south of Peninsula.

It would be your loss if you came to Cuyahoga Valley National Recreation Area and only rode the towpath. The Canal Visitor Center contains exhibits on the history of the area. Additionally, the Boston Store Visitor Center is directly adjacent to the Towpath Trail and contains interactive exhibits and the partial replica of a canal boat. The exhibits detail the history of boat building along the canal. Several historical places are worth seeing as well: Wilson's Mill, the last operating mill on the canal; Hale Farm, a restored brick farmstead belonging to one of the earliest settlers in the area; and across the street from the farm, a restored village containing blacksmiths, potters, weavers, candlemakers, and their crafts. The old canal town of Peninsula is another popular tourist area filled with shops and restaurants. In the summer, you might consider spending an evening at the Blossom Music Center, listening to the Cleveland Orchestra under the stars. If you're a theater buff, you might attend summer stock at the Porthouse Theater. There are also several parks within Cuyahoga Valley where you can hike rock ledges and waterfalls, swim, golf, cross-country ski, downhill ski, and sled. There are plenty of attractions to keep you entertained no matter what time of year you come.

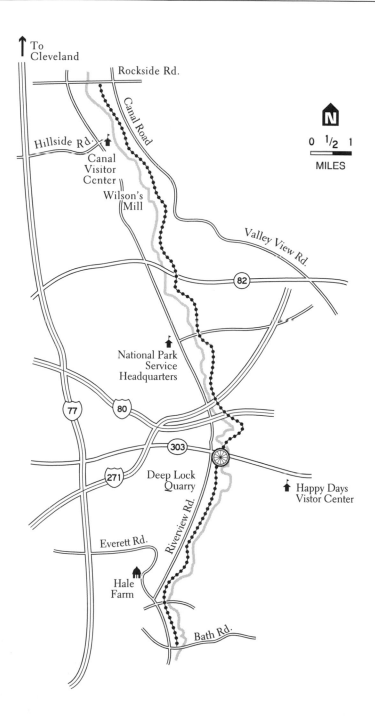

To
Cleveland

Rockside Rd.

Canal Road

N

0   1/2   1

MILES

Hillside Rd.

Canal
Visitor
Center

Wilson's
Mill

Valley View Rd.

82

National Park
Service
Headquarters

77   80

303

271

Deep Lock
Quarry

Happy Days
Vistor Center

Riverview Rd.

Everett Rd.

Hale
Farm

Bath Rd.

General location: Eight miles south of Cleveland.

Elevation change: Negligible.

Season: Enjoy this trail all year long; it's fun any time.

Services: The town of Peninsula has all services, as do Cleveland and Akron.

Hazards: Proceed with caution on some bridges and on the boardwalk when it's freezing. Keep an eye out for other bikers, joggers, and hikers on this popular trail.

Rescue index: The trail is heavily used, so encountering other people won't be a problem.

Land status: National park service and now part of the recently established Ohio and Erie Canal National Heritage Corridor.

Maps: Cuyahoga Valley Recreation Area will send you a map of the area and its attractions. Write them at the address below. The USGS 7.5 minute quads are Northfield and Peninsula.

Finding the trail: From the intersection of I-80 and OH 21, go south on OH 21 about 1.5 miles to I-77. Take I-77 south for about 3 miles to I-271. Then take I-271 north for 3.5 miles to OH 303, and take OH 303 for about 2 miles to Peninsula. In Peninsula, turn left at the traffic light by Fisher's Restaurant. Go 1 block and turn left again. You'll see the parking area for the trail and signs directing you to the trailhead.

Contact Cuyahoga Valley National Recreation Area for additional places to pick up the trail.

Sources of additional information:

Cuyahoga Valley National Recreation Area
15610 Vaughn Road
Brecksville, OH 44141-3097
(440) 526-5256
www.nps.gov/cuva

Happy Days Visitor Center
(330) 650-4636 (local calls only)

Canal Visitor Center
(216) 524-1497 (local calls only)

Notes on the trail: Peninsula isn't at either end of the towpath, but this is a good place to start because of the convenient parking, restaurants, shops, and other services.

The trail endpoints are at Rockside Road and Bath Road, but plans are under way to extend the trail in both directions.

RIDE 7 · Alum Creek State Park

AT A GLANCE

Length/configuration: One 2-mile and one 5-mile single-track loop.

Aerobic difficulty: Easy

Technical difficulty: Easy to challenging, depending upon the loop you ride.

Scenery: Streams, ravines, deer, some small animals, and waterfowl.

Special comments: Advanced riders can depart the main trail and tackle the user-made spurs, which are steeper and rockier.

The military once used this area for practicing tank maneuvers. You'll be able to make some maneuvers here, too, as you ride the narrow single-track trails. Officials at Alum Creek State Park, working in conjunction with local bike shops who helped with fund-raising for the parking lot and signage, have developed a two-part trail. There's a two-mile loop designed for beginning riders and a five-mile connecting loop for intermediate riders. The trail resembles what Dan Negley, manager of Break Away Cycling and Fitness, rode in his home town. "This reminds me of back where I'm from in Nebraska down by the river—single-track trails with lots of curves and overgrowth."

You'll like testing your skills on the winding trails. There are no serious switchbacks, but ruts, roots, stumps, ditches, and a stream crossing will challenge you without being too menacing.

Among the highlights is a ridge that runs along a ravine overlooking a swampy area at the tip of a cove. On one part of the ridge, you'll take a fast curve down and, before you know it, you're on a bridge followed by a few ditches. If you take one user-made trail, you can visit a wonderful old "carpeted" tree, hollowed out like Winnie-the-Pooh's house and probably used by hunters. I didn't see Pooh, but you will find deer, groundhogs, and waterfowl.

General location: Twelve miles north of Columbus from the I-270 beltway.

Elevation change: You'll find a few minor climbs, but the elevation change is not great.

Season: The best time to ride is in the winter because the trail is more heavily traveled in the summer. Also, from May to late summer, you may be besieged by ticks and poison ivy.

Services: You can camp at Alum Creek State Park. All services are available in Delaware and Columbus. For bike service, try Break Away Cycling in Delaware.

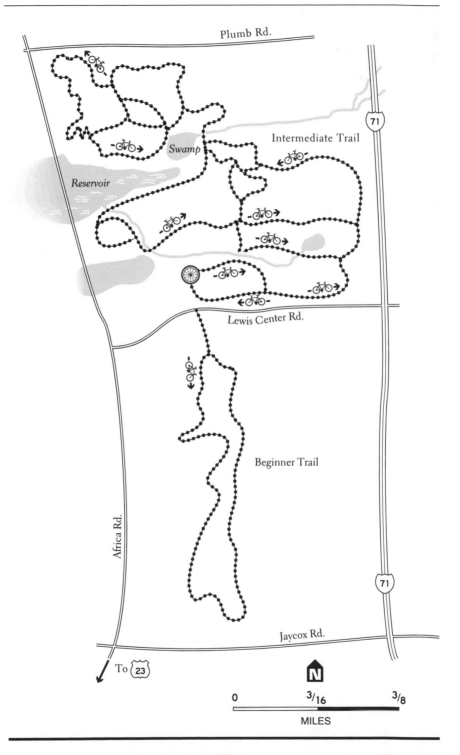

Plumb Rd.

Intermediate Trail

Swamp

Reservoir

Lewis Center Rd.

Africa Rd.

Beginner Trail

71

71

Jaycox Rd.

To 23

N

0   3/16   3/8

MILES

Dan whizzes hrough the single-track at Alum Creek State Park, one of only a handful of exclusive mountain bike trails.

Hazards: Look for stumps, roots, and a few tricky bridge crossings.

Rescue index: The area is basically a square mile surrounded by roads, so you're never more than a half mile from a road. There is a park office on the east side of the lake.

Land status: State park

Maps: Alum Creek State Park has a map of the entire park, but the current mountain bike trail is not too detailed on it. The state park is working on a more detailed map. The USGS 7.5 minute quad is Galena.

Finding the trail: From the I-270 beltway north of Columbus, take US 23 north for 6 miles to Lewis Center Road. Turn right on Lewis Center Road and go 4.5 miles to the 4-way stop at Africa Road. Turn left onto Africa Road and go a short distance until Lewis Center Road picks up again. Turn right on Lewis Center Road and follow that for 0.5 mile to the sign for Alum Creek State Park Mountain Bike Trail. The 5-mile connecting loop begins at the end of the parking area. The 2-mile trail is on the other side of the road.

Sources of additional information:

Alum Creek State Park
3615 South Old State Road
Delaware, OH 43015
(740) 548-4631

Break Away Cycling
17 West William Street
Delaware, OH 43015
(740) 363-3232

Notes on the trail: The main trail is marked, but feel free to explore the user-made spurs and dead ends. If you get turned around, listen for the traffic on I-71 and head in that direction. Then you can walk north or south to the first road.

SOUTH CENTRAL OHIO

L ike Indiana and Illinois, Ohio tends to be flatter in the north and hillier in the unglaciated, river-carved south. For the most extreme riding, try the southeast corner of the state. For the easiest, stay up around the lake.

I focused my efforts on the south-central region for several reasons. First, it should, in theory, be representative of the middle ground of riding in the state. As it turned out, it's not. It favors the more demanding southern terrain with only a few beginner trails. Second, the area is accessible to lots of people, being an easy drive from Dayton, Cincinnati, and Columbus and a not-so-bad drive from Toledo and Cleveland. Third, I aimed at the middle because it's where the best and worst of mountain bike trails come to life.

And what are the best? Those recently developed trails that benefited from some research and engineering, such as Paint Creek State Park. The worst? Those "grandfathered" into the state's trails system simply because they were there. The best example of bad trails: Great Seal State Park. Trails should not redefine the land on which they exist. That concept escaped the people who blazed this mess of erosion.

To their credit, the decision makers in Ohio decided to move ahead with trails on state property early in the 1990s. At the beginning of that decade, they were no more enlightened than their neighbors in Indiana. Within five years, Ohio had blown past the foot-draggers in the Hoosier state to establish trails on most state land.

Also unlike neighboring states of Indiana and Kentucky, Ohio is more open to the use of motorized ATVs on their trails. Although I've never had a conflict while riding there, you're advised to ride aware and yield to these riders. You can hear and see them far better than they can hear and see you.

Despite a progressive attitude, there are places where you cannot ride. If in doubt, ask. And ask someone in authority. One popular book on mountain biking in Ohio has a Web site where enthusiasts can post new trails they've discovered. We ran into a group of riders who had driven several hours to a trail they'd seen on the site, only to be told by park police that bikes were absolutely not permitted on those trails. That incident occurred near Tar Hollow State Park, but could have been at any number of sites around the state.

In general, Ohio is a bike-friendly place. There are several major road tours here, sponsored by clubs throughout the state. Mountain biking is well accepted, and there's a long history of good bike shops, dating back to the Wright brothers' store (before they got on that crazy flying idea).

RIDE 8 · Paint Creek State Park, North Loops

AT A GLANCE

Length/configuration: 3-mile main loop with 2 miles of optional, tighter single-track (total of 5 miles). This trail is wide in the fields, narrow in the woods.

Aerobic difficulty: The main loop is easy; an excellent introduction for a rank beginner, and a good place to take the family or any other group with widely disparate skill levels. The optional sections are moderately challenging, with some short, steep hills.

Technical difficulty: The main loop is easy; it's basically a path mowed through the prairie grasses. The optional sections are moderate, with hills, tight technical sections, and occasionally loose traction, which could challenge even an accomplished rider who chooses to take them at speed.

Scenery: The main loop is mostly fields with some brush; the options throw in some wooded single-track.

Special comments: Paint Creek State Park gets my recommendation for base camp. Big camp sites. A lake. Plenty of showers. A well-stocked store. And, as of this writing, a staff member who rides and races and has assumed responsibility for the trails. The talent and dedication show.

Paint Creek State Park tries hard to be a lot of things to a lot of people, and it succeeds. In the week my buddy Joe and I camped there, the park staff held a bean supper and a pancake breakfast. It was just before Halloween, and as that day approached, the campgrounds filled with families and retirees trying to outdo each other with Halloween decorations. Some even rented a second site adjacent their RV and made it into a graveyard or other spooky hokum. Early in the week, we did some star gazing from our site; by the end of the week, the place was so lit up you couldn't find a star.

The long and short of it is that this park does a good job with kids and families. If you're looking for a wilderness experience, you'll only get it here by peering through the windows of the neighbor's RV and watching a National

RIDE 8 • Paint Creek State Park, North Loops

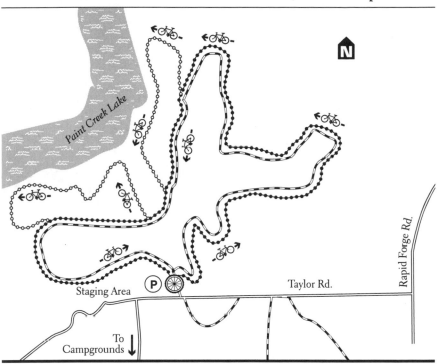

Geographic special on their big-screen TV. But if you want a place where the kids aren't bored on day two, this may be it. This is the place you come to if you want to try a lot of things, but aren't particularly proficient at any of them. Camping. Canoeing. Fishing. Hiking. Mountain biking.

The trails reflect this beginner-friendly philosophy, especially the north loops. If you stay on the main trail, you get a gently undulating ride through the field. Nothing scary here. The only downside is that like most field trails, this one has a slight washboard ride. It's a minor annoyance, however.

This is not to say other riders won't have fun here. They will. Once the kids have done a lap of the main loop, the masters category racer in the family can go back and hit the optional loops. The tight, technical single-track here will keep the adrenaline pumping.

General location: About 12 miles east-northeast of Hillsboro in south central Ohio

Elevation change: 300 feet, but only on the roller-coaster optional loops. The main loop is purt-near flat.

Season: All year, with prime time in May and June, and again in September and October

Joe Ernst navigating a shallow stream crossing.

Services: There's a camp store at the park. The inventory varies from kooky gifts to traditional campground carbohydrates like marshmallows. Bainbridge has most things, including a couple of convenience stores and 1 or 2 hometown restaurants where the food's not bad, but the cigarette smoke rolls across the ceiling like a funeral shroud. Both Hillsboro to the west and Chillicothe to the east have hotels, grocery stores, and shopping centers. The nearest bike shop is in Chillicothe.

Hazards: Basically none

Rescue index: Help can be found at the state park office or with park security.

Land status: State park

Maps: Trail maps are available from the state park office or a box at the trailhead.

Finding the trail: From Highway 50, turn north on Rapid Forge Road. There are signs there directing you to the Paint Creek State Park. In about 3 miles, you'll turn left onto Taylor Road. There are signs there, as well. When the park road goes left off of Taylor Road and into the campground (you'll see signs for the campground), turn right into the parking lot. There are maps on the bulletin board. From there, just follow the signs.

Source of additional information:

Paint Creek State Park
14265 US 50
Bainbridge, OH 45612

(937) 365-1401, park office
(937) 981-7061, camp office

Notes on the trail: This is a dandy beginner's trail. The field sections can be a bit lumpy, but are otherwise undemanding. The more technical parts come in 2 pieces, so a beginner can try just one or both, depending on how high the confidence meter reads. For intermediate riders, the long option is fun, fast, and not at all overwhelming even though it's a bit tight and technical in spots. There are a few rocks, some loose soil, maybe a couple of linear feet of mud here and there. There are also a few short, moderately steep little hills on the optional sections. If the beginners in your group have tired of riding in the field, these single-track options offer the next step in their mountain biking education. Try them out on the first one and see how it goes. If they like it, take in the second option, too. If not, let them return on the main loop in the field.

RIDE 9 · Paint Creek State Park, South Loops

AT A GLANCE

Length/configuration: My computer didn't agree with the park maps. I clocked 4 and 2.5 miles for the main trail plus the optional single-track (for a total of about 6.5). The park map says 3 miles for the main plus an additional 5 for the optional (for a total of 8 miles). Like the north trails, these are mostly single-track; wide in the fields, narrow in the woods.

Aerobic difficulty: The field sections could be ridden by almost anyone. The optional sections have a few short uphill grunts that I'd rate moderate.

Technical difficulty: The main loop is easy, although some parts are moderate compared to the north trail. This trail rolls a little more. Some of the optional single-track is moderate, even difficult on the short climbs. It can be tough to find traction here.

Scenery: Fields with some brush; more woods than the north trail, and there are a few spurs that provide nice views of Paint Creek reservoir.

Special comments: When your beginner tires of the north trail, this is the next logical step. Both the open and single-track sections are more demanding than those of the north trail; the single-track especially is tougher—hillier and more technical.

Joe Ernst is treated to some ridgetop views before following the trail downhill to the lake.

So, the north loops have grown familiar, and you're ready to head on to another location. Well, hold on there, pardner. You owe it to yourself to make a lap of the south loops first. They're more challenging than the north loops. They're longer. The hills are steeper. There are more rocks and a few roots. There's also more woods.

These south loops have an almost endless appeal. You could ride them over and over all day without tiring of them. There are little spurs that go off to picnic tables by the lake. The trails twist and turn so sight distances are kept short, which is a good way to hold a rider's attention.

There's a crossover point so you can really cut this ride short. You'll see it on the trail map the park provides. You won't see it on the map in this book because I recommend against taking it. If you do, you'll miss the best riding. Besides, if you want to do a short ride, do the north trail.

General location: About 12 miles east-northeast of Hillsboro in south central Ohio

Elevation change: 300 feet, although most of the trail has much less. The only time you'll see that much climbing is when you come back up from the lake, about halfway through the ride, and that's a gentle climb.

Season: All year, with prime time in May and June, and again in September and October

Services: There's a camp store at the park. The inventory varies from chintzy gift-baubles to traditional campground carbohydrates like marshmallows. Bainbridge

RIDE 9 · Paint Creek State Park, South Loops

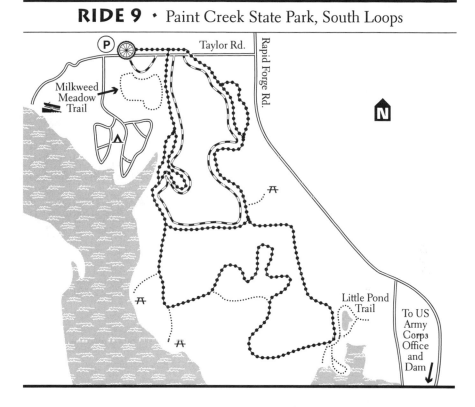

has most things, including a couple of convenience stores and 1 or 2 home-town restaurants where the food's not bad, but the cigarette smoke rolls across the ceiling like a funeral shroud. Both Hillsboro to the west and Chillicothe to the east have hotels, grocery stores, and shopping centers. The nearest bike shop is in Chillicothe.

Hazards: Basically none, although less-experienced riders may find the op-tional sections—especially the first one—a bit intimidating. That section has some logs and a few steep ravines; the same things exist on the other optional sections, although in less menacing form than on that first option.

Rescue index: Help can be found at the state park office or with park security.

Land status: State park

Maps: Trail maps are available from the state park office or a box at the trail-head. You won't need them to find your way; if you get lost on this trail, you have no business being in the woods. But the maps will show where the spurs to the lake are, where you can find a picnic table, and how far it is to the next chunk of optional single-track.

Finding the trail: From US 50, turn north on Rapid Forge Road. There are signs there directing you to the Paint Creek State Park. In about 3 miles, you'll turn left onto Taylor Road. There are signs there, as well. When the road goes down into a dip, watch for the trailhead on the left. Continue driving to where the park road goes left off of Taylor Road and into the campground (you'll see signs for the campground). Turn right into the parking lot. Park, then ride the short piece of Taylor Road back to the trailhead. (Go down the hill, past the entrance for the hiking trails, then up the other side, still on the road. Look for the sign on your right. It's easy to mistake the hiking entrance for the biking entrance. Don't turn onto a trail until you've gone down the hill and most of the way back up the other side.) There are maps on the bulletin board at the parking area.

Source of additional information:

Paint Creek State Park
14265 US 50
Bainbridge, OH, 45612
(937) 365-1401, park office
(937) 981-7061, camp office

Notes on the trail: The first optional section comes up quickly on the right after you get off the road and onto the trail. If you're not confident of your off-road abilities, you may want to skip this first option; it's the most demanding of the 3 optional segments on this trail. The second option, which peels off to the left about halfway through the ride, and the third option, which goes to the right less than a mile from the end, are worth exploring even for somewhat timid riders. If you're looking for spot for a picnic, there are several. My suggestion is to ride down to the lake. To do this, keep your eyes open after the second optional segment returns to the main trail. You'll go down a hill; the trail turns sharply left at the bottom and begins climbing. At that point, you can turn right onto a secondary trail and follow it a 100 yards or so to the lake. You'll have to climb after you've finished eating, but the trail is wide, and the grade reasonable, so it's not a problem.

RIDE 10 · Pike State Forest APV Area, Outer Loop "A" *

AT A GLANCE

Length/configuration: 5.5-mile loop. Mostly wide single-track.

OH

Aerobic difficulty: Challenging; there are frequent steep climbs. My riding partner rode every one of them; I walked about a third.

Technical difficulty: Moderate to challenging; surface is loose in spots and there are some tough climbs. Virtually no rocks, roots, or other traditional challenges, though. Combination of aerobic and technical demands make this a good expert loop.

Scenery: Mostly woods, but with a feel like something out West, maybe Summit County, Colorado. I'm not sure why.

Special comments: This outer loop will be too long for all but the strongest riders. Those who are up to the challenge will be rewarded with plenty of fast downhills.

Pike State Forest APV Area was designed for and built by motorcyclists. Motorized use is still common here, although there were few users present when we showed up. As new trail-building methods are implemented and new erosion control becomes necessary, the trail changes. It is in a constant state of being reinvented. There's lots of up and down, with brutal climbs and thrilling descents. (Some of the redesigning may bypass the steepest sections.) Traction was incredible in the dry conditions we enjoyed, but was sketchy in the few places where the trail was covered in talus.

This area is great fun; don't let the steep hills prevent you from riding here. And don't avoid this longer option. The area is a spiderweb of trails, so if you get too tired to continue, hop a connector back to the parking lot.

Much of what's here will be rebuilt in time. I really hope they keep the descent at the end. It's not as wide as the other sections, and it's filled with fast whoops. It's a rocket ride that dumps you out right back at the parking area.

General location: About 7 miles east of Sinking Springs on OH 124 in south-central Ohio

Elevation change: Once you leave the parking area and begin the first climb, there isn't a flat stretch to be found. Most climbs are on the order of 200 feet or so; you only get the full altitude change of 400 feet at the beginning and end.

Season: The area is closed December 1 through April 1. Traction can be a real

* My designation, it's not signed as such.

RIDE 10 • Pike State Forest APV Area, Outer Loop "A"

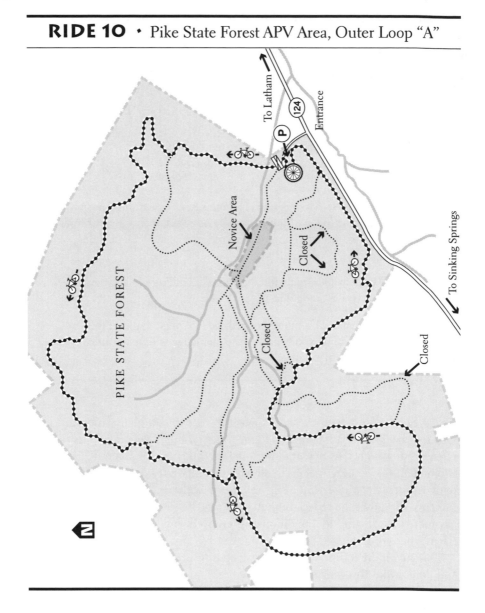

problem when the trail is wet, so the dry season (late summer and early autumn) is best.

Services: There are convenience stores and minimal services in Latham and Sinking Springs. Get your water and whatever else you need before you arrive, as there are no services on site. The nearest bike shop is in Chillicothe.

Hazards: Way steep, and sometimes loose. If fast descents scare you, find someplace else to ride. Also, yield to ATVs. We asked the state employee we

A rare stretch of relatively flat trail allows Joe Ernst to recover before attacking the next climb.

met if they were more prevalent one time than another. We got the expected reply: weekends and in summer. Was there ever a time mountain bikers should avoid the area altogether? No.

Rescue index: Don't ride alone, this place can be a ghost town. The nearest phone is in Latham.

Land status: State forest

Maps: From the state forest office; they're in need of (and in the process of) updating, so ask about any changes that may not appear on your copy.

Finding the trail: The area is on the north side of OH 124 about 7 miles east of Sinking Springs. Watch for signs at the entrance.

Sources of additional information:

Pike State Forest Office
334 Lapperell Road
Latham, OH 45646
(614) 493-2441

Notes on the trail: Following this loop is easy—always bear right. Start from the parking area and bear right at the gate. Keep right to enjoy this perimeter loop of the area. After the initial climb, you'll be rolling pretty much the whole time. As you get farther along, there will be spots where the trail has loose rock on it. This talus makes traction tough, especially because it tends to show up on climbs. If you run out of steam, there's another trail that comes up to meet this one roughly halfway through. Turn left onto it and you'll return to the APV Novice Area. Ride through that area back to the gate and—just beyond and to the right—the parking lot. Otherwise, stay on the perimeter loop, always bearing right, and you'll be rewarded with that roller-coaster descent at the end.

RIDE 11 · Pike State Forest APV Area, Middle Loop "B"*

AT A GLANCE

OH

Length/configuration: 3.5-mile loop. Mostly wide single-track.

Aerobic difficulty: Challenging, due to frequent steep climbs. My partner bagged all of them; I walked a few sections near the tops of the tougher climbs.

Technical difficulty: Moderate to challenging; surface is loose in spots and there are some tough climbs. No rocks, roots, or other traditional challenges, though.

Scenery: Mostly woods, with a little creek bottom and a creek crossing near the beginning.

Special comments: This is one of the intermediate loops offered here; "intermediate" not because it's easier than the outer loop, but because it's shorter.

Pike State Forest APV Area was designed for and built by motorcyclists. Motorized use is still common here, although there were few users present when we showed up. As new trail-building methods are implemented and as new erosion control becomes necessary, the trail changes. It is in a constant state of being reinvented. There's lots of up and down, with brutal climbs and thrilling descents. (Some of the redesigning may bypass the steepest sections.) Traction was incredible in the dry conditions we enjoyed, although there were stretches of loose rock on a few of the climbs.

This middle loop offers most of the appeal of the outer loop, but in an abbreviated version. If you're not sure you're ready for the rigors of the longer outer loop, try this one first. We rode all three in the same day. We came away tired, but we did complete the entire system.

General location: About 7 miles east of Sinking Springs on OH 124 in south central Ohio

* Once again, my designation.

RIDE 11 · Pike State Forest APV Area, Middle Loop "B"

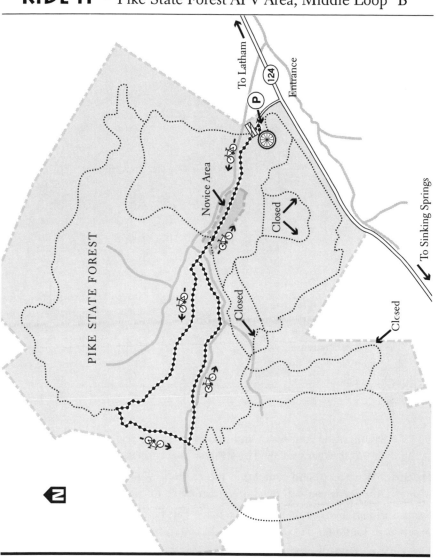

Elevation change: Under 400 feet. You'll see that at the beginning and end. Most of the rest of the trail is rollers with about 200 feet of change; some are much more shallow, maybe 50 feet up and down.

Season: The area is closed December 1 through April 1. Traction can be a real problem when the trail is wet, so the dry season (late summer and early autumn) is best.

Services: There are convenience stores and minimal services in Latham and

Built for all-terrain vehicle use, these trails are wide, smooth, and fast, as Joe Ernst demonstrates.

Sinking Springs. Get your water and whatever else you need before you arrive, as there are no services on site. The nearest bike shop is in Chillicothe.

Hazards: Way steep, and sometimes loose. Hone your descending skills elsewhere. The speeds you can reach here can make for ugly wrecks.

Rescue index: Don't ride alone, this place can be a ghost town. The nearest phone is in Latham.

Land status: State forest

Maps: From the state forest office; they're in need of (and in the process of) updating, so ask about any changes that may not appear on your copy.

Finding the trail: The area is on the north side of OH 124 about 7 miles east of Sinking Springs. Watch for signs at the entrance.

Source of additional information:

Pike State Forest Office
334 Lapperell Road
Latham, OH 45646
(614) 493-2441

Notes on the trail: This loop basically cuts out the extreme right and left sections of the outer loop. Where the outer loop goes right at the gate at the end of the parking area, this one goes through the gate and into the APV Novice Area, beyond. Go straight through the Novice Area to marker #6. (Marker numbers were current as of this writing, but may change.) You're heading straight through the Novice Area, across the creek, and up the hill.

At the top (at marker #5), go left. You'll ride a section of more shallow hills, rollers, really. Veer left again at marker #10. When the trail splits, veer left again. (There's no marker here. Go down the hill, not up.) Continue to the Novice Area, then turn right to return to the parking area.

RIDE 12 · Pike State Forest APV Area, Short Loop "C" *

AT A GLANCE

Length/configuration: 1.5-mile loop. Mostly wide single-track.

Aerobic difficulty: Challenging due to steep climbs. The first one is especially brutal. Even my partner walked this one.

Technical difficulty: Moderate to challenging; surface has loose rock in spots, and there are some tough climbs.

Scenery: Mostly woods. There's a stretch immediately after leaving the Novice Area that runs along a little creek.

Special comments: This loop is slated for rebuilding. As it is, it's a brutal little gem with a brief warmup followed by a sobbing, gasping climb. It is another of the intermediate loops offered here; "intermediate" not because it's easier than the outer loop, but because it's shorter.

OH

Pike State Forest APV Area was designed for and built by motorcyclists. Motorized use is still common here, although there were few users present when we showed up. Traction was incredible in the dry conditions we enjoyed, although there were stretches of loose rock on a few of the climbs.

This trail has a really pretty section along a creek before things turn uphill and ugly. My partner and I both walked this climb. It was late in the day, and we'd already ridden the other two loops, but even if we'd attempted this right off, with fresh legs, we'd have been hoofing it.

If you go and ride all of it, there are two explanations: 1) you're a world-class rider with no body fat, genetically altered lungs, and pistons in your thighs. 2)

* Once again, my designation.

RIDE 12 · Pike State Forest APV Area, Short Loop "C"

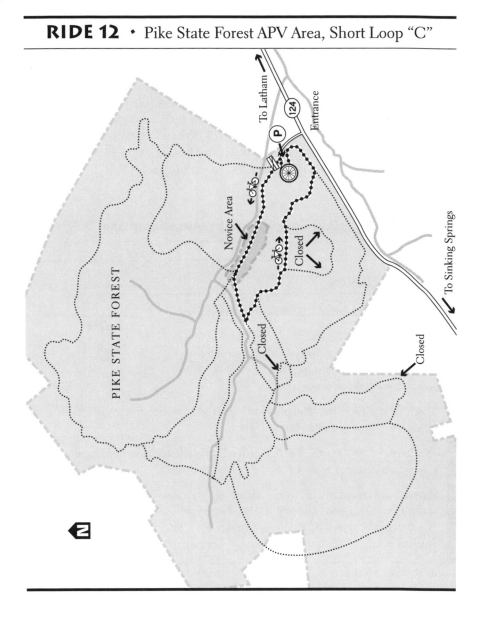

you've arrived after this trail has been reconfigured. As it is, the pitch is too steep. Erosion is a problem. The trail's slated to be rebuilt, with a much more mellow ascent.

General location: About 7 miles east of Sinking Springs on OH 124 in south central Ohio

Elevation change: Under 400 feet, but that comes all at once just before the halfway point. This trail is one huge climb, followed by a few smaller downs and ups, with a fast, fun descent at the end.

Joe Ernst catches his breath between a brutal climb and a white-knuckle descent.

Season: The area is closed December 1 through April 1. Traction can be a real problem when the trail is wet, so the dry season (late summer and early autumn) is best.

Services: There are convenience stores and minimal services in Latham and Sinking Springs. Get your water and whatever else you need before you arrive, as there are no services on site. The nearest bike shop is in Chillicothe.

Hazards: Way steep, and sometimes loose. The biggest hazard is the risk of going into cardiac arrest on the initial climb.

Rescue index: Don't ride alone, this place can be a ghost town. The nearest phone is in Latham.

Land status: State forest

Maps: From the state forest office; they're in need of (and in the process of) updating, so ask about any changes that may not appear on your copy.

Finding the trail: The area is on the north side of OH 124 about 7 miles east of Sinking Springs. Watch for signs at the entrance.

Sources of additional information:

Pike State Forest Office
334 Lapperell Road
Latham, OH 45646
(614) 493-2441

Notes on the trail: Start as you did with Loop B by going past the gate at the end of the parking area and into the APV Novice Area. At the end of the Novice Area, turn left at marker #8 (marker numbers are subject to change). (Where you went straight through the creek for Loop B, turn left for this loop.) You'll ride through a clump of trees, with a creek on your right. The trail will curve to the left, then bend back to the right. At that point, turn left. (This is the first left after leaving the Novice Area. It had marker #15 when we visited.) Climb like a monkey. Or a mule. Continue straight and descend to the parking area. Masochists may repeat.

RIDE 13 · Great Seal State Park, South Loop

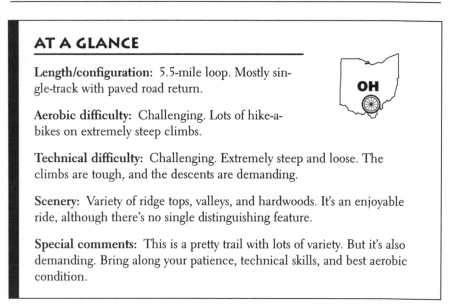

AT A GLANCE

Length/configuration: 5.5-mile loop. Mostly single-track with paved road return.

OH

Aerobic difficulty: Challenging. Lots of hike-a-bikes on extremely steep climbs.

Technical difficulty: Challenging. Extremely steep and loose. The climbs are tough, and the descents are demanding.

Scenery: Variety of ridge tops, valleys, and hardwoods. It's an enjoyable ride, although there's no single distinguishing feature.

Special comments: This is a pretty trail with lots of variety. But it's also demanding. Bring along your patience, technical skills, and best aerobic condition.

This is one of those trails grandfathered into the state's system. Horses and motorcycles had been going straight up and down the fall line for years. Little was done to make these into official trails when the time came. No grading or rerouting, just someone with a can of paint spraying blazes alongside the existing mess. The bad news: this is a brutal system to riders and to the environment. Knee-deep erosion gullies. Miles of loose rock.

The good news: it's a great place to hone technical skills. If you have a low frustration threshold (I'm guilty), this is not the trail for you. If, on the other hand, you're willing to concentrate and work hard, this trail will reward your deepest yearning for technical riding and climbing.

General location: 5 miles northeast of Chillicothe

Elevation change: Under 400 feet. You'll start with a paved climb with maybe

RIDE 13 · Great Seal State Park, South Loop

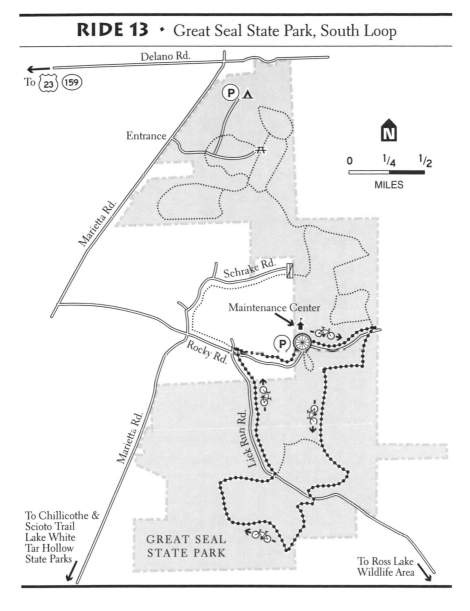

150 feet of elevation gain. After a flat stretch, you'll descend to Lick Run Road. Crossing the road, you'll climb about 400 feet to the top of Mount Ives. (It's not a real mountain, but it feels like it when you're climbing.) After you descend back to Lick Run Road, the only climbing that remains is on paved Rocky Road back to the parking lot.

Season: All year, depending on snow cover and mud, both of which are unreliable even in an "average" year. Refer to the general introduction. Your best bet is during the dry season of late summer to late fall.

Threading his way between boulders and trees, Joe Ernst sets up for the next descent.

Services: Everything, including bike shops, in Chillicothe. "Everything" means restaurants, shopping centers, grocery stores, hotels, and emergency medical care. Camping is available.

Hazards: Extremely steep and loose in spots. Other than that, nothing unusual.

Rescue index: Good; although Chillicothe is nearby, hedge your bets and ride with someone and/or take a phone.

Land status: State park

Maps: From the state park. Check with the people in Just North of Daytona bike shop in Chillicothe. They'll annotate your map for you. You may want to chuck the map and go riding with them.

Finding the trail: Take Bridge Street north from downtown Chillicothe to Marietta Street. Turn right. At the 4-way stop, turn right onto Rocky Road (there's a white clapboard church at this corner). Parking is at the state park lot about 1 mile up Rocky Road on the left. If you reach the crest of the hill on Rocky Road, you've gone too far.

Sources of additional information:

Great Seal State Park
825 Rocky Road
Chillicothe, OH 45601
(614) 773-2726

Better yet,

> Just North of Daytona bike shop
> 51 East Main Street
> Chillicothe, OH 45601
> (740) 775-7873

Even if you don't want or need advice, stop by and chat. Really nice people. By the way, these folks love the technically demanding nature of these trails and don't necessarily agree with my assessment of the quality of those trails. I see them as environmental nightmares; they see them as fun and challenging opportunities.

Notes on the trail: Leave the parking lot and continue ascending Rocky Road. At the top (about 0.5 mile), turn right onto the trail. (It's not the gravel road, but the single-track to the right of it.) You'll ride up a small swale, after which the radio towers will be on your left. At 1 mile, go straight, not right. (This is the first split you encounter on the trail.) At about 1.5 miles, you'll go straight down the hill. Be careful; this is a demanding, technical descent. At the bottom, follow the blazes. At about 2 miles, turn left onto Lick Run Road for about 50 yards, then right into the woods. (Watch for the blazes, although the trail is distinct and you won't miss it.) You'll begin climbing. The climb is gradual at first, then murder to the top of Mount Ives. At 3 miles you're on the ridge top. You'll get a break here on a fairly flat stretch before the descent back to Lick Run Road. This one is also tricky, so take your time and focus. Turn left on Lick Run to Rocky Road, then right back to the parking lot. If you loathe pavement, you can turn right on Lick Run Road instead and go back the way you came in. But remember that descent? Do you really want to shoulder your bike all the way to the top?

RIDE 14 · Great Seal State Park, North Loop

AT A GLANCE

Length/configuration: 8-mile loop. Mostly single-track with paved road return.

Aerobic difficulty: Challenging. Lots of hike-a-bike, both up and down. An aerobic downhill? Don't doubt it. Shouldering your bike down a quarter mile of talus on a 15% grade will have you huffing and puffing plenty.

Technical difficulty: Challenging. Extremely steep and loose. Not for the timid.

Scenery: Incredible variety: ridge tops, valleys, hardwoods, creek bottoms, rock formations, an abandoned roadbed.

Special comments: This ride is more demanding but also more scenic than the South Loop. Because the trail is so technical, this is a good place for platform pedals and hiking boots.

The North Loop is another of those trails grandfathered into the state's system. The bad news: this is a brutal system to riders and to the environment. Knee-deep erosion gullies. Miles of loose rock. Much as I admire the state of Ohio for opening up trails on many of its properties, I wonder about the wisdom here. In my opinion, the trail should be closed until sections of it can be rerouted or rebuilt.

But they don't care about my opinion, so the trail is open and legal to ride. If you think your technical ability is good, here's the litmus test. Challenge your buddies to see who can ride up (or down) the farthest without hopping off the bike. Navigating this loop is much tougher than the south loop.

This trail is a workout, but it rewards you with some stunning scenery—and the chance to be alone. We were startled by the voices of children playing near the north end of this loop. They were on the hiking trails across the creek. We hadn't seen another soul the whole time we were on the trail system (we did the south loop first), and the return of humanity was a bit jarring. Solitude is a nice feature for a trail.

General location: 5 miles northeast of Chillicothe

Elevation change: Under 400 feet. There's lots of incidental climbs, but the 2 toughest are to the top of Bald Hill and Sugarloaf Mountain. Both of these offer the full 400 feet of gain.

Season: All year, depending on snow cover and mud, both of which are unre-

RIDE 14 · Great Seal State Park, North Loop

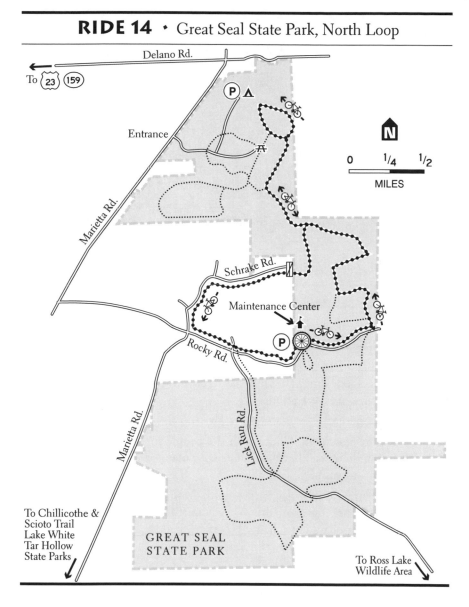

liable even in an "average" year. Refer to the general introduction. Your best bet is during the dry season of late summer to late fall. This also makes the creek crossings on the north end more manageable.

Services: Everything, including bike shops, in Chillicothe. "Everything" means restaurants, shopping centers, grocery stores, hotels, and emergency medical care. Camping is available.

Hazards: Extremely steep and loose in spots. Other than that, nothing unusual.

This trail is much steeper than the photo indicates, and every bit as technical as Joe Ernst's body position suggests.

Rescue index: Good; although Chillicothe is nearby, hedge your bets and ride with someone and/or take a phone.

Land status: State park

Maps: From the state park. Check with the people in Just North of Daytona bike shop in Chillicothe. They'll annotate your map for you. You may want to chuck the map and go riding with them.

Finding the trail: Take Bridge Street north from downtown Chillicothe to Marietta Street. Turn right. At the 4-way stop, turn right onto Rocky Road (there's a white clapboard church at this corner). Parking is at the state park lot about 1 mile up Rocky Road on the left. If you reach the crest of the hill on Rocky Road, you've gone too far.

Sources of additional information:

> Great Seal State Park
> 825 Rocky Road
> Chillicothe, OH 45601
> (614) 773-2726

Better yet,

> Just North of Daytona bike shop
> 51 East Main Street
> Chillicothe, OH 45601
> (740) 775-7873

Even if you don't want or need advice, stop by and chat. Really nice people. By the way, these folks love the technically demanding nature of these trails and don't necessarily agree with my assessment of the quality of those trails. I see them as environmental nightmares; they see them as fun and challenging opportunities.

Notes on the trail: Leave the parking lot and continue ascending Rocky Road. At the top (about 0.5 mile), turn left onto the trail. (It's directly across the road from the South Loop trailhead.) Go about 1 mile to the second left, which threads between several huge boulders. Begin a steep descent. At the T, turn right onto Old Shrake Road. It's closed to traffic. The pavement soon turns to dirt, then the trail goes left. Climb up over Bald Hill; at the bottom, veer right at marker "C." More descending—and good luck on this sketchy hill. At the bottom, turn right. You'll soon come to marker "B." Bear right to go up and over Sugarloaf Mountain. After descending Sugarloaf, go left at the T intersection (marker "A"). From there, retrace your route to marker "C," where you turn right and begin a descent (follow the blazes). At the end, turn right onto the remains of Shrake Road. Go over the barricade into the housing addition. At the first T, turn left. Follow this road to the 4-way stop at Rocky Road, where a left will take you back to the parking lot.

SCIOTO TRAIL STATE FOREST

Scioto Trail State Forest lies in the lower Scioto Valley. While this area was one of the first regions in Ohio to be settled, the hilly territory where the state forest is located saved it from agricultural development. After the Civil War, though, the area was heavily cut. Now this reforested region is a wonderful gem for some challenging mountain biking. Scioto Trail State Forest, just west of the Scioto River on the Allegheny Plateau, contains some rugged topography. The hills on some rides will test your endurance, but we've also thrown in a couple of beginner trails. This is a fun area to visit, and the inclusion of some easier rides means the whole family can play in the dirt. Also, there's free primitive camping during the annual mountain bike campout, usually the third weekend in June. Call the State Forest Service at (614) 663-2523 for more information.

Mountain biking is permitted on the bridle trail network that weaves throughout the forest. On some of these trails, you'll feel as if you're climbing forever, even though it may be only half an hour. Other rides are designed for those who would rather get a workout on the sparsely traveled forest roads— roads with spectacular views of the surrounding hills.

RIDE 15 · Scioto Trail State Forest—Bridle Trails

AT A GLANCE

Length/configuration: 34 miles of dirt trails, primarily out-and-backs.

Aerobic difficulty: Challenging. There isn't a single trail here that doesn't have a climb.

Technical difficulty: Easy to moderate

Scenery: Reforested woods, many hills but no sweeping vistas.

Special comments: Equestrians do not use Scioto Trail State Forest as much as they use other state parks, so you won't find too many horse divots here.

You're not likely to encounter the old tomahawk-carrying hermit who used to live in a cave in this forest—he died over 160 years ago—but you will find over 34 miles of trails available at Scioto Trail State Forest. The various bridle trails and hiking trails are open to mountain bikers. Most are out-and-backs, but if you combine them with the forest roads, you can create loops of varying length, depending on your tastes. Every trail will take you back to a road. The dirt trails are wide, but you will find a few obstacles. Overall, the trails don't require much in the way of technical ability. Your endurance will likely be tapped on a couple of rides that even local mountain bikers consider challenging, and inexperienced riders will walk their bikes quite a bit. Long Branch, for instance, can be especially tough. For 2.5 miles, you'll ride in a relatively flat area along a creek and a ridge, but the last half mile has a difficult climb. The Headquarters Trail has a lengthy uphill heading into Cutoff Road. There is now one three-quarter- mile nature trail open only to hikers and disabled people.

General location: Off Highway 23, 9 miles south of Chillicothe. If you're coming from Chillicothe, watch for signs and get in your left lane. The entrance requires a left turn off of US 23; the turn comes up soon after you crest a hill.

Elevation change: Between 300 and 400 feet of change on the bridle trails

Season: You can ride here all year, but the fall colors are particularly striking. The spring and the fall are busier, and spring can be wet and muddy.

Services: Camping is available. All services, including bike shops, restaurants, shopping centers, grocery stores, hotels, and emergency medical care can be found in Chillicothe.

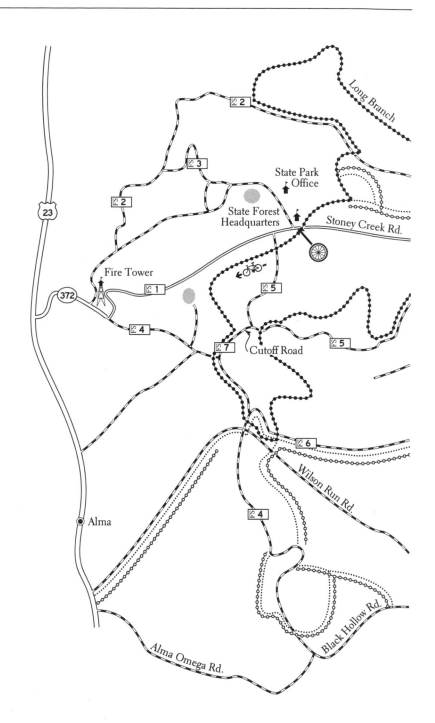

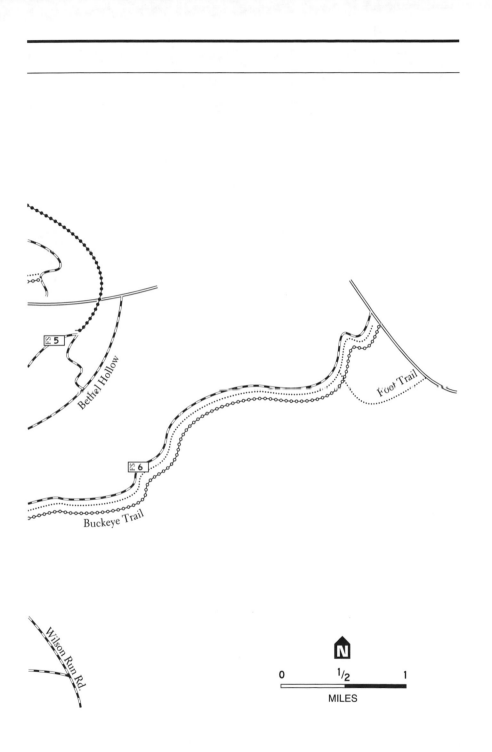

FS 5

Bethel Hollow

FS 6

Buckeye Trail

Foot Trail

Wilson Run Rd.

N

0   1/2   1

MILES

The bridle trails, with little horse traffic, make for a great mountain bike ride.

Hazards: Besides the usual trail obstacles, watch out for hikers and occasional equestrians.

Rescue index: The Forest Headquarters and the state park office are usually staffed. The area usually has enough visitors around to provide assistance. Chillicothe is the nearest source for medical care.

Land status: State forest. There is also a state park contained within the forest boundaries. The trails in the park have recently opened to bicycles.

Maps: You can get a map of the forest from the office and at the fire tower. The USGS 7.5 minute quad for Scioto Trail State Forest is Waverly North.

Finding the trail: From Chillicothe, take US 23 south about 9 miles. At State Highway 372, you'll see the entrance for Scioto Trail State Forest. Follow the signs to the park office and park there or, if you like, at any of the other parking areas you see. If you park at the office, you can begin your ride on the Headquarters Trail, right off Forest Service Road 1.

Sources of additional information:

Just North of Daytona bike shop
51 East Main Street
Chillicothe, OH 45601
(740) 775-7873

Scioto Trail State Forest
2731 Stoney Creek Road

Chillicothe, OH 45601
(740) 663-2523

Notes on the trail: The trails are marked and easy to follow, so you're not likely to get lost. Stick to the bridle paths. The Buckeye Trail also passes through Scioto Trail State Forest.

RIDE 16 · Scioto Trail State Forest—Forest Road 2

AT A GLANCE

Length/configuration: 8.5-mile loop of gravel and paved road.

OH

Aerobic difficulty: Moderate to challenging

Technical difficulty: Easy

Scenery: Stunning views of the surrounding hills.

Special comments: The scenery is magnificient all along this ride. Climb to the top of the fire tower for a panoramic picture of the forest.

If you're visiting Scioto Trail State Forest but you don't wish to ride the bridle trails there is an easier scenic ride. This route, traveling mostly along FS 2, contains spectacular vistas of the surrounding hills so gorgeous that they should be illegal. Many oaks, especially chestnut oaks, can be found along the ridges, and you may spot wild turkeys as well. Five miles of this 8.5-mile loop is gravel and fairly isolated. It should take the average rider about an hour and a half to make the trip. FS 2 winds to an elevation of roughly 300 feet before descending near the start of the Cemetery Bridle Trail. This isn't a technical ride, but it may require some endurance on the climb.

General location: Off US 23, 9 miles south of Chillicothe. If you're coming from Chillicothe, watch for signs and get in the left lane. The entrance requires a left turn off US 23; the turn comes up soon after you crest a hill.

Elevation change: The elevation change is around 300 feet.

Season: The fall colors in the panoramas you find will delight you.

Services: Camping is available. All services, including bike shops, restaurants, shopping centers, grocery stores, hotels, and emergency medical care in Chillicothe.

Hazards: Traffic is light on FS 2, so you won't find many hazards.

RIDE 16 · Scioto Trail State Forest / Forest Road 2

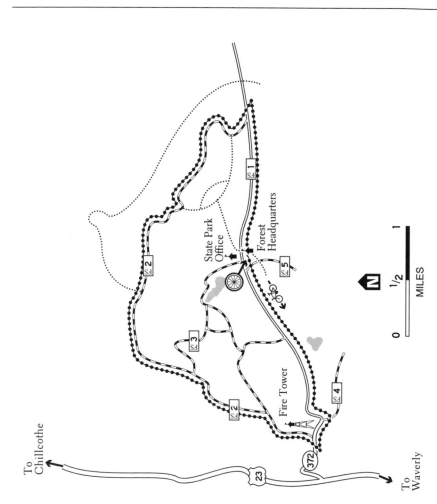

Rescue index: The Forest Headquarters and the state park office are usually staffed. You may be able to flag down the occasional car on FS 2, but the area is fairly remote.

Land status: State forest

Maps: You can get a map of the forest from the office and at the fire tower. The USGS 7.5 minute quad for Scioto Trail State Forest is Waverly North.

Finding the trail: From Chillicothe, take US 23 south for about 9 miles. At

Forest Road 2 provides many spectacular views of the hills in southern Ohio.

OH 372, you'll see the entrance for Scioto Trail State Forest. Follow the signs to the park office and park there.

Source of additional information:

Scioto Trail State Forest
2731 Stoney Creek Road
Chillicothe, OH 45601
(740) 663-2523

Notes on the trail: From the state park headquarters, turn right onto FS 1. This will intersect with OH 372 in 2 miles. Turn right at the "Forest Headquarters" sign. The gravel starts here, and the fire tower is located by the headquarters. Follow the gravel through the buildings and keep going on the one-way for 1.5 miles. At the intersection of FS 2 and FS 3, take FS 2 for 3.5 miles. When you get to FS 1, turn right and follow that back to your vehicle. The trail intersections have numbers marked on posts corresponding to the new courtesy map, which can be picked up at the fire tower and also at the Scioto Trail State Forest Trails office.

RIDE 17 · Scioto Trail State Forest, Trail "A" *

AT A GLANCE

Length/configuration: 10-mile loop; it's a mix of single- and double-track, gravel and paved roads.

Aerobic difficulty: Moderate, and challenging on the few steep climbs.

Technical difficulty: Challenging due to some very sketchy descents and some demanding single-track. Linking those sections are stretches deserving a pleasant "moderate" rating.

Scenery: Eastern hardwoods, pines, lakes, some stream crossings, a few nice overlooks.

Special comments: This route can be hard to follow, even with a map. There are lots of "social" (unofficial) trails. Getting really lost is unlikely, but making small, unintentional detours may be a problem. A demanding ride, but doable by most intermediate riders.

Buddy Joe and I rode a lot of good-to-great trails while visiting Ohio. This is the one for which I'll go back. Most of the climbs were rideable for me. (The bulk of my walking was done on the bridle trail at the beginning.) The lake is a nice feature. But what I liked best was the variety of scenery and trail type. There were tough climbs, creek bottoms, gradual climbs, technical descents, gentle single-track. I'd no sooner get tired of threading my way down a demanding drop than I'd be out on a paved road, climbing back to single-track. This trail packs more features into fewer miles than anything I've ridden in a long time. It compares favorably with the best trails in the Chattahoochee National Forest in northern Georgia, one of my all-time favorite places to ride.

Navigating is troublesome because of the number of social trails, but the problem is more of a nuisance than a threat. We detoured onto several of these trails and found they often paralleled the trail we wanted. To really deviate from the correct trail would require a deliberate move, like a sharp turn. Otherwise the worst you'll suffer is a momentary sidetracking.

General location: The entrance is off of US 23, about 9 miles south of Chillicothe. If you're coming from Chillicothe, watch for signs and get in the left lane. The entrance requires a left turn off of US 23; the turn comes up soon after you crest a hill.

Elevation change: 400 feet. The bridle path at the beginning has some short, intensely steep climbs, which are followed by a gradual climb—the only place

---

* My designation, it's not signed as such.

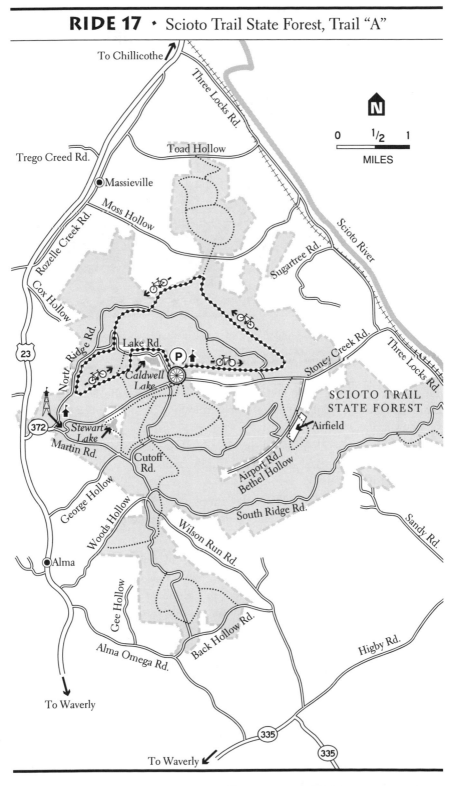

To Chillicothe

Three Locks Rd.

N

0   1/2   1
MILES

Trego Creed Rd.

Toad Hollow

Massieville

Moss Hollow

Scioto River

Rozelle Creek Rd.

Sugartree Rd.

Cox Hollow

North Ridge Rd.

Lake Rd.

Stoney Creek Rd.

Three Locks Rd.

P

Caldwell Lake

SCIOTO TRAIL
STATE FOREST

23

372

Stewart Lake

Airfield

Martin Rd.

Cutoff Rd.

George Hollow

Airport Rd./
Bethel Hollow

Sandy Rd.

Woods Hollow

South Ridge Rd.

Alma

Wilson Run Rd.

Gee Hollow

Back Hollow Rd.

Higby Rd.

Alma Omega Rd.

To Waverly

To Waverly

335

335

After cleaning this technical, demanding trail, Joe Ernst takes it easy beside the lake on the way back to the parking area.

you'll see the full 400 or so feet of gain. Then there's a long descent, with a paved-road climb (about 200 feet of gain). After that, it's single-track all the way back down.

Season: All year, weather permitting. Expect to see some mud after snow or rain in spring, but this area drains well, and the trails here can be ridden when others are still too muddy.

Services: Everything, including bike shops, in Chillicothe. "Everything" means restaurants, shopping centers, grocery stores, hotels, and emergency medical care. Camping is available.

Hazards: Generally demanding; watch out for hikers and equestrians.

Rescue index: Although this is a popular area, it's also large; ride with someone. The state park office has an outdoor pay phone. There's usually someone in that office during normal business hours. At other times, you may find help at the Forest Service office near the entrance. (It was on the left after you drove up the hill coming in.) Chillicothe is the nearest source for medical care.

Land status: State forest. There is also a state park contained within the forest boundaries. The trails in the park have recently opened to bicycles.

Maps: From the Forest Service. Be sure to get the Forest Service map, not the State Park Trail Guide, which is confusing and does not show the whole ride. The USGS 7.5 minute quad is Waverly North.

Finding the trail: Take the main road (FS 1/Stoney Creek) to the state park office on Lake Road. Park near the office or at Caldwell Lake. Ride Back to FS 1/Stoney Creek and turn left. The trail starts on the east side of the pole barn/equipment shed there (watch for blazes).

Sources of additional information:

Just North of Daytona bike shop
51 East Main Street
Chillicothe, OH 45601
(740) 775-7873

Scioto Trails State Park
144 Lake Road
Chillicothe, OH 45601
(740) 663-2125

Scioto Trail State Forest
124 North Ridge Road
Waverly, OH 45690-9513
(614) 663-2523

Notes on the trail: Follow the bridle trail. After a brief warmup, you'll begin a tough climb. After dropping down again, you'll cross FS 2. When the trail Ts into a double-track, go left onto a long climb. From this trail are a number of social trails, but the main trail is usually obvious because it's more well traveled. From the high point you'll do a sketchy descent to FS 2/North Ridge Road. Turn right. Follow the trail when it leaves FS 2/North Ridge Road and turns left back into the woods. Now comes a really white-knuckle, technical descent to FS 3/Lake Road. Turn right and climb.

Note: Lake Road is a one-way the other way; watch for traffic! Near the top of the climb, follow the trail left into the woods again. Bear left at the first fork, right at the second. This is a wonderful stretch of single-track; after the earlier technical single-track, this is a cruise through the woods by comparison. When you reach FS 3/Lake Road, turn right, then right again onto the trail behind the lake to return to the parking area.

RIDE 18 · Scioto Trail State Forest, Trail "B" *

AT A GLANCE

Length/configuration: (Approximately) 7-mile loop; it's a mix of single- and double-track, gravel and paved roads.

Aerobic difficulty: Moderate; this ride is designed so that nearly all of the climbing is done on pavement.

Technical difficulty: Moderate in most places, although the final descent has a few tricky spots.

Scenery: Eastern hardwoods, pines, a nice view of Stewart Lake and some ridge top overlooks.

Special comments: A somewhat less demanding ride than the Scioto "A," this one's good for intermediate riders. The highlight comes at the end on a long descent with just the right mix of speed and technical terrain.

One of the reasons Joe and I wanted to do this trail was because there was a lot of single-track on it. Surprise. Much of the early single-track had been closed. Not only was that trail closed but the trail that remained open took us up a tough climb. Worst of all, it bypassed Stewart Lake altogether. We decided to skip the remaining sections of that first piece of single-track and ride the road to start. The road is nice, but not fabulous—but we salvaged the single-track ride along the backside of the lake for later. It was a tough call, but we think the end result was a net gain. Want to do your own comparison? It's simple. To take the beginning section we did not do, go right on Stoney Creek Road from the parking area, then almost immediately left on FS 5. Take the first single-track to the right; it comes up within a quarter mile. Stay on this to the top. You'll join Cutoff Road there, and can follow the route we selected from that point.

General location: Entrance is off of US 23, about 10 miles southeast of Chillicothe. Watch for the signs. If you're coming from Chillicothe, watch for signs and get in the left lane. The entrance requires a left turn off of US 23, which comes up soon after you crest a hill.

Elevation change: You'll climb gently along the back of Stewart Lake. There's a stiff climb on (paved) Martin Road and some uphill on (gravel) Cutoff Road.

Season: All year, weather permitting. See the general introduction for a discussion on snow and mud. This area drains well, and little of the trail would be affected by rain, so this can be ridden when other area trails are still too muddy.

* Again, my designation.

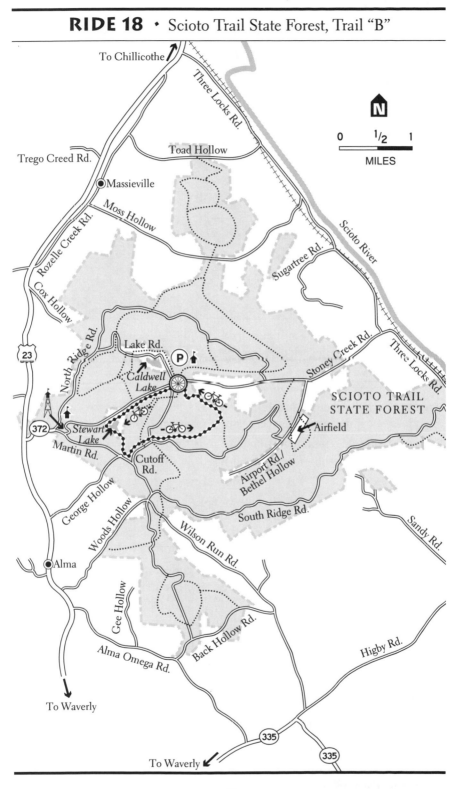

To Chillicothe

Three Locks Rd.

Trego Creed Rd.

Toad Hollow

N

0   1/2   1
MILES

Massieville

Moss Hollow

Rozelle Creek Rd.

Sugartree Rd.

Scioto River

Cox Hollow

Lake Rd.

P

North Ridge Rd.

Caldwell Lake

Stoney Creek Rd.

Three Locks Rd.

23

SCIOTO TRAIL
STATE FOREST

372

Stewart Lake

Martin Rd.

Cutoff Rd.

Airfield

Airport Rd./
Bethel Hollow

George Hollow

Woods Hollow

South Ridge Rd.

Sandy Rd.

Alma

Wilson Run Rd.

Gee Hollow

Back Hollow Rd.

Higby Rd.

To Waverly

Alma Omega Rd.

To Waverly

335

335

This is a great ride that ends with a singletrack descent that's fast, but not too fast, technical, but not too technical. Joe Ernst quotes Goldilocks when he proclaims it "Just right."

Services: Everything, including bike shops, in Chillicothe. "Everything" means restaurants, shopping centers, grocery stores, hotels, and emergency medical care.

Hazards: Nothing exceptional. When we rode this, there were quite a few hoof prints on the upper section near Cutoff Road, so you might watch for horses.

Rescue index: Although this is a popular area, it's also large; ride with someone. The state park office has an outdoor pay phone. There's usually someone in that office during normal business hours. At other times, you may find help at the Forest Service office near the entrance. (It was on the left after you drove up the hill coming in.) Chillicothe is the nearest source for medical care.

Land status: State forest. There is also a state park contained within the forest boundaries. The trails in the park have recently opened to bicycles.

Maps: Be sure to get the Forest Service map, not the State Park Trail Guide, which is confusing and does not show the whole ride.

Finding the trail: Take the main road (FS 1/Stoney Creek) to the state park office on Lake Road. Park near the office or at Caldwell Lake. Ride Back to FS 1/Stoney Creek and turn right. In about 0.75 mile, just before the road goes uphill, bear left into the parking lot. The trail starts from the end of the lot.

Sources of additional information:

Just North of Daytona bike shop
51 East Main Street

Chillicothe, OH 45601
(740) 775-7873

Scioto Trails State Park
144 Lake Road
Chillicothe, OH 45601
(740) 663-2125

Scioto Trail State Forest
124 North Ridge Road
Waverly, OH 45690-9513
(614) 663-2523

Notes on the trail: Follow the trail along the back of Stewart Lake. This is a really nice section of single-track of varying width. It's fairly flat, although you're climbing a bit. At the end, there's a short, steep, uphill kick to Martin Road. Turn left on Martin Road and go up the hill. Near the top, turn sharp left onto Cutoff Road. When the road forks, bear right onto Hatfield Road. Watch for the bridle trail, which comes up soon on your left. Follow the bridle trail from the ridge top. You'll be treated to a hugely fun descent back to Stoney Creek road. It's a mix of fairly tight, technical sections and fast, straight pieces. It's a bit steep in spots, but not white-knuckle steep. On a trail with lots of reasons to recommend it, this descent stands out as the highlight. Once you've landed on Stoney Creek Road, turn left, then right onto Lake Road to return to the parking area.

RIDE 19 · Scioto Trail State Forest, Trail "C" *

AT A GLANCE

Length/configuration: (Approximately) 2-mile loop; about half single-track, half open field and/or paved road.

Aerobic difficulty: Easy. There's a bit of climbing, but it's short and shallow.

Technical difficulty: Easy. All the mountain bike hazards are here — rocks, roots, creek crossings — but in their most benign forms.

Scenery: Eastern hardwoods, open fields (including an abandoned airstrip), some stream crossings.

Special comments: Though this isn't the right choice for someone riding off-road for the very first time, it would be a good choice for the beginner who wants just a little challenge.

* Again, my designation.

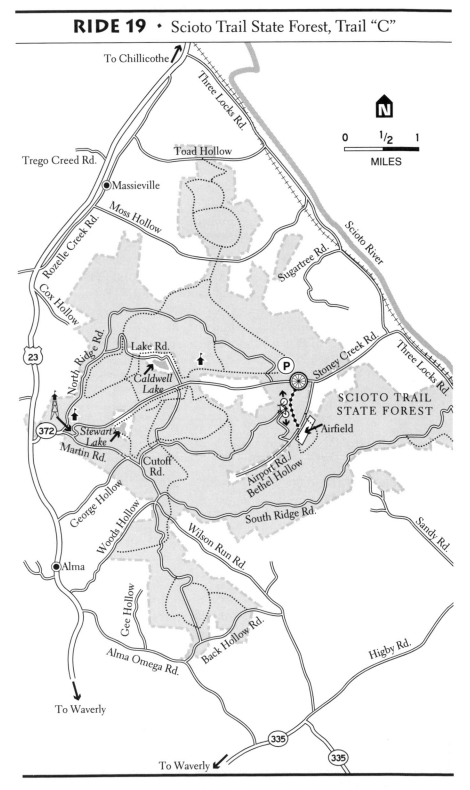

To Chillicothe

Three Locks Rd.

Toad Hollow

Trego Creed Rd.

Moss Hollow

Massieville

Rozelle Creek Rd.

Sugartree Rd.

Scioto River

Cox Hollow

N

0   1/2   1

MILES

North Ridge Rd.

Lake Rd.

Caldwell Lake

23

Stoney Creek Rd.

Three Locks Rd.

P

SCIOTO TRAIL
STATE FOREST

372

Stewart Lake

Airfield

Martin Rd.

Cutoff Rd.

Airport Rd./
Bethel Hollow

George Hollow

Woods Hollow

South Ridge Rd.

Sandy Rd.

Alma

Wilson Run Rd.

Gee Hollow

Back Hollow Rd.

Higby Rd.

Alma Omega Rd.

To Waverly

To Waverly

335

335

Here's a sweet little trail that will introduce a relative newcomer to all that mountain biking has to offer. An absolute first-timer may find it a bit challenging, while an accomplished rider like Joe Ernst will still have fun.

In this rugged part of Ohio, it's tough to find beginners' trails. This one qualifies. It's an excellent place for a beginner to work on skills beyond merely staying upright. There's a chance to practice on miniature versions of everything a rider might encounter on any trail. This isn't to say an intermediate rider should avoid this trail. Ratchet up the pace and what was a simple ride becomes much more demanding. In fact, local riders and racers warm up on this before going off to tackle more challenging terrain, such as Scioto Trail State Forest, Trail "A."

General location: Entrance is off of US 23, about 10 miles southeast of Chillicothe. If you're coming from Chillicothe, watch for signs and get in the left lane. The entrance requires a left turn off of US 23, which comes up soon after you crest a hill.

Elevation change: There's a little climb when you leave the old airstrip, some shallow rollers in the middle, a small drop to a creek, and an equally small climb back up out of the creek.

Season: Year-round, weather permitting. See the introduction for a discussion on snow and mud. The challenge after a rain would be the creek crossings, the worst one of which can be avoided by returning through the field instead of the road. The field itself gets pretty boggy when it's wet. None of this would prevent an intermediate rider from completing the loop, but it should be taken into account if this is the day you take a beginner for a ride.

Services: Everything, including bike shops, in Chillicothe. "Everything" means restaurants, shopping centers, grocery stores, hotels, and emergency medical care.

Hazards: There are a few shallow ravines There are also sections of rock and a few roots, but these show up mostly on flat, level stretches.

Rescue index: Although this is a popular area, it's also large; so ride with someone. This part of the forest gets less use than the rest. There are homes along Airport Road, and a volunteer fire department where you turn from Stoney Creek Road onto Airport Road. The state park office has an outdoor pay phone. There's usually someone in that office during normal business hours. At other times, you may find help at the Forest Service office near the entrance. (It was on the left after you drove up the hill coming in.) Chillicothe is the nearest source for medical care.

Land status: State forest. There is also a state park contained within the forest boundaries. The trails in the park have recently opened to bicycles.

Maps: Be sure to get the Forest Service map, not the State Park Trail Guide, which does not show this area.

Finding the trail: Follow FS 1/Stoney Creek all the way through the park. As you come out the other side, watch for Airport Road to the right (there's a volunteer fire department building on the left at the intersection). Turn right onto Airport Road. There's a pulloff and small parking area 0.5 mile up on the left.

Sources of additional information:

Just North of Daytona bike shop
51 East Main Street
Chillicothe, OH 45601
(740) 775-7873

Scioto Trails State Park
144 Lake Road
Chillicothe, OH 45601
(740) 663-2125

Scioto Trail State Forest
124 North Ridge Road
Waverly, OH 45690-9513
(614) 663-2523

Notes on the trail: Ride through the creek (or across the bridge), then go straight back, skirting the edge of the airfield. When you reach the far corner, bear right to continue following the perimeter. Take the third trail entrance into the woods; it has a bridle trail blaze on a Carsonite marker. You'll immediately begin a short climb. The trail soon levels out. This begins the best part of this loop. There are multiple shallow ravines, which are dry except right after a rain. There are sections of rocks and a little bit of roots. After less than a mile, the trail dips down, then angles right and climbs a bit. It drops again onto some wide single-track that will take you back to the old airstrip. Angle to the right (about a 30-degree angle, if that helps) across the field. You should be able to see where the trail crosses the field and where it breaks through the brush on the far side to cross the creek. If it's not clear, you can simply ride clockwise around the perimeter of the airfield until you find the creek crossing. Once there, you can cross the creek and return on the road. If the creek is too high or your beginner too timid, you can also continue along the edge of the airfield. Either option gets you back to your vehicle.

RIDE 20 · Scioto Trail State Forest, Trail "D" *

AT A GLANCE

Length/configuration: 1.2-mile out-and-back (0.6 miles each way); all single-track.

OH

Aerobic difficulty: Easy.

Technical difficulty: Easy.

Scenery: Eastern hardwoods.

Special comments: Someone astride a mountain bike for the first time can conquer this little gem and have a lot of fun in the process.

What a splendid little trail. It's perfect for kids or first-timers. It would also be the ideal place to convert a non–mountain biker into a rabid enthusiast. A borrowed bike and a trip or two across this trail will do the trick. Interestingly, it's also the only place I crashed while we were in Ohio. How? Joe and I were supposed to meet someone in Chillicothe and were running late, so I was really honking on this thing. My front tire washed out on a slight turn, and down I went. It's an example of how haste can overpower skill, even in the friendliest setting.

General location: Entrance is off of US 23, about 10 miles southeast of Chillicothe. If you're coming from Chillicothe, watch for signs and get in the left lane. The entrance requires a left turn off of US 23, which comes up soon after you crest a hill.

Elevation change: Minimal, probably not a total of 100 feet of climbing over the whole thing.

Season: Year-round, weather permitting. See the general introduction for a discussion on snow and mud. This loamy soil drains well, so the real consideration

* Again, my designation.

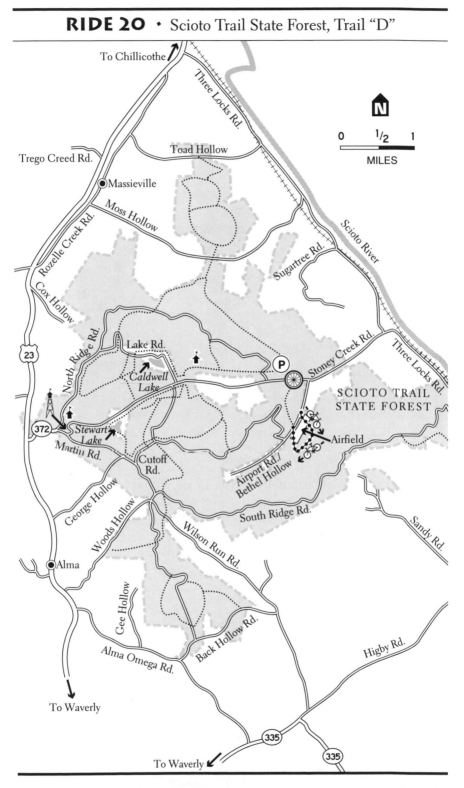

To Chillicothe

Three Locks Rd.

Toad Hollow

Trego Creed Rd.

Massieville

Moss Hollow

Rozelle Creek Rd.

Sugartree Rd.

Scioto River

Cox Hollow

23

North Ridge Rd.

Lake Rd.

Caldwell Lake

P

Stoney Creek Rd.

Three Locks Rd.

SCIOTO TRAIL STATE FOREST

372

Stewart Lake

Airfield

Martin Rd.

Cutoff Rd.

Airport Rd./ Bethel Hollow

George Hollow

Woods Hollow

South Ridge Rd.

Sandy Rd.

Wilson Run Rd.

Alma

Gee Hollow

Back Hollow Rd.

Higby Rd.

Alma Omega Rd.

To Waverly

335

335

To Waverly

N

0   1/2   1

MILES

whether your beginner is open to the idea of getting muddy. If not, wait a day for things to dry out.

Services: Everything, including bike shops, in Chillicothe. "Everything" means restaurants, shopping centers, grocery stores, hotels, and emergency medical care.

Hazards: A few little roots and rocks; enough to give a rank beginner the feel of mountain biking without being intimidated.

Rescue index: Although this is a popular area, it's also large; ride with someone. Just up the road from this trail's start point is a volunteer fire department, although there's rarely anyone there. The state park office has an outdoor pay phone. There's usually someone in that office during normal business hours. At other times, you may find help at the Forest Service office near the entrance. (It was on the left after you drove up the hill coming in.) Chillicothe is the nearest source for medical care.

Land status: State forest. There is also a state park contained within the forest boundaries. The trails in the park have recently opened to bicycles.

Maps: From the Forest Service. Be sure to get the Forest Service map, not the State Park Trail Guide, which does not show this area.

Finding the trail: Follow FS 1/Stoney Creek all the way through the park. As you come out the other side, watch for a parking area on the left before you get to Airport Road. Right across Stoney Creek Road from the parking area, the trail goes into the woods. (The parking area has a creek on one side.)

Sources of additional information:

Just North of Daytona bike shop
51 East Main Street
Chillicothe, OH 45601
(740) 775-7873

Scioto Trails State Park
144 Lake Road
Chillicothe, OH 45601
(740) 663-2125

Scioto Trail State Forest
124 North Ridge Road
Waverly, OH 45690-9513
(614) 663-2523

Notes on the trail: Ride across Stoney Creek Road. The trail starts with a little dip, then a quick rise. It has numerous gentle turns around trees and rocks. Eventually it turns hard left and brings you out to Airport Road. (Across the road from this point is the parking area for Ride 15.) Turn around and head back.

RIDE 21 · Hocking Technical College

AT A GLANCE

Length/configuration: Your choice. We did 12 miles in a pattern like the veins in a leaf, with numerous spurs and some backtracking. It's easy to put together 10 or 15 miles from this jumbled mass of trail spaghetti.

Aerobic difficulty: Moderate, except that the initial climb from the saddle barn is kind of tough. You can make the whole thing tough by repeatedly going up and down the ridges, or do as we did and make it mostly easy by staying on the ridge tops.

Technical difficulty: Moderate with a few loose or rocky parts. Intermittent tree roots. Otherwise, these trails would rate an "easy."

Scenery: Eastern hardwoods and a tiny college campus

Special comments: Two caveats—park only where it's clearly legal to do so (marked as "Visitors Parking"), and *do not* ride the walking trails. How can you tell if a trail is a walking trail? They're usually wide, signed, smooth, and have stairs at the ups and downs.

I hesitated to include this trail system. It doesn't meet the usual criteria. It's not an "official" mountain bike facility, although riding is permitted on the horse trails. No maps exist, and describing a route would be futile since new trails are formed almost weekly while others are abandoned. But I'd heard good things about the area and decided to come and give it a try. If I felt the fun factor outweighed the other, negative elements, I'd include this trail in the book. As you can see, the fun won.

This is the kind of riding we did when we were kids. No maps. No markers. No big plans or goals. Just a bunch of yelling juveniles having fun in the woods. Our reward was an afternoon of simple fun and occasional surprises, like the old oil well.

General location: Just outside Nelsonville, which is about 15 miles northwest of Athens

Elevation change: With some planning and a willingness to double back occasionally, you can escape the steepest uphills everywhere but at the initial climb. The remaining occasional climbs are mostly short and gain only 50 feet or so of elevation. Of course, if you're a masochist or racer in training, you can go up and down until your lungs burst.

RIDE 21 · Hocking Technical College

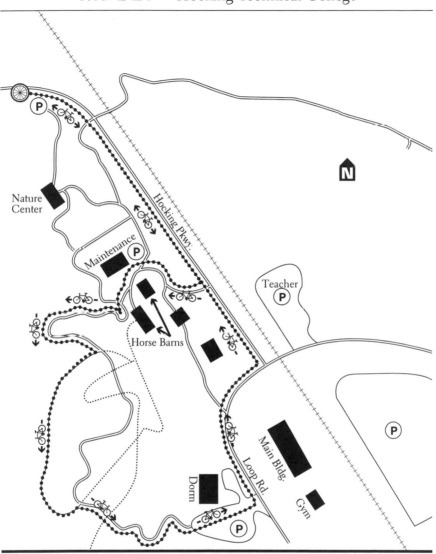

Season: Year-round, weather permitting. See the general introduction for a discussion on snow and mud. Joe and I rode on a weekend during school, but saw few other users. On the other hand, the school has the trails for their use, so you may want to call ahead and confirm that there's not another activity—horseback riding classes or a mountain bike race—going on when you want to visit.

Services: Convenience stores, motels, groceries, and such in Nelsonville. The nearest bike shop is in Athens.

Once away from the saddle barns, Joe Ernst finds solitude and easy cruising.

Hazards: Getting lost is a risk, since virtually nothing is marked. Just keep in mind which direction it is back to the campus, and you'll be okay.

Rescue index: Few folks venture far from the horse barns, so don't ride alone. In the event of an emergency, head to the security office, located beside the bookstore, in front of John Light Hall.

Land status: Mixed; mostly college property with some that belongs to the county.

Maps: The college has a map showing the horse and walking trails, but that's only about 10% of the trail inventory here.

Finding the trail: Enter the college by Hocking Parkway from OH 691. (That intersection is immediately south of the bridge over the Hocking River, and less than 0.25 mile south of US 33.) Follow the Hocking Parkway over the railroad tracks, past the horse barns, to the parking area for the Nature Center. (Wherever you decide to park, make sure it is plainly labeled as public parking.) Ride back and between the 2 horse barns. The trail starts where the road ends.

Sources of additional information: None. The college people we talked to, from students to a security guard to someone in administration, were clueless about mountain biking on these trails. The one thing they all confirmed is that it is legal.

Notes on the trail: The climb from the horse barns is steep, and made unpleasant by abundant hoof divots and occasional piles of manure. But it didn't take long in this network for the horse traffic to disperse, and soon a hoof print or road apple was a rarity. We climbed to the top on the trail from the horse barns, then veered right. We stayed on the ridge top, exploring maybe a dozen side trails. At one point we encountered a paved road, so we turned around and went back. Our return required some backtracking, although less than we'd expected. We weren't sure how far we had to go back before heading down. As it happened, we overshot the most direct trail and came down some technical single-track behind the Hocking Heights residence hall. From there, we rode the road back to the parking area.

WAYNE NATIONAL FOREST

If you want some truly challenging riding, head out to the Ironton District of Wayne National Forest. This national forest consists of two districts and one unit. Each has its own policies regarding mountain bike usage. Here at the Ironton District and at the Athens District, mountain bikes are not permitted on the hiking trails. That's okay. They are permitted on the off-road vehicle (ORV) trails. Trust me: these trails will keep you occupied. Former astronauts John Glenn and Neil Armstrong are from Ohio, and it wouldn't suprise me at all if they both came to the Ironton area to train for the rigors of spaceflight. Hanging Rock will throw steep downhills, moguls, curves, and ruts at you—the whole nine yards. Pine Creek, though a little easier, is still nothing to brush aside. Because of the ORV use, the trails are fast—at least on downhills and straightaways. The uphill climbs are a different matter.

Wayne National Forest, located in southeastern Ohio, is the hilliest region described in this book. Located in the foothills of the Appalachian Mountains, the forest does not have the long, 1,000-plus foot climbs and descents you'll find in central Appalachia, but for those who like to tackle shorter climbs and rapid descents, this is the place.

Another thing you'll appreciate about all three areas of Wayne National Forest is the remoteness. While trails in other parts of the state are populated by various user groups, on my mid-week trip to these trails I found little use, even by ORVs. This is truly a place of hidden treasures.

RIDE 22 · Pine Creek ORV Trail

AT A GLANCE

Length/configuration: 40-mile out-and-back ORV trail.

Aerobic difficulty: Moderate

Technical difficulty: Moderate to challenging

Scenery: Deciduous forest

Special comments: The area is remote, so don't go it alone.

This 20-mile one-way (40 miles total) out-and-back ORV trail is excellent for those who enjoy cycling on ORV trails but aren't up to the challenges of Hanging Rock. And this trail is good for that beginning hammerhead who wants to hone those technical skills. Similar to Hanging Rock, this trail requires some skills for the moguls, tire ruts, gullies, and loose dirt. The average mountain biker, though, will find this trail doable and will have fun hammering down the hard-packed, wide trail. You'll encounter about six hills to test your endurance. On the trip, you'll see rock ledges and shelters as well as a bridge over Pine Creek.

The trail branches at a **Y** intersection, and you have your choice of heading to either the Lyra or Wolcott trailhead. Since the climb out of either trailhead is steep, take your choice, but be warned that the Wolcott branch is longer. You'll hit splashes of pine in this otherwise deciduous forest. Also, keep your eyes and ears peeled for wild turkey and the occasional bear. There have been rare reports of bears in the area, so consider yourself extremely lucky (or unlucky) if you get the chance to see one.

General location: Wayne National Forest, 22 miles north of Ironton

Elevation change: The overall elevation change is about 300 feet.

Season: The spring and fall colors are pleasing, and the temperatures are more moderate then.

Services: Bring your own water. Camping is available at Lake Vesuvius Recreational Area. Food and lodging are available in Ironton. Huntington, West Virginia, has bike service.

Hazards: Look out for ORVs on the trail as well as tire ruts and loose dirt.

Rescue index: This area is isolated and receives few visitors. State Highway 93 has traffic, but of course, the further you ride down the trail, the further away it is.

Land status: Wayne National Forest—Ironton Ranger District

RIDE 22 • Pine Creek ORV Trail

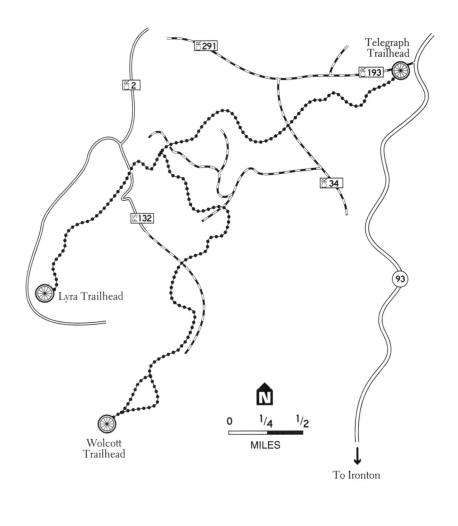

Maps: The Ironton Ranger District has a map for this trail. Write for one at the address below. The USGS 7.5 minute quads covering this area are Pedro, South Webster, and Gallia for the trailhead.

Finding the trail: From Ironton, take OH 93 north for 23 miles. You'll see a sign for Off Road Vehicle Trailhead—Telegraph. Turn left there onto County Road 193 (not identified). Go ⅛ mile and you'll see the parking area on your left. The marked trailhead is on the right side of the parking area.

Riding through the pines provides a refreshing change from the moguls and gullies.

Source of additional information:

Ironton Ranger District
Route 2, Box 203
Pedro, OH 45659
(740) 532-3223

Notes on the trail: The trail is marked with brown carsonite signs. However, the Forest Service does have a problem with people vandalizing signs, and there are several user-made trails that might confuse you. Therefore, you might wish to carry a topo map and a compass. Please stick to the designated route and stay off the user-made trails.

RIDE 23 · Hanging Rock ORV Trail

AT A GLANCE

Length/configuration: 9 ORV trails, totaling 26 miles.

Aerobic difficulty: Everything from easy to challenging.

Technical difficulty: Again, everything from easy to challenging, but far more trails approach the "challenging" designation than the "easy." Expect steep downhills, moguls, curves, and ruts.

Scenery: Some areas have nice river views.

Special comments: The trails are well marked and even coded to their difficulty level.

There are 26 miles of ORV trails to tackle at Hanging Rock—and "tackle" isn't a strong enough word. I warmed up on Gas Well, one of the easiest trails, enjoying the speed I could attain on the hard-packed trail. But later as I was riding Copperhead, a more difficult trail, I had to stop for a moment to remove my heart from my mouth and put it back where it belongs. The trail contains a steep downhill with several obscene moguls, curves, and ruts. You'll need to borrow technical skills to make it through this area, as it could be dangerous. Ride this only if you know what you're doing! If you're nervous, portage. When you see a sign that says "hill" and shows a curvy arrow, believe it. As you make your way down that hill, somewhere in the back of your mind, you know there's going to be an equally hard uphill.

Copperhead is just one of the nine trails that blanket the area. Since the trails are designed for ORV use, they are wide and you can pick up speed on many of them. But beware of potholes, ruts made by ORVs, and washouts. Also, this is southern Ohio, so flatlanders take care: you will need to climb hills. Multiple loop options are available to you as the trails connect to one another, so feel free to make a short loop or a long one. There are trails for all ability levels, but most of them are designated "moderate." Hanging Rock, the trail that gives this area its name, is one of the steepest trails, especially on its west and east ends. As a general rule, as you approach a bridge, expect a downhill followed by an uphill. Where Copperhead leaves High Knob, you'll get a nice view of the river. This is a great area to spend the day. Bring a map and plenty of water, and have at it.

General location: Wayne National Forest, about 10 miles north of Ironton

Elevation change: You'll experience about 300 feet of elevation change at Hanging Rock.

RIDE 23 · Hanging Rock ORV Trail

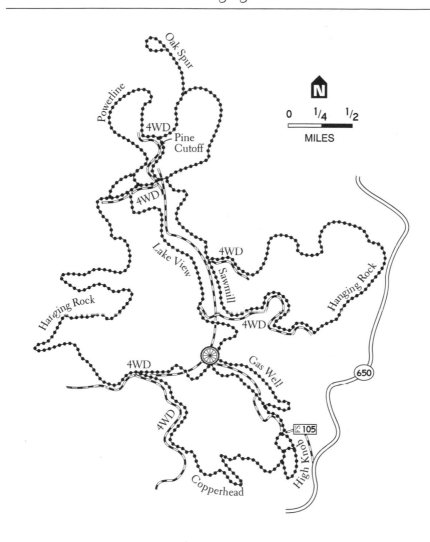

Season: Late September is a good time because the mornings and evenings are cool, and the days are warm. On weekdays, few people are around, but on weekends, it can get crowded.

Services: Bring your own water. Camping is available at Lake Vesuvius Recreational Area. Food and lodging are available in Ironton. Huntington, West Virginia, has bike service.

Hazards: Of course, keep an ear out for ORVs. Sections of the trail have potholes, tire ruts, and occasional rocks. Be careful on washouts where the ORVs

You'll need all your concentration on the fast downhills.

have torn up the hardpack; this stuff is like riding through a patch of sand and you may lose your traction.

Rescue index: The area is remote. You might pass a rare vehicle on Forest Service Road 105; OH 650 is busier.

Land status: Wayne National Forest—Ironton Ranger District

Maps: The Ironton Ranger District has an adequate map of this area. Write to the address below. The USGS 7.5 minute quad is Ironton.

Finding the trail: From Highway 52 and OH 650 north of Ironton, take OH 650 north for 0.75 mile. Just before a coal tipple, turn left on FS 105. Go 1.5 miles to the trailhead.

Source of additional information:

Ironton Ranger District
Route 2, Box 203
Pedro, OH 45659
(740) 532-3223

Notes on the trail: From the trailhead, you have 2 choices. You can go back up the road a bit to where Gas Well and Hanging Rock cross each other. Start with Gas Well if you like, or go with the more difficult Hanging Rock.

WAYNE NATIONAL FOREST—
ATHENS DISTRICT AND
ZANESVILLE

The Athens District of Wayne National Forest has only one area open to mountain bikes: Monday Creek Off-Road Vehicle Area. As with the Ironton District, hiking trails are off-limits, but Monday Creek, with over 70 miles of trails, will more than satisfy your mountain biking appetite. "Ohio" is Iroquois for "something great," and you'll be muttering "Ohio, Ohio, Ohio!" on these trails. Its reputation as one of the top spots for dirt bike riding in the country should tell you something about what you can expect for our less motorized sport. Monday Creek still has relatively little mountain bike use, though dirt bikers frequently ride in this fabulous area. Unlike the conflicts between equestrian groups and mountain bikers, I haven't found similar tensions with dirt bikers. Obviously, it's a lot easier for a cyclist to hear an oncoming dirt bike than it is for an equestrian to hear a mountain bike. If you want more privacy, stay away on the weekends, when the dirt bikers are more prevalent. The area, though, is vast, and you're not likely to meet many other users.

Heading out of Wayne National Forest to the north and east, you'll find several rides for bikers of differing abilities. On the northern border of the forest is Perry Trail Campground, a private campground popular with horses; it will give those beginning and intermediate riders a good experience. Perhaps one of the most challenging areas I've found is a trail on private property south of Zanesville. Zanesville was the hometown of the famous adventure writer Zane Grey, and riding the trails at Tom Hayes Farm is definitely a thrill. While the trails in the ORV areas are formidable, the narrowness of the trails here tests mountain bikers of all abilities with equal ferociousness.

Not wanting to be responsible for "challenge overload," I'll add that the final trail in this section slows things down a bit. Ohio Power Recreation Land, a popular fishing and camping area, contains several gravel roads perfect for catching your breath.

Ridden hard or easy, the trails in Wayne National Forest and the Zanesville area offer some of the best mountain biking options in the state.

Thanks to Scott Williams for information about Monday Creek ORV Area, and Dan German for information about Perry Trail Campground and Tom Hayes Farm.

RIDE 24 · Monday Creek ORV Area

AT A GLANCE

Length/configuration: Over 70 miles of wide, hard-packed ORV trails.

Aerobic difficulty: Moderate

Technical difficulty: Moderate to challenging

Scenery: Thick forests, some historic kiln structures, and a waterfall — though it's not visible from the trail.

Special comments: The trails are marked, but there have been problems with vandals stealing the signs, so keep a topo map with you.

Serious mountain bikers will love the ORV trails in the Monday Creek area. Scott Williams, the owner of Camp Ohio, puts it succinctly and elegantly when he says, "There are a lot of whoop-de-doos here — some jumps where you can get some air time." Over 70 miles of trails run throughout this area, a whole network of which can be found in the Dorr Run section. The trails are wide and hard-packed, but they are challenging. In fact, *Dirt Wheels*, a major dirt bike magazine, rated this area in the top ten in the nation for dirt bike riding. So imagine what that must mean for mountain bikers! You'll have to match your wits against fallen logs, rocks, moguls, gullies, tire ruts, mud, gas pipelines (don't ride on them), steep climbs, and whatever else Mother Nature can think of to throw at you.

The area has a lot of history and scenery as well. You'll find strip pits off the trail, especially on the Main Corridor. There is a waterfall in the Dorr Run area, but you won't be able to see it from the trail. This region was once home to the world's largest brickyard with the first continuous kiln, and you may find evidence of this on the trails. (I found a few bricks half buried in the dirt here and there.) Off the trail, there are still remants of a kiln south of the New Straitsville area.

If you ride in the winter, you'll get to see some sites off the trail that you can't spot through the summer foliage, including old gas wells, shacks, foundations, sand dug wells, and caves. You may also see steam rising from underground vents.

Rock cliffs are one of many fascinating features found at Monday Creek.

The three-mile New Straitsville loop is the easiest section, but it gets increasingly difficult as you make your way down the Main Corridor. The most challenging section is Long Ridge, but Snake Hollow and Dorr Run can get complex, too. Dorr Run has steep ridges and good climbs. Monday Creek contains thick forests full of turkey, deer, woodchuck, grouse, and beaver. This area is a good place to spend a few days camping and riding. Carry a topo map and a compass and plan to get lost.

General location: Wayne National Forest, about 15 miles northwest of Athens.

Elevation change: Although the elevation ranges only between 800 and 1,000 feet, the climbs you find are steep.

Season: October, with its fall colors, is a good time to ride. Also, mountain bikers might wish to come out on the weekdays to avoid the many dirt bikers on the weekends.

Services: Bring your own water. You'll find a phone in New Straitsville, and all services are available in Athens. There are 2 campgrounds off State Highway 595 near the trails. I found the folks at Camp Ohio to be quite friendly and helpful.

Hazards: Look out for the steep climbs, ruts, and other obstacles noted above. Watch out for ORV users, too.

Rescue index: Some of the sections are remote, but you're likely to find traffic on OH 595, OH 278, Highway 33, and County Road 24.

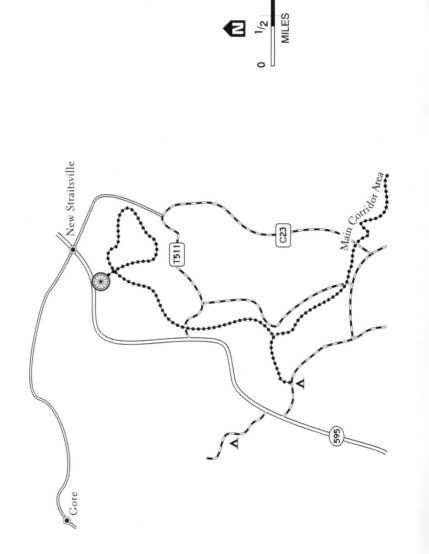

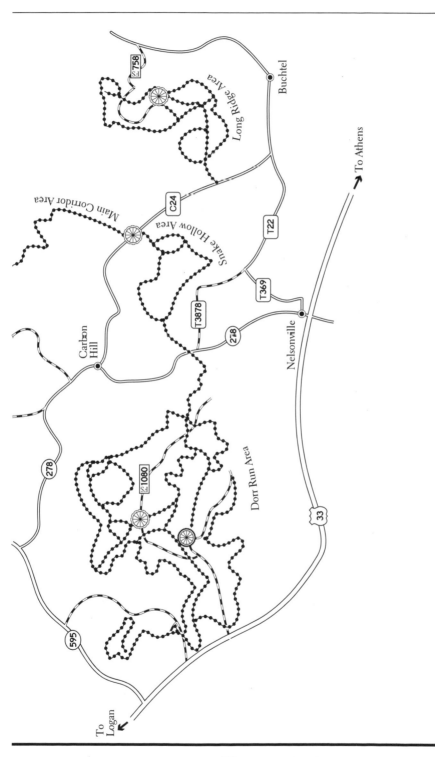

Land status: Wayne National Forest—Athens Ranger District

Maps: The Athens Ranger District has a map of the area with topographical markings. Write to the address below to get one. The USGS 7.5 minute quads for this area are Gore, New Straitsville, Union Furnace, and Nelsonville.

Finding the trail: For the New Straitsville Trailhead: From US 33, take OH 595 north. Go about 8.5 miles and you'll see the sign for the New Straitsville trailhead. As you begin your ride, you'll see a sign marked "MC" for the Main Corridor. Go a bit further and you'll come to the entrance for the 3-mile loop.

For the Dorr Run Trailhead: At the junction of US 33 and OH 595, go south on US 33 for 1.5 miles. Turn left at the sign for the Dorr Run Trailhead. In 1.3 miles, you'll come to an intersection where you can go straight or branch off to the left. Head straight to the additional parking sign and in another 0.5 mile, you'll find a parking area and a sign for the Dorr Run Loop. If you like, you can take the left branch to another parking area.

Sources of additional information:

Athens Ranger District
219 Columbus Road
Athens, OH 45701
(740) 592-6644

Camp Ohio
12063 Gore-Greendale Road
Logan, OH 43138
(740) 753-2303

Notes on the trail: The trails are marked with their level of difficulty. From the Dorr Run trailhead, you can follow the outer perimeter loop marked by brown signs with blue stickers. This will give you a 15-mile ride. Vandals stealing signs is a problem, so be aware of missing signs. Some of these areas are isolated; ride with a companion.

RIDE 25 · Perry Trail Campground

AT A GLANCE

Length/configuration: 11-mile loop of single- and double-track trails with some spurs.

Aerobic difficulty: Moderate

Technical difficulty: Moderate

Scenery: Pine-and-oak forest, some ponds, and the remains of an old coal mining operation.

Special comments: Nearby New Lexington, a historic coal mining town, makes an interesting side trip.

OH

Beginner and intermediate mountain bikers will like this 11-mile loop located in the Perry Trail Campground. The single-track and double-track trails form a loop with a few spurs and are wide and well maintained. Consequently, there arc only a few ditches and moguls to worry about. The few climbs and descents are not too difficult, especially since the trail surface is smooth. You'll even find one stream crossing, and you'll pass several ponds along the trail. Also, you might come across a few scenic high walls from an old coal-mining operation. The woods are mainly pine forest and white oak, and you're likely to see many spots where the beavers have redesigned the trees.

General location: Off OH 345, 3.5 miles north of New Lexington

Elevation change: There are some hills, but nothing dastardly.

Season: The summer and fall, when the ground is drier, are best. In June, there are several scheduled events for horse riders.

Services: Camping is available at Perry Trail Campground, but bring your own water. For bike service, go to The Wheel and Spoke Bike Shop in Zanesville.

Hazards: Be aware of horses, especially coming around blind turns. The horse tracks shouldn't be a problem since the trails are often groomed.

Rescue index: There are several roads in the area where you could flag down traffic. You'll also find a clear-cut where a buried gas pipeline runs. Follow the clear-cut to Possum Run Road, which will take you to OH 345. From there, it's less than a mile back to the campground.

Land status: Private property. The day fee is $2.50 to use the trails. If you camp here, trail use is included with the camping fee.

Maps: The USGS 7.5 minute quad map is New Lexington.

RIDE 25 • Perry Trail Campground

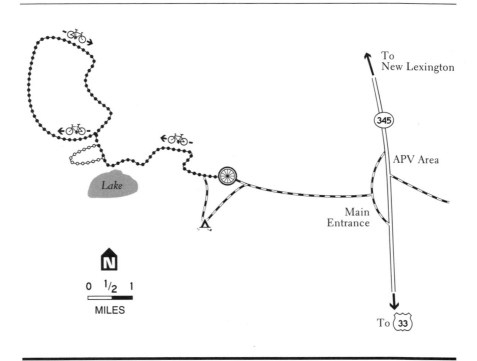

Finding the trail: From Interstate 70 and OH 13, take OH 13 south about 15 miles into New Lexington. Take a left in New Lexington at the traffic light onto OH 345. Take OH 345 north for 3.5 miles to the campground. The folks at the campground will direct you to the trailhead.

Sources of additional information:

Perry Trail Campground
5200 State Route 345 NE
New Lexington, OH 43764
(740) 342-0601

Wheel and Spoke Bike Shop
634 Main Street
Zanesville, OH 43701
(740) 453-3438

Notes on the trail: The trail is well marked. The markings will be on your left side going out and your right side coming back. The main loop is blazed in orange. Pink blazes will take you down the more difficult spurs and blue blazes will take you to the ponds (if you want to water your bike with the horses).

WAYNE NATIONAL FOREST—ATHENS DISTRICT AND ZANESVILLE **99**

RIDE 26 · Tom Hayes Farm

AT A GLANCE

Length/configuration: 6.5-mile dirt loop with several spurs.

Aerobic difficulty: Challenging

Technical difficulty: Challenging

Scenery: Hardwood forest inhabited by coyote, deer, and game birds.

Special comments: Take spurs seriously. If you're only pretty sure you're experienced enough, or are having an off ride, don't go there.

OH

"This is training ground for West Virginia," says Tom Hayes, owner of the land on which this trail is found. I've never ridden in West Virginia, but I think I have an idea of what he means. Dan German, a local mountain bike racer, explains the ride more simply: "It's really hard, one of the most difficult in the state." This I understand. In fact, I don't mind telling you that I took the worst spill I've ever had here at Tom Hayes Farm—but I enjoyed the ride anyway. The elevation increases about 400 feet on this fast course, requiring strong technical ability and stamina to pedal up long and steep hills, jump ditches (I can still feel my ribs ache), fly over moguls, and avoid rocks and ruts. You'll fight to keep your balance on sections where the trail is off camber along the hillside. No wonder this place is a popular spot for local mountain bike races.

The main loop is for those who know what they're doing, but the spurs off the main loop are for those who know even more. For instance, in one spot on the main trail, you'll see a cutoff for the experts at the bottom of a steep hill. If you take that, you'll need to hike-a-bike in spots where the trail is only a foot wide and drops four feet straight down. Then you'll ride up a creek bed of loose shale before hitting another hike-a-bike section up a steep ravine. Of course, if you have wings, you won't need to do this part.

The area has historical significance as well. From an overlook on the trail, you'll be able to see the kiln fire walls of an old coal-burning power plant that supplied all the power from Columbus to Kentucky, as well as a little of Indiana and West Virginia. In fact, the plant is listed in German archives as a bombing site in World War II. There are also a few Indian mounds toward the end of the trail. In the fall when the leaves are down, you can see the churches and buildings of the small town of Philo.

Bear tracks have been spotted out here, but not the bears. However, you are likely to spy coyote, deer, grouse, and pheasant among the buckeye, hickory, white oak, blue gum, elm, ash, and maple trees.

Dan won't have time to relax after fighting this uphill climb. On the other side, the fast downhill will throw a series of ditches at him.

General location: Off OH 60, 10.5 miles south of I-70 in Zanesville.

Elevation change: The elevation begins around 830 feet and gains between 350 and 400 feet.

Season: The fall is a nice time to ride; the weather is cooler and the leaves are starting to turn. When the leaves are down, you'll get a better view of the towns of Philo and Duncan Falls.

Services: Bring your own water. Blue Rock State Park and Campground is located 6 miles away and offers swimming, hiking, and limited biking. All services can be found in Zanesville. For bike service, check out The Wheel and Spoke Bike Shop or Southside Cycle at 2924 Maysville Pike.

Hazards: The numerous rocks, ruts, ditches, and moguls will definitely challenge your technical skills.

Rescue index: Make your way to OH 60 and flag someone down. The town of Duncan Falls is only 1 mile away.

Land status: Private property. Before you ride, please check with The Wheel and Spoke Bike Shop about current availability. You ride at your own risk!

Maps: Since the trail is recent and likely to vary as the local riders work on it, you're best bet is to contact The Wheel and Spoke Bike Shop. The USGS 7.5 minute quad for this area is Philo.

Finding the trail: From the intersection of I-70 and OH 60 in Zanesville, take OH 60 south for 9.5 miles. After you pass the turn-off for Blue Rock State Park

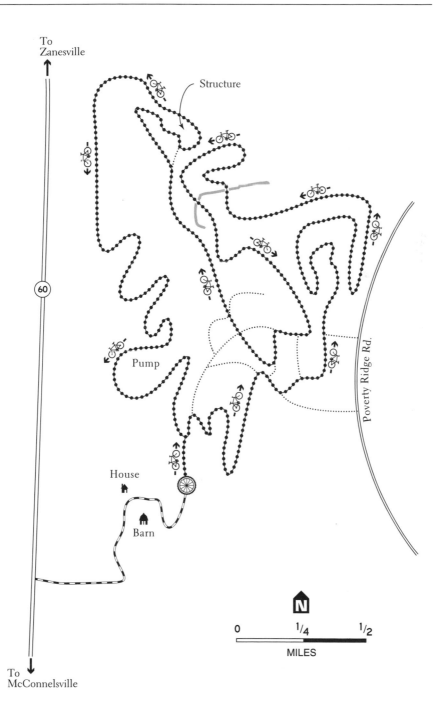

To
Zanesville

Structure

60

Pump

House

Barn

Poverty Ridge Rd.

To
McConnelsville

N

0   1/4   1/2

MILES

just outside Duncan Falls, go another 0.8 mile and look for a rock outcropping on your left. Turn left into the gravel entrance by this rock outcropping, and eventually you'll come to a farmhouse and a barn. Curve to the right and head toward the barn. Go past it to where the road turns into dirt double-track. You can park along the trees or in the field area. You'll see a break through the trees at the back of the clearing where you can begin the ride.

Source of additional information:

The Wheel and Spoke Bike Shop
634 Main Street
Zanesville, OH 43701
(740) 453-3438

Notes on the trail: The trail is marked, but if you get turned around, follow the arrows backward. They will return you to your car.

RIDE 27 · American Electric Power's Recreation Land

AT A GLANCE

Length/configuration: 25 miles of gravel and paved roads

Aerobic difficulty: Easy to moderate

Technical difficulty: Easy

Scenery: Lush tree-covered valleys, rock cliffs, some fine fishing, and a covered bridge.

Special comments: This is a fun ride for a family outing, but you won't produce much adrenaline along these trails.

If you want to take a family vacation where you can camp, fish, hike, and go out for some easy mountain biking; American Electric Power's Recreation Land is the place for you. This area, covering 30,000 acres, is a reforested coal strip mine area. There are over 350 lakes and ponds stocked with fish, so bring along a fishing pole. The ride I describe below is a mix of gravel and paved roads, so your serious mountain biker won't find it too challenging. However, this 25-mile ride, including the distance along the main loop and the out-and-back spurs, does maximize the gravel roads, most of which head in and out of the various camping areas. This is ideal for the family that owns mountain bikes and wants an easy place to ride them.

RIDE 27 · American Electric Power's Recreation Land

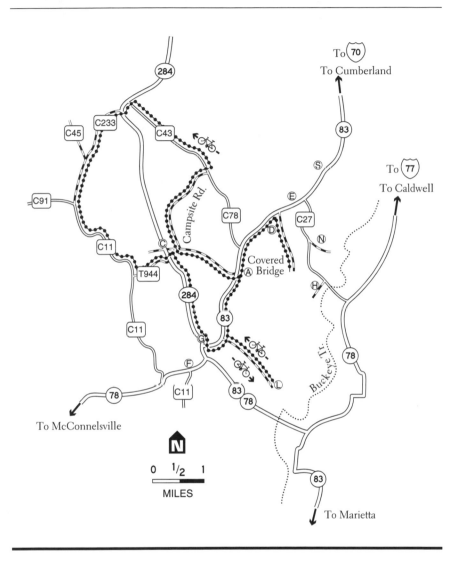

You won't need much in the way of technical skills, just enough to dodge a little traffic on the major roads, which, unfortunately, make up a couple of legs on this ride. You will need a modest amount of energy. While the gravel roads around the park site areas are flat, OH 78 and OH 83, the primary paved roads, have rolling hills, so be prepared.

The scenery in this area is worth the trip. You'll pass along the border of the restricted strip mine area, which offers an intriguing view of the mining operations.

One of Ohio's small covered bridges can be found on a quiet gravel road at Recreation Land.

In addition, you'll ride by several scenic views of tree-covered valleys. In some areas, you'll get the chance to look back 300 million years at steep rock cliffs exposing layers of clay, sandstone, shale, limestone, and slate. Down park site D, Sawmill Road, you'll even find a small covered bridge. Among the animals you might see here are largemouth bass, channel catfish, northern pike, and chain pickerels. If you don't bring your fishing pole and an Ohio fishing license, then you'll have to be content with the blue heron, woodchucks, beaver, fox, and deer. In short, come for the camping and stay for the cycling. AEP's Recreation Land Bike Trails can be enjoyed for no charge.

General location: In Morgan, Muskingum, and Noble Counties, 22 miles southeast of Zanesville and 28 miles northwest of Marietta

Elevation change: The elevation change is negligible on most of the gravel roads, and the paved roads contain gently rolling hills.

Season: Ride here during any season, but the alders, sycamores, silver maples, poplars, and ash will look fantastic in the fall.

Services: You can camp at the park sites, which have water and sanitary facilities, but no electricity. Reinersville has a few food shops. All services can be found in Zanesville.

Hazards: You should pay attention to vehicular traffic, especially on OH 83 and OH 78.

Rescue index: There's a phone at park site E. Otherwise, you can flag down traffic on any of the major roads. You'll frequently find campers down the park site roads.

Land status: The land is owned by American Electric Power, under a cooperative agreement with the Ohio Department of Natural Resources. You'll need to get a free permit from Ohio DNR or any AEP office if you plan on camping, hunting, or fishing in the area. Write them at the address below.

Maps: You can get a map of the Recreation Land area showing the boundaries and the restricted areas for Ohio DNR by writing the Department of Natural Resources at the address below. The USGS 7.5 minute quad for this area is mostly Reinersville, with a little of the area in the Cumberland, Ruraldale, and McConnelsville quad maps.

Finding the trail: From I-77: Take Exit 25, OH 78, west for 10 miles. Turn left on CR 27 (3 miles before the junction of OH 83). Take CR 27 for 3.5 miles, and turn left onto OH 83. Almost immediately you'll see park site E, Windy Hill, on your right.

From Zanesville: From I-70, take OH 146 east for 21 miles to OH 83. Take OH 83 south 8 miles to parksite E.

Sources of additional information:

Department of Natural Resources
Fountain Square
Building B
Columbus, OH 43224-1327
(740) 265-6659

American Electric Power
P.O. Box 328
McConnelsville, OH 43756
(740) 962-1208

Notes on the trail: The park sites and roads are marked. You can begin your ride from park site E. Turn right out of the parking area and take OH 83 for a half mile to Sawmill Road, park site D. Make sure to check out the covered bridge at the end of this 1-mile-each-way spur. Come back up Sawmill Road and turn left onto OH 83 again. Take OH 83 for 1.5 miles to park site A, Hook Lake. Across from park site A, on the other side of OH 893, there's a gravel road that you should take for about 1 mile. You'll find this stretch to be rather scenic, passing tree-covered valleys and rock outcroppings. When you get to Camp Site Road, turn right and travel along a cattailed wetland area for approximately 2 miles. When you reach CR 43 at the T intersection, turn left. You're now traveling along the border of the restricted area, which affords a view of the strip mine operation. Take CR 43 for 2.5 miles and turn left on OH 284. Go for a few yards and then turn right on CR 233 (also called Young Hickory). You're now skirting the border of the Recreation Land area. The scenery changes here—you'll notice trees on your left and pleasant farmlands in the distance to your right. As you pass into Morgan County, CR 233 changes to CR 11. When this road dead-ends in 2 miles, take a jog to the left. CR 11 will take you to Bristol Township Road 944 (also called Bristol Church Road) 2.5 miles later. Turn left on TR 944 and go 1 mile to OH 284. Go right on OH 284 for 2 miles to OH 83. When you get to OH 83, turn left and take that 0.5 mile to Horse Run, the road for park site L. Go down the spur for parksite L, a meadow area with abundant wildflowers, before heading back out to OH 83. Turn right on OH 83 and take that 4 miles back to park site E, where you parked your vehicle.

This is just one recommended route for AEP's Recreation Land. Feel free to shorten it if you like or explore some of the other park sites not included here, such as park site N. The area is picturesque. Don't let the fact that you'll need to ride on some paved roads deter you.

The Buckeye Trail also passes through Recreation Land.

WAYNE NATIONAL FOREST— MARIETTA UNIT

Marietta, which follows along the banks of the Ohio River, is the oldest organized American settlement in the old Northwest Territory. It was founded in the summer of 1788. The Ohio River itself has been described as the "highway of settlement," "the avenue of frontier commerce," and "the dividing line between the North and the South." Call it what you will, the trails in this region are mastered only by the best riders.

The Marietta unit of Wayne National Forest has a different policy than the other two units regarding mountain bike usage. Here at Marietta, mountain biking is allowed on the hiking trails. If you are up for the challenge, head to this area, which features both covered and natural bridges, as well as caves and coves.

Since these trails have been designed for hikers, they are generally narrower than those at the other two districts. Also, the numerous trail obstacles will prevent all but the best riders from gaining significant speed. These trails are not for the faint of heart. The switchbacks are formidable; the trail width often pernicious. In fact, several of these trails are so remote and isolated, if something were to happen to you, it could be days before you would be found.

Scare tactics and caveats aside, the persistent mountain biker will enjoy the sheer physical exertion required to ride here. Also, the Appalachian foothills are most prominent in this area—quite a contrast to the flatter lands in the northern part of the state.

Every now and then, the U.S. Congress does something right. Take Public Law 96-199, for instance. This law authorized the development of the North Country National Scenic Trail (NCT), which passes through or near several of the rides in this area. In Ohio, parts of the NCT follow the Buckeye Trail. When completed, the NCT will cover approximately 3,200 miles, beginning near Lake Champlain in New York, dipping across the northeast corner of Pennsylvania, and looping around Ohio. It leaves Ohio through the northeast corner and continues on through eastern Michigan, northern Wisconsin, and central Minnesota before finishing at the Missouri River in North Dakota. Needless to say, this will rival the Appalachian, Continental Divide, Trail of

Tears, Pacific Crest, Iditarod, and Oregon Trails in terms of distance. If you would like more information about the NCT, write to:

North Country National Scenic Trail
1709 Jackson Street
Omaha, NE 68102

RIDE 28 · Lamping Homestead Trail

AT A GLANCE

Length/configuration: A 5-mile, single-track, mostly dirt trail comprised of two connecting loops.

Aerobic difficulty: Fairly easy, the longer loop is more challenging than the shorter.

Technical difficulty: Moderate, and there are areas that may require a portage.

Scenery: Colorful wildflowers make for a pretty finish to this trail.

Special comments: This is the trail for the mountain biker with good bike handling skills who wants only a dash of technical challenge and more opportunities to ride a little easier.

Of the traditional hiking trails in the Marietta district, this one is perhaps the easiest. It will still require good bike-handling skills, though, to navigate around rocks and travel up small hillsides. This mostly dirt single-track consists of two connecting loops; one is 3.2 miles long and the other is 1.8, for a total distance of 5 miles. The elevation doesn't change more than 200 feet, but you may have to portage over some deadfall. The 3.2-mile loop is a little steeper and longer than the 1.8-mile loop. You'll even find a few stream crossings to spice things up a bit on the smaller loop, but if it hasn't rained, the beds might be dry.

The trail begins in a section of pine that winds around the pond. Soon you'll be traveling along a creek and winding up the hill on the other side. This is a placid ride, and even the coyote and her pup scampering off into the brush didn't seem too disturbed by my presence. The end of the trail is punctuated by purple, yellow, white, and orange wildflowers.

General location: One and a half miles from the junction of State Highway 260 and OH 537, about 35 miles from Marietta

Elevation change: The net gain is about 200 feet.

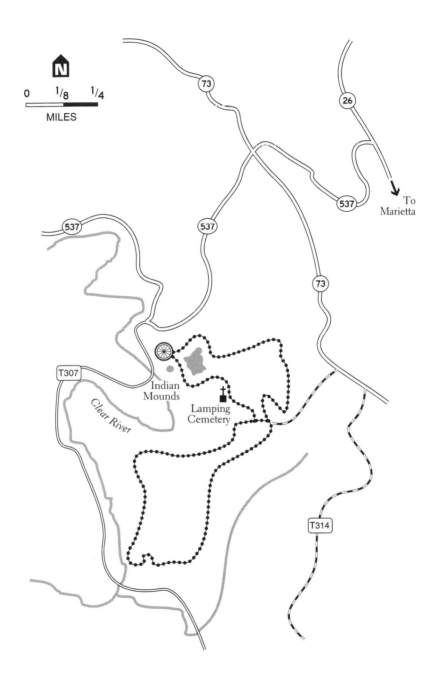

The wildflowers flanking the end of the Lamping Homestead Trail salute you as you finish the ride.

Season: The weather is drier in the fall, and the Indian summers have moderate temperatures. Ticks can be a problem in May.

Services: Primitive camping is available at Lamping Homestead; you will need to bring your own water. All services are available in Marietta

Hazards: You'll find some rock obstacles. Be careful, too, that you don't slip going up a hillside.

Rescue index: The nearest phone is at a gas station in Graysville on OH 26, about 3 miles north of the intersection of OH 26 and OH 537. There is light traffic on OH 537.

Land status: Wayne National Forest—Marietta Ranger District

Maps: For 50 cents, the Marietta Ranger District will send you a map showing the topographical markings of the 5 trails in their district; write to the address below. The USGS 7.5 minute quad for this area is Graysville.

Finding the trail: From Marietta, take OH 26 approximately 30 miles north. When you get to OH 537, go west. (OH 537 is 10 miles from the junction of OH 26 and OH 260.) Take OH 537 for 1.7 miles and follow the signs from there.

Source of additional information:

U.S. Forest Service
Route 1, Box 132
Marietta, OH 45750
(740) 373-9055

Notes on the trail: The trail begins through the pine trees by the picnic tables and is well marked by white diamonds. You won't miss the point where the 2 loops connect.

RIDE 29 · Archers Fork Trail

AT A GLANCE

Length/configuration: 9.5-mile loop of narrow dirt single track.

OH

Aerobic difficulty: Moderate

Technical difficulty: Moderate. You'll need your bike-handling skills for the usual hiking-trail obstacles.

Scenery: Wooded hollows, caves, and the Irish Run natural bridge.

Special comments: A camera-worthy ride.

This nine-and-a-half-mile loop has much to offer those who like to cycle and explore. On the cycling side, the narrow dirt single-track passes through Irish Run and Jackson Run, with excellent views of the wooded hollows deep below. As you wind around, you'll need bike handling skills to traverse deadfall, rocks, and similar obstacles. You'll see your share of rock outcroppings on this steep trail, which cuts into the hillside in places. You'll even find a few stream crossings if the weather hasn't been too dry.

On the exploring side, you'll not only see (and smell) a few old oil and gas wells but a couple of natural formations, too. Consider exploring a cave at the bottom of a hollow. Signs will point the way. More unusual is the Irish Run Natural Bridge, which you'll find further up the trail. You can't ride across it, but it's definitely worth getting off your bike to see. The arch is 51 feet long, 16 feet thick, and 39 feet to the rocky bottom below.

General location: Wayne National Forest, about 4.5 miles from the junction of OH 26 and OH 260, roughly 30 miles northeast of Marietta

Elevation change: You'll experience about 300 feet of elevation change.

Season: The weather in the fall is more moderate and the ground is drier than at other times of the year. In May, ticks are prevalent.

Services: Bring your own water. All services can be found in Marietta.

Hazards: Keep your eyes peeled for deadfall, rocks, and other hiking trail obstacles.

Archers Fork Trail, on the way to the natural bridge.

Rescue index: This trail is very remote, so travel with a partner. Even if you make your way to one of the intersecting roads, you may have to wait a while to flag down traffic.

Land status: Wayne National Forest—Marietta Ranger District

Maps: For 50 cents, the Marietta Ranger District will send you a map showing the topographical markings of the 5 trails in the district. Write to the address below. The USGS 7.5 minute quad for this area is Rinard Mills.

Finding the trail: From OH 26 and OH 260, take OH 260 east. Go 3 miles to Ludlow Township Road 34 and turn right. TR 34 is easy to miss, so pay attention. Take TR 34 for 1.3 miles and you will come to an entrance labeled "North Country Trail." Turn in and park near the cemetery.

Source of additional information:

U.S. Forest Service
Route 1, Box 132
Marietta, OH 45750
(740) 373-9055

Notes on the trail: Start the ride by traveling down an old dirt access road by the parking area. Soon you'll see a trail off to the left marked by the blue diamonds for the North Country Trail, which encompasses this section of Archers Fork. In a bit, you'll reach the intersection that takes you into the loop. Go to the right if you would like to visit the cave and the natural bridge on the first half of your loop.

RIDE 29 · Archers Fork Trail

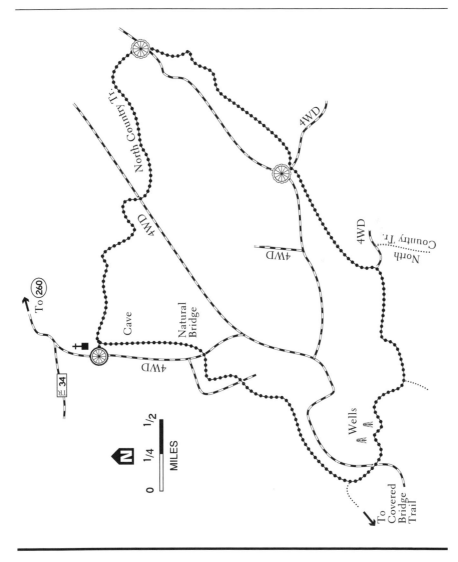

The North Country Trail is marked in blue. The sections where the North Country Trail and Archers Fork run together are marked by blue and white diamonds. The sections that are strictly Archers Fork are marked by white diamonds.

If you break away from Archers Fork on the south end of the loop, you can follow the North Country Trail. Also, there is a connector trail that joins Archers Fork with the Covered Bridge Trail on the southeast end of the loop. The connector trail is marked by white blazes with a powder-blue dot in the middle.

RIDE 30 · Covered Bridge Trail

AT A GLANCE

Length/configuration: 10-mile (5 each way) out-and-back dirt single track.

OH

Aerobic difficulty: Easy

Technical difficulty: Easy to moderate

Scenery: Essentially, you're following a stream bed that meanders through both fields and woods. Covered bridges begin and end the trail, and wildflowers bloom along the way.

Special comments: This trail is among the easiest in the Marietta district, but good bike handling skills are still needed for the narrow trails, deadfall, and rocky stream crossings.

Perhaps the most interesting attractions of this trail are not on the trail itself but at either end of it: covered bridges, one of which is still in use. Built over 100 years ago, these bridges over the Little Muskingum River take you back to a time when life was simpler. Beginning with a couple of stream crossings, the trail makes its way out of the woods and into a field where the trail turns to grass flanked by beautiful wildflowers. Soon you'll enter the woods again, still following the creek. Enjoy the numerous stream crossings, but take care—some of them are rocky. After you cross over a pipeline, you'll start to climb. The last stretch of the ride puts you in a pine thicket. Then you travel downhill, eventually reaching the Hune Covered Bridge.

General location: Wayne National Forest, about 22 miles northeast of Marietta on OH 26

Elevation change: The overall gain is about 300 feet.

Season: Early spring and early fall are best, when fewer deerflies will annoy you and the weather is cooler. Avoid the ticks in May.

Services: Primitive camping is permitted at both trailheads, but bring your own water. All services are available in Marietta.

Hazards: Rocky creek crossings and deadfall may challenge you. Expect to portage your bike on occasion.

Rescue index: The nearest phone is at a general store in Wingett Run, 1.5 miles south of Haught Run Recreation Area on OH 26. Otherwise, traffic could be flagged down on OH 26.

Land status: Wayne National Forest—Marietta Ranger District

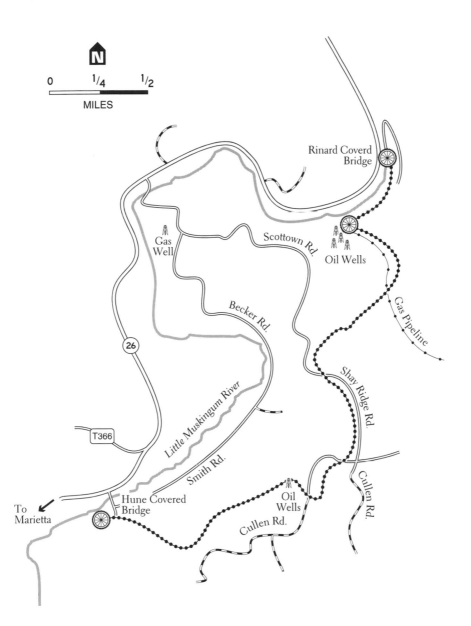

N

0   1/4   1/2
MILES

Rinard Coverd
Bridge

Gas
Well

Scottown Rd.

Oil Wells

Becker Rd.

Gas Pipeline

26

Shay Ridge Rd.

Little Muskingum River

T366

Smith Rd.

Hune Covered
Bridge

To
Marietta

Oil
Wells

Cullen Rd.

Cullen Rd.

Between the covered bridges, this trail offers single-track and numerous stream crossings.

Maps: For 50 cents, the Marietta Ranger District will send you a map showing the topographical markings of the 5 trails in the district. Write to the address below. The USGS 7.5 minute quads for this area are Rinard Mills and Dalzell.

Finding the trail: From the intersection of OH 7 and OH 26 in Marietta, you'll go 22.3 miles north and turn right on County Road 406. After about a block, turn right into the Haught Run Recreation Area. You'll see the Rinard Covered Bridge right off OH 26 as a marker. Note: A few miles before the Haught Run Recreation Area, you'll pass the Hune Bridge trailhead access, but parking is better further up at Haught Run.

Source of additional information:

U.S. Forest Service
Route 1, Box 132
Marietta, OH 45750
(740) 373-9055

Notes on the trail: As you pull into the camping area, follow the little loop around, and to the left of the toilet facility, you'll see the white diamonds marking the trail through the trees.

This trail has a connector trail to the Archers Fork Trail, which in turn links up to the North Country Trail. The connector trail is marked by white blazes with a powder-blue dot in the center. To get to the connector trail, go up a hill to a road, where you'll see a sign directing you further up the road a little bit to the NCT connector on your left. To keep on the Covered Bridge Trail, you simply cross the road and ride straight through.

SOUTHWESTERN OHIO

Southwestern Ohio is not exactly a hotbed of mountain biking activity, but it is home to several great recreational sites—Kings Island Amusement Park and a water slide park among them. The two rides listed in this section are just up the road from Cincinnati.

The trails highlight two opposite types of riding. The Little Miami Scenic River Trail is a rail-trail conversion offering easy riding in a historical area. Seven miles southeast of Lebanon is Fort Ancient State Memorial, a Hopewell Indian site on a bluff overlooking the Little Miami River. The park surrounds a series of earthen walls ranging in height from 4 to 25 feet. It's worth heading over to Fort Ancient State Memorial to learn more about the Hopewell culture, which was active between 100 B.C. and A.D. 500.

The trail at Caesar Creek State Park is completely different. Here, you'll appreciate the efforts of the Dayton Bicycle Club, along with Bellbrook bike pro shop, Centerville bike store, Wilmington College, and West Chester Cyclery, who have been maintaining the trail for the last two years. With the cooperation of park officials, they have developed a trail system through the woods that will challenge many riders' abilities.

When I first explored Ohio, these were the first two trails I visited. Not far apart in terms of distance, but polar opposites on the technical meter. Try whichever type of riding grabs you.

RIDE 31 · Little Miami Scenic River Trail

AT A GLANCE

Length/configuration: 100-mile out-and-back, most of which is paved.

Aerobic difficulty: Easy

Technical difficulty: Easy

Scenery: Forests and farmland interspersed with gorges. An old Native American fort provides some historical interest, as well.

Special comments: This is a pretty ride for the whole family, and a good day trip from Cincinnati.

If you like family rides, this multi-purpose trail is perfect for you. This 50-mile each way (100 miles total) out-and-back follows the Little Miami River along an abandoned railroad line. Forty-seven of these miles are paved, and three are gravel. This wide trail doesn't require any technical skill. As far as stamina is concerned, travel as many of the miles as you're able. You won't be disappointed by the scenery as you meander past farmlands and forests, and occasional gorges and cliffs. The area has historical value as well. Fort Ancient, located on the high bluffs along the river, was built by the Hopewell Indians centuries ago. In addition, Daniel Boone spent a good deal of time along the river. You'll find many songbirds along this trail. (I took great relish as two goldfinches followed me, flitting from branch to branch.) If you're vacationing in the Cincinnati area, consider taking the family here for a relaxing day of riding.

General location: From Milford to Xenia to Spring Valley, following the Little Miami River

Elevation change: Negligible

Season: Ride this trail all year. Spiders spinning their webs across the trail in the summer can be a bit nerve-wracking to the faint-hearted.

Services: The trailheads have water, including the Morrow trailhead listed below. Bed-and-breakfasts and motels can be found in Lebanon, Morrow, Loveland, and Milford. I found a quaint shop in Morrow called "Capricorn," which serves refreshments and has a few basic bike essentials. Stop in and talk with the owner. Loveland, Corwin, Spring Valley, Xenia, and Milford have some nice shops and places to eat.

Hazards: Be careful as you cross the street intersections: stop at all stop signs.

Rescue index: The trail passes several towns and houses. You'll find phones at

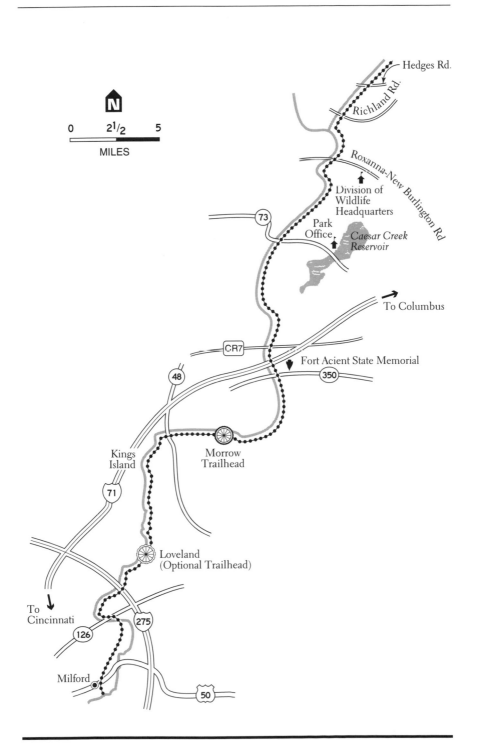

Along this relaxing trail, there's plenty of time to reflect upon the Hopewell Indians, who lived along the Little Miami River.

the Loveland, Morrow, Xenia, Spring Valley, Corwin, South Lebanon, Kingville, Miamiville and Milford trailheads.

Land status: State park

Maps: The map available from the state park at the address below should meet your needs, as this trail is easy to follow.

Finding the trail: To get to the Morrow trailhead: from Interstate 71, take the Morrow Exit 32, State Highway 123. Turn right on OH 123 and take that 6 miles into Morrow. When you get to the junctions of OH 123, Highway 22, and OH 3, turn right at the stoplight onto Pike Street. Go past the next light and turn right on Center Street. Go barely a block and you will see a grassy area where you can park your car.

Contact Caesar Creek State Park for additional places to pick up the trail. Xenia, Spring Valley and Corwin are all excellent starting points.

Sources of additional information:

Little Miami State Park
c/o Caesar Creek State Park
8570 East State Route 73
Waynesville, OH 45068-9719
(513) 897-3055

Green County Recreation and Parks
651 Dayton-Xenia Road

Xenia, OH 45385
(937) 376-7440

Notes on the trail: I prefer starting from the Morrow trailhead. If you to choose to ride the entire 50 miles there and back, you can start from either the Milford trailhead in the south or the Hedges Road trailhead (just south of Xenia) in the north.

Begin your ride out of Morrow, heading north down the paved street from where you parked your vehicle. Cross over a wooden bridge and you'll see where the trail splits off.

RIDE 32 · Caesar Creek State Park

AT A GLANCE

Length/configuration: 12 miles of dirt single-track out-and-back.

Aerobic difficulty: Moderate, the elevation changes aren't major, but there are many of them along the ride.

Technical difficulty: Moderate due to some gullies and bumps in places where you'll likely be moving along at a fast clip.

Scenery: Woodlands, but they're not the reason to ride this trail.

Special comments: This trail has some wonderful earthen stairs which I haven't yet figured out how to ride up.

A park officer told me the local mountain bikers were tired of riding on flat terrain—they wanted an area where they could hike-a-bike. Well, they got it here. This out-and-back trail is 6 miles one-way (12 miles total), and you won't be disappointed. Most of the trail is wide dirt single-track with a few grassy sections. The trail is challenging—especially the ups and downs and gullies in the area between Harveysburg Road and Ward Road. The section north of Ward Road is a little flatter, but even it has some steep downhills. Because the climbs and descents aren't long, you can do some fast cranking on this curvy trail, but keep an eye out for roots and rocks. Red-tailed hawks, box turtles, and red fox are among the animals you might see in these oak-hickory and beech-maple woodlands.

General location: Northeast of I-71, just outside of Harveysburg.

RIDE 32 · Caesar Creek State Park

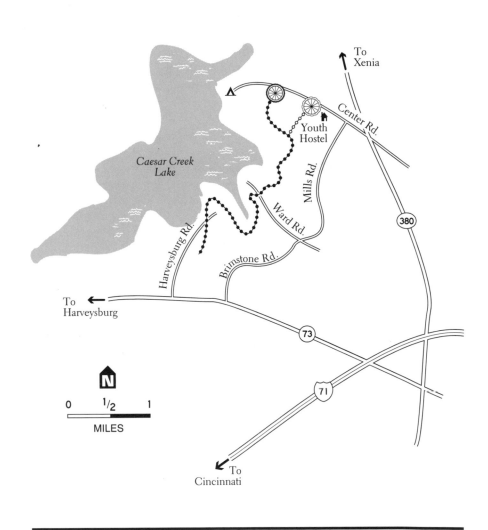

Elevation change: The climbs and descents are occasionally steep, but the overall elevation change is not significant.

Season: Any time of year. In the fall, you will enjoy the foliage, but it's also hunting season.

Services: Water is available at the campground. All services are available in Harveysburg.

Hazards: Be on the lookout for rocks, roots, and other common trail obstacles. Watch out for the occasional hiker as well.

This single-track is a piece of cake after portaging over the earthen stairs.

Rescue index: The entrance to the campground is staffed in the summer only. You should also be able to flag down traffic on Ward Road, Brimstone Road, Harveysburg Road, and, of course, OH 73. The area is fairly secluded, so always ride with a partner. Also, there is a railhead on Harveysburg Road. You will pass the local life squad building on your right on Harveysburg Road. There is an emergency telephone on the building.

Land status: State park

Maps: The USGS 7.5 minute quad for this area is New Burlington.

Finding the trail: From I-71, take Exit 45 for OH 73. Turn right, go about 1 mile to OH 380, and turn left. Go 3 miles to Center Road and turn left again. This will take you directly to the campground where you can park your vehicle.

Source of additional information:

Caesar Creek State Park
8570 East State Road 73
Waynesville, OH 45068
(513) 897-3055

Notes on the trail: From the campground, ride back to Center Road. Go up Center Road a few yards and you'll see the entrance through the grass on your right. The trail begins on a wide grass path, passing an algae-covered pond. Soon you'll enter the woods and the trail will be signed.

Beware of one tricky spot where the trail enters a clearing with the lake to your right (before Ward Road). Ride uphill in the clearing and you'll find the entrance back into the woods on the side of the clearing around a pumping station. If you get lost on the trail, head downhill toward the stream, which will take you to Harveysburg Road, Ward Road, or Brimstone Road, depending on where you are.

There is one main trail, but plans are under way to put in spurs around the more difficult sections to accommodate less skilled riders. Check with the park first to verify their access.

As of summer 1999, the volunteers who maintain the trail will be putting up better trail markers, trail head information boards, and printing maps. They will also be re-routing some of the more eroded sections.

NORTHERN INDIANA

The slogan for a popular Indiana amusement park says, "There's more than corn in Indiana." That's true. There are also soybeans. The idea of mountain biking through an Indiana cornfield is not exactly a cyclist's image of daring adventure. After all, it's called mountain biking, not crop biking. (But if that ever catches on, remember, you heard it here first.) If you think mountain biking opportunities are few and far between in northern Indiana, well, you're right. There are two reasons for this. First, much of the area is relatively flat, agricultural land. The second reason is Indiana's Department of Natural Resources (DNR) mountain bike policy: mountain bikes are not allowed on DNR property. Perhaps someday we'll see an easing of this strict policy, but for now, it officially limits mountain bike opportunities in the state.

However, it is possible to find the occasional exception. Huntington Reservoir is one of them. Though the land is managed by DNR, the property is owned by the U.S. Army Corps of Engineers, and they permit mountain biking here. Located outside of Huntington, known for its Romanesque Revival architecture and as the hometown of a former U. S. Vice President Dan Quayle, the reservoir area has a trail that will test your technical skills—especially if you manage to ride there after the water level in the reservoir has dropped and the trail is littered with deadfall.

Not all potential mountain bike areas are state-run, as evidenced by France Park, one of the parks in Cass County. Park officials tell me that mountain biking is increasingly popular here and that riders often come up from the Indianapolis area. Most trails in this system are easy to ride, but a few spots will test your ability.

If you're looking for perhaps the liveliest trail in northern Indiana, you have to move away from public land and look at private land. Outside Syracuse, local mountain bikers have taken matters in their own hands and created their own trail—a popular spot for races—at the Wellington Farm. If you want a definition for the term "switchback," go out there.

Thanks to Joe Fritsch, who helped supply information about the Wellington Farm, and to Keith Meyers, who assisted with Huntington Reservoir.

RIDE 33 · Wellington Farm

AT A GLANCE

Length/configuration: Four-mile loop of dirt and grass single-track.

Aerobic difficulty: Moderate, with no major elevation changes, but some uphills are home to switchbacks that will give your lungs and legs a fine test.

Technical difficulty: Challenging, with many white-knuckle switchbacks.

Scenery: Not that you'll notice much of it, but there are woods and fields in addition to all the hills.

Special comments: This trail was developed by mountain bikers for mountain bikers and the adrenaline you'll produce on this ride may last you the better part of week.

Switchback after switchback after switchback after switchback . . . Don't be deceived by this short, four-mile loop, which is dirt and grass, narrow single-track trail developed by local mountain bikers and used for area races. Your front wheel will be turning constantly from side to side on this one. You'll encounter switchbacks on uphills, switchbacks on downhills, and switchbacks just for the heck of it. "We wanted to make a course that was challenging to ride and challenging to finish," says Joe Fritsch, a local mountain bike racer. He adds, "This trail is much more like how mountain biking was four or five years ago when mountain biking was just starting. People would make it technical and challenging. Nowadays, so many courses are just wide open. Many mountain bike races follow dirt roads, so basically they're road races instead of mountain bike races. That's why we've gone to this style."

And challenging it is. On a dry day, you'll fight to maintain your balance. On a wet day, I shudder to think. You will enjoy the white-knuckle switchbacks, especially the ones heading downhill. And no one will laugh if you decide to walk it around some of the intimidating ones. There are no major climbs, but that's no guarantee you won't be tested for endurance. I can think of one climb in particular that will cause you to struggle since you'll get no speed rounding a 180-degree turn.

The trail winding through the woods is narrow with lots of climbs, descents, and gullies; look out for trees on those curves. When you get to the field, the trail is much wider, but it still winds its way through the grass. You'll have so

RIDE 33 · Wellington Farm

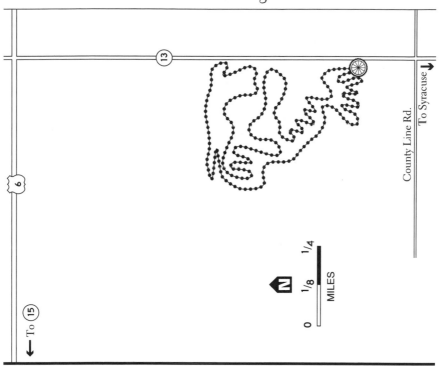

much fun trying to negotiate this trail, you probably won't even notice the flora and fauna. If you do get off and portage, perhaps you'll see the many leopard frogs inhabiting this area. This ride is for the serious cyclist—in northern Indiana, of all places.

General location: Off State Highway 13, 1 mile south of Highway 6 in Syracuse

Elevation change: The hills are short and the overall elevation change is nominal, but the constant up-and-down will tire you eventually.

Season: Late spring and early fall, whern there isn't as much overgrowth, are the best.

Services: Bring your own water. Syracuse has food and lodging. Goshen has all services. For bike check, go to Hollinger Bicycles in Goshen.

Hazards: Look out for the trees on the narrower sections, especially the switchbacks. Obstacles on the trail are not as significant in comparison.

Rescue index: The area is not very large, so if you run into trouble, making your way back to IN 13 won't be difficult.

Joe dashes to the next switchback, fighting to win the race.

Land status: Private property. Before you ride, please check with Hollinger Bicycles about current availability. You ride at your own risk.

Maps: Since the trail is new and likely to vary as the local riders work on it, your best bet is to contact Hollinger Bicycles. The USGS 7.5 minute quad for this area is Millford.

Finding the trail: From IN 15 and US 6, go east on US 6 for 5 miles. Turn right on IN 13 and go 1 mile. You can park at the church at the corner of IN 13 and South County Line Road. To find the trailhead, ride back up IN 13 the way you came, and just past the guardrail, you'll see an opening through the trees for the trailhead on your left.

Source of additional information:

Hollinger Bicycles
1410 South 10th Street
Goshen, IN 46526
(219) 534-2274

Notes on the trail: As you enter the trail, it's best to keep traveling forward. This is the direction that local riders traditionally go. You can ride the other direction, but if there are other people out there, you might run into someone. The trail is cut so that it often parallels another section of the trail. There are no intersections, however, so you won't make a wrong turn. Even though the trail is easy to follow, if you miss a turn you may end up on a part of the trail on which you would have been in a few moments or, perhaps, were on earlier. (I once did that on a golf course fairway.) If you do get lost or if you come to the field section and choose to cut your ride short, you can always head east, and in no time you'll be on IN 13.

RIDE 34 · Huntington Lake—Kekionga Trail

AT A GLANCE

Length/configuration: 11-mile single-track dirt loop around the lake. The trail is more complicated on the south side of the lake than the north.

Aerobic difficulty: Easy

Technical difficulty: Easy to moderate on the north side, moderate to difficult on the south side.

Scenery: Masses of wildflowers make the area a truly beautiful ride.

Special comments: Glacier riding is a treat. Time your winter visit after a flood and you can make your own trail over the ice.

IN

Huntington Lake is used for flood control by the U.S. Army Corps of Engineers, so riding here can be a different experience every time you come. When the water levels are high, portions of this 11-mile loop dirt trail can be literally underwater. After the water recedes, you won't know what to expect. Deadfall washed up by the floodwaters can present challenging obstacles to test your bike handling skills. Park workers clear the trails about three times a year, so there are times when it's easier to get through. Just before my first visit to Huntington, the disastrous Mississippi River flood of 1993 had peaked in the Midwest. The water was kept high at this reservoir to minimize water that would eventually make its way into the Mississippi River. I rode the trail just after the water had receded and was impressed by the extraordinary number of branches deposited there.

Discounting the deadfall, the trail on the north side of the lake is straight and easy to follow, presenting just enough gullies to keep it interesting. The south side of the lake, though, is more complicated and technical since the single-track is narrower and rougher. There's a lot of heavy brush on this side and one tough creek crossing strewn with boulders. If you're looking for some technical riding, this is the side for you.

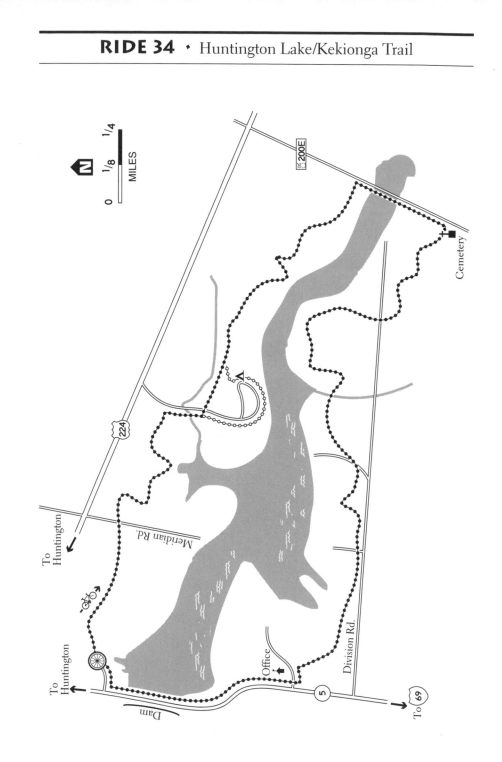

Keith relaxes on a short grassy section after tackling the deadfall around the reservoir.

If you come in the winter, you might be lucky enough to experience what local mountain biker Nick Hancock refers to as "glacier riding." On occasion, the reservoir floods in the winter and then freezes. When the Corps of Engineers lets the water down, the "glacier" drops, causing the ice to crack and split. The ice covers the underbrush, and you can make your own trail through the trees. The area is home to deer, opossum, owls, and redheaded woodpeckers. Wildflowers like Queen Anne's lace, blue phlox, mayapple, and pasture rose add to the beauty of the area.

Oh, and how could I forget—Huntington is also the home of the Dan Quayle Museum. Need I say more?

General location: Off IN 5 in Huntington

Elevation change: The short hills don't add significantly to the overall elevation change.

Season: The best riding is from mid-summer to late fall, when the area is not as muddy or flooded as other times of year. The trails could be completely underwater after lengthy periods of rain.

Services: There's water by the Observation Mound. Camping is permitted at Huntington Lake. All services are available in Huntington. For bike service, check out Summit City Bicycles in Fort Wayne.

Hazards: Creek crossings and logs will cause you the most problems. Since the trail frequently changes with flooding, don't expect to find the same obstacles each time you ride.

Rescue index: You may find DNR staff by the beach entrance. Otherwise, you can flag down traffic on US 224 or Division Road.

Land status: The U.S. Army Corps of Engineers owns the land, but it's operated and maintained by the Indiana Department of Natural Resources. If you enter at the park entrance, the admission fee is $2.

Maps: You can get a map at the park entrance. The USGS 7.5 minute quad for this area is Majenica.

Finding the trail: From US 24 and IN 5, take IN 5 south through the town of Huntington, cross the Huntington (J. Edward Roush) Dam until you see the sign to the Little Turtle Beach; turn left into the entrance, pass the gatehouse, and drive straight ahead for about 0.25 mile, watching for the mountain bike trailhead sign. When you see the trailhead sign, turn left and park. Registration cards, trail maps, recreation guides, and rules of the trail are available there.

Sources of additional information:

Huntington Lake
517 North Warren Road
Huntington, IN 46750
(219) 468-2165

Summit City Bicycles
3615 North Clinton
Fort Wayne, IN 46805
(219) 484-0182

Notes on the trail: You'll begin the ride on the south side of the reservoir and follow the trail in a counterclockwise direction. Ride back toward the gatehouse, where you came into the Little Turtle Beach area. At the entrance to the little campground (just before reaching the gatehouse), turn left and then take an immediate right and ride along the treeline into the woods. Follow the orange Carsonite sign markers. The south side of the trail winds through areas that are open to hunting during certain hunting seasons, so wear hunter orange to let the hunters know that you are riding the trail.

On the north side after coming off of County Road 200E, you will have an easy ride, but be careful through the curves. After numerous curves, you will cross a small wooden bridge. Make a sharp right turn and ride through the pine trees. After crossing another bridge you'll start on a long straightaway. You'll ride through a small creek, go another 0.5 mile, and come out onto the paved campground access road. Turn right for 100 yards, turn left at the bottom of the hill and you're back on the trail for a ride through fields back to IN 5. Take IN 5 south across the dam to the entrance of the Little Turtle Beach and you're almost done.

RIDE 35 · France Park

AT A GLANCE

Length/configuration: 4.5 miles of primarily dirt trails loop around the park

Aerobic difficulty: Trails A–D and F are easy to moderate; trail E is another matter altogether, with steep, rocky sections.

Technical difficulty: Again, trails A–D and F are easy to moderate; trail E takes some real skill.

Scenery: There are two ponds, a rock quarry, and some cliffs along the trail.

Special comments: Summer can make for a wet ride, but if you want a water slide, that's the time to go.

This is a nice place for the recreational cyclist who's looking to get a taste of what mountain biking is like on some easy trails. The various trails, labeled A–G, form a loop around and across the park area. Even though there are only four and a half miles of mostly dirt trails, you'll get plenty of variety: some bends in the trail, occasional root and rock obstacles, a few short hills, and views of the rock cliffs. After you try some of the easier trails, you can tackle Trail E, which is considerably more challenging. In fact, don't be surprised if you end up portaging your bike up a few steep, rocky areas. Despite the trail's short length, you may feel compelled to make a couple of laps around the park.

After you're finished riding, there's plenty more to do. Besides the fishing and swimming at France Park, you'll enjoy the miniature golf. The more adventurous can attempt scuba diving (bring your own gear). Among the mulberry, dogwood, and pine, look for badgers, fox, skunks, and raccoons. On second thought, don't look too hard for the skunks.

General location: On US 24, 4 miles west of Logansport

Elevation change: You'll experience a few hills, but nothing to write home about. Trail E, though not long, is steep.

Season: I'd go in the summer, although the ice fishing and ice skating are nice activities in the winter.

Services: All services are available in Logansport. Camping and a store are also available at the park.

Hazards: You'll find a few roots and rocks. Take care while crossing the bridges, and remember, Trail E is rocky and steep.

RIDE 35 · France Park

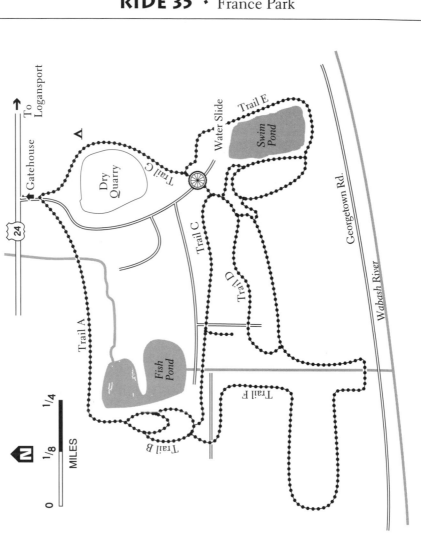

Rescue index: The gatehouse is staffed and has a pay phone. Usually, you'll find other users on the trail and at the other recreational sites.

Land status: Cass County Park and Recreation Board. General admission is $1.50, $5 for mountain biking and scuba activities.

Maps: You can get a map from the Cass County Park and Recreation Board at the address below. The USGS 7.5 minute quad for this area is mostly Lucerne, except for a small portion covered in Clymers.

With a water slide and miniature golf available at France Park, you just might want to leave your bike for some non-cycling fun!

Finding the trail: From the intersection of US 24 and US 35 west of Logansport, the park is 3 miles west on US 24. Once you're in the park, follow the main road around to the parking areas just west of the beach.

Source of additional information:

France Park
4505 W. US 24 West
Logansport, IN 46947
(219) 753-2928
www.francepark.com

Notes on the trail: The trails are well marked, especially at intersections, and are easy to follow. Look for a yellow triangle trail marker or a silhouette of a hiker. You can begin your ride on Trail G at the east side of the parking area. This trail is mostly limestone gravel, but becomes dirt once you get up to Trail A. Trail F makes its way through the pines, and Trail E is the toughest, as it's narrow and steeper than the others.

MADISON, INDIANA

Madison's stock-in-trade is history. Virtually the entire downtown—some 133 blocks—is on the National Register of Historic Places. Dozens of homes have been maintained in or restored to their mid-nineteenth-century splendor.

The city celebrates its history with a number of home tours and garden tours every year. Other festivals include a Chautauqua of the Arts in September and a regatta every July. This race is for unlimited hydroplane boats. Powered by helicopter engines and measuring over 30 feet long, these monsters reach speeds of over 200 miles per hour on the Ohio River.

While the city has long cherished its historic nature, it's only been in recent years that Madison has enjoyed a minor renaissance beyond preservation. There are finally some coffee shops, decent restaurants, art galleries, and other amenities in the downtown area.

Madison's hilltop, meanwhile, is home to fast food outlets, car dealerships, grocery stores, and several small strip malls. Chain hotels (Best Western, Holiday Inn) are up there; mom-and-pop hotels and bed-and-breakfast places are mostly downtown.

All these features add to the area's appeal, but you wouldn't need them as an excuse to come ride here. Though there is no single-track, there is a vast network of county roads weaving together streams, hills, and valleys. Hidden deep within these contours are dozens of stone buildings, many more than 150 years old. Built mostly by Scottish immigrants, these homes, churches, schools, and other structures have met varying fates. Some have been refurbished into lavish country homes; other roofless, windowless shells try to stand up to one more winter storm.

Wildlife abounds here. You're likely to see deer, turkeys, turkey vultures, hawks, foxes, and an assortment of snakes and turtles. Birds are abundant. Cardinals fly erratically through the brush along the road, while pileated woodpeckers thunk-thunk-thunk against dead wood in the distance. Watch closer and you may see an eagle or two, maybe a bobcat—and, along the river, herons. The naturalist at Clifty Falls State Park, (812) 265-1331 or (812) 265-1324, can tell you more.

Don't let the fact that these rides are on county roads fool you. They're roads, yes, but roads through the most rugged, remote countryside the state has to offer. Be as prepared here as anywhere. You'll need plenty of water, something to eat, a compass and map, a first aid kit, and whatever tools and parts you need to keep a sweet ride from turning into a hellish hike. Nice additions to that list include a camera and some pepper spray for the occasional loose dog. My motto: better to have it and not need it, than need it and not have it.

The roads themselves can be hard-packed clay, loose gravel, bare bedrock, or any combination. Stream crossings may be by bridge or a simple concrete slab over which the water flows. Be cautious on the slabs. They're often covered with treacherously slippery algae. Ride them s-l-o-w-l-y and try to stay in the car tracks, where some of the algae has been scrubbed off.

The best bike for these roads is a hardtail with a suspension seatpost and a supple suspension fork. There are few big hits out here, but the washboard and gravel can get annoying on a full rigid rig. Full suspension? Doggy on the many climbs, but ideally suited to the fast, wide, sweeping downhills.

Riding season is pretty much year-round. Winter can bring rain, sleet, snow, ice, sunshine, 70 degrees above or 17 degrees below zero, sometimes all in the same week. Summer can be hot and absurdly humid. The best riding seasons are May and June and again in September and October.

More information can be had from the Madison Area Convention and Visitors' Bureau, (800) 559-2956; the Jefferson County Historical Society, (812) 265-2335; the Madison Area Bicycle Club, (812) 265-3620, ext. 7006; or from local bike shops:

Madison Schwinn
2034 Lanier Drive
Madison, IN 47250
(812) 273-4278

Fizz'z Bike Shop
311 West Street
Madison, IN 47250
(812) 273-3499

Enjoy the rides. Enjoy Madison. If, during your visit, you don't consider moving here at least once, you'll be the first tourist to be so jaded.

RIDE 36 · Bloody Run Ramble

AT A GLANCE

Length/configuration: 20-mile loop, about a third of which is paved. The rest is flat to gently rolling gravel roads.

IN

Aerobic difficulty: Easy; mostly flat with a single 1-mile climb near the end that rates a solid "moderate."

Technical difficulty: Mostly easy, except that loose gravel and occasional stream crossings may test your skills.

Scenery: Lush, densely wooded bottomland with streams and occasional small farms, both working and abandoned.

Special comments: During snowmelt, after heavy rains, or whenever flash flood warnings are posted, *do not* ride this route. The stream crossings will be too fast and deep. One curious observation that has held true for years: this route, particularly the stretch on the lower part of Bloody Run and Barbersville roads, is a magnet for butterflies.

This is one of my favorite rides in this area. The paved beginning and end have low traffic and great scenery. The gravel road middle portion is as pretty and deserted as you're likely to find. While on that middle part, you're never far from Indian-Kentuck Creek, which runs all the way to the Ohio River.

While much of the county is seeing new homes, many of the homes here have been in place for more than a century. Some still hunker in the shadows of ancient barns, which have been tilted back by the prevailing southwesterly winds. Cattle occasionally graze, often with horses for companionship. More common animals are turkey vultures, red-tailed hawks, and butterflies.

There's little traffic on this route. What there is arrives mostly in early morning or midafternoon, as people commute to factory jobs in Madison and across the river in Kentucky.

The gravel roads cans be muddy and rough, but are passable at all times. My least favorite time to ride is the week after the roads have been graded, when the gravel is loose and deep. That happens twice, maybe three times each year. Soon after, the cars pack things down again and riding is much smoother and faster.

General location: Starts and ends in Canaan, about 17 miles east of Madison on State Highway 62. Turn left off IN 62 onto Locust Street, which turns right onto Main Street. Go up a couple of blocks to the firehouse, which will be on

RIDE 36 · Bloody Run Ramble

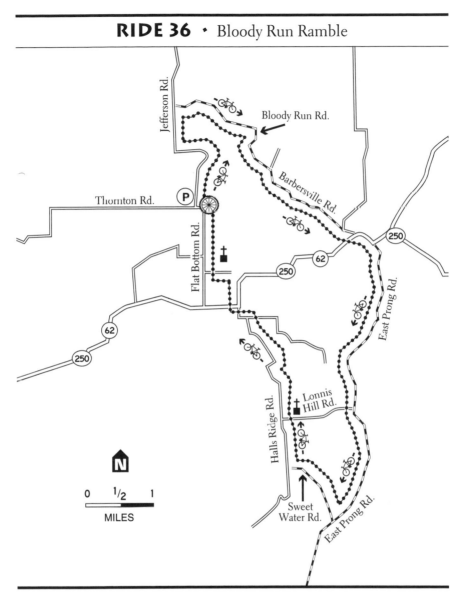

your left. Park across the street. As you're facing the firehouse, you'll be leaving to your right.

Elevation change: Mostly flat except for a 400-foot descent near the beginning and a corresponding 400-foot climb near the end.

Season: Year-round, though fall is best because it's generally dry and the turning leaves are spectacular. Spring is good, but be cautious about high water.

Services: Indian Trails Restaurant in Canaan offers genuine home cooking, but irregular hours; plan on bringing everything you need from Madison. Everything, including hotels, restaurants, groceries, and 2 bike shops, is located in Madison.

Hazards: Potential for fast, deep water and slick slab bridges. Otherwise, pretty benign.

Rescue index: Madison has a good regional hospital, but getting there depends on someone finding you. There are a few homes along this route, but you may not see another person all day.

Land status: If you're not on the road, you're on private property. Get off! You'll be tempted to trespass in order to take photos. Get permission first.

Maps: The county highway map, available from the highway garage on Clifty Drive/IN 62 or from the courthouse, is large, clear, and distinguishes between gravel and pavement.

Finding the trail: Facing the Canaan firehouse, you'll leave to your right (north) on Main Street. Within 2 blocks, Main Street ends and you must turn left onto Clay Street.

Sources of additional information:

Madison Area Convention and Visitors' Bureau
(800) 559-2956

Jefferson County Historical Society
(812) 265-2335

Madison Area Bicycle Club
(812) 265-3620, ext. 7006

Local bike shops:

Madison Schwinn
2034 Lanier Drive
Madison, IN 47250
(812) 273-4278

Fizz'z Bike Shop
311 West Street
Madison, IN 47250
(812) 273-3499

Notes on the trail: After turning left onto Clay from Main, follow Clay about a half mile until it Ts into Flat Bottom Road. Turn right. Take the first right, Jefferson Road, which is about 1.5 miles from where you turned onto Flat Bottom Road. Once you're on Jefferson Road, it's just over 2 miles to the right turn onto Bloody Run, which is gravel. At the bottom of this 1-mile descent, Bloody Run takes a sharp, unexpected right turn. It looks like the road goes straight, but that's a private lane. A half mile after that surprise right turn is your first stream crossing.

In 2 more miles a paved road comes in from the left. That's Barbersville

Road. Veer right. You're now on Barbersville Road (Bloody Run Road ends when it meets Barbersville Road). A half-mile farther is your first bail-out point; turn right here and right again on IN 62 if you need to get back to Canaan for an emergency. Otherwise, continue straight.

In 1.5 miles, the gravel ends. Turn right onto the paved Hicks Ridge Road (not straight and up the paved hill road). In another 0.5 mile is the second bail-out point; turn right on IN 62 and climb back into Canaan if necessary. Otherwise, continue straight. Be careful: this road (IN 62) occasionally carries a fair amount of traffic, and drivers aren't expecting a cyclist to pop out of the woods.

Within 0.1 mile, paved IN 62 turns left. Go straight onto the gravel East Prong Road. You're about halfway through the 20-mile loop at this point.

Continue on East Prong. It's not tricky to follow; as long as you don't go up any hills, you're on it. You'll encounter a couple of slab bridges. In dry weather, they're just concrete. In wet weather, they're booby traps with fast-flowing water, hidden holes and drop-offs, and zero traction. Be careful.

At about 15 miles, turn right onto Sweet Water Road. It's easy to spot. There's a field on the near side, a row of trees on the far side, and a small slab bridge at the base. Grind your way to the top, where you'll turn right onto paved Hall's Ridge Road.

About 3 miles after you turn right onto Hall's Ridge Road, it goes hard left (Risk's Ridge Road is to the right). Stay on Hall's Ridge until it joins IN 62; go straight 0.5 mile on IN 62 to Locust Street and back into Canaan.

RIDE 37 · Double Drop with a Comley-Fagg Option

AT A GLANCE

Length/configuration: 23- or 31-mile loop, about half of which is paved, half gravel roads. (The percentage of gravel is a little higher on the long option.)

Aerobic difficulty: Moderate, with some climbing on either option, and an extra climb on the long one.

Technical difficulty: Mostly easy, except for 2 wicked-fast descents (WFDs) (3 WFDs on the long option).

Scenery: Breathtaking ridge-top vistas, dense woods, a smattering of historic buildings.

Special comments: If you have a need for speed, this route will give you 3 chances to approach nirvana. Or you could just slow down and enjoy the splendor of this remote corner of the state.

There's more pavement on this one than I'd like, but the payoff is three wonderful downhills: fast, long freefalls off the side of the earth with sweeping turns and plenty of runout room at the bottom. Other attractions include pastoral scenery, a 150-year-old stone home where Comley Hill and Vernon Ridge Roads meet at the bridge, and a tranquil farmstead with a log home as its centerpiece about halfway up Manville Hill Road on the left.

The climbs are mostly gradual and mostly paved, so this ride isn't particularly difficult. The challenge is to ride within your limits on the downhills. Speeds of 40 to 50 miles per hour are possible, so make sure you and your equipment are ready.

One variable to consider is when the gravel portions were last graded—the longer ago, the better, since grading loosens the gravel and makes for a sketchy ride with lots of vibration through the handlebars.

Another variable is the chance to knock out about three miles of pavement by parking a car at the junction of IN 56 and Eagle Hollow Road and starting the ride from there.

General location: Starts and ends in downtown Madison

Elevation change: There's a 400-foot climb near the beginning and again near the end. Both of these climbs are on long, gentle, paved roads. The long option has another paved climb of roughly 400 feet, as well as some short, steep climbs on Comley Hill Road.

RIDE 37 · Double Drop with a Comley-Fagg Option

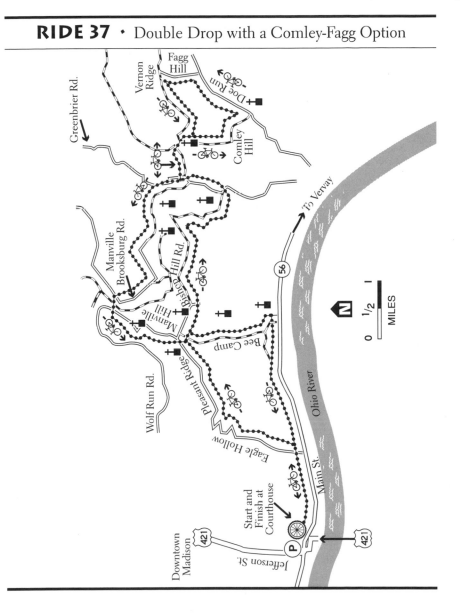

Season: Year-round. Fall is best; winter offers great views through leafless trees; summer is sticky. Spring is okay except after heavy rains, when the slab bridges and creek crossings get tricky.

Services: Everything, including hotels, restaurants, groceries, and 2 bike shops, is located in Madison. Get a boost late in the ride by stopping at the Manville country store.

Hazards: Fast downhills all the time; slippery slab bridges and deep water in stream crossings after a rain or snowmelt.

Rescue index: Madison, which has a hospital and clinic, is nearby. Traffic volume on most of this route varies from a few cars per hour to 1 or 2 per day.

Land status: Stay on the roads; everything else is private property.

Maps: The county highway map, available from the highway garage on Clifty Drive/IN 62 or from the courthouse, is large, clear, and distinguishes between gravel and pavement.

Finding the trail: Simple, since it's all on public roads. You'll start from the courthouse at the corner of Main (IN 56) and Jefferson (Highway 421) streets in downtown Madison.

Sources of additional information:

Madison Area Convention and Visitors' Bureau
(800) 559-2956

Jefferson County Historical Society
(812) 265-2335

Madison Area Bicycle Club
(812) 265-3620, ext. 7006

Madison Schwinn
2034 Lanier Drive
Madison, IN 47250
(812) 273-4278

Fizz'z Bike Shop
311 West Street
Madison, IN 47250
(812) 273-3499

Notes on the trail: Begin on the Main Street (north) side of the Jefferson County courthouse. (If street parking is filled, off-street parking is available in the city lot just south of the courthouse at the corner of Jefferson and Second.) Proceed east on Main Street/IN 56.

About 2 miles out, turn left onto Eagle Hollow Road; it's your first left after you leave the city limits. A mile later you'll begin a 1.5-mile climb. Soon after you reach the top, Eagle Hollow Road turns into Pleasant Ridge Road. Pleasant Ridge Road and Bishop Hill Road (which you'll soon be on) both have wonderful vistas, with the Ohio River on one side and rural countryside tucked into a valley on the other.

A couple of miles later you'll pass Pleasant Ridge church. Just beyond the church, Pleasant Ridge Road goes right. You'll bear left onto gravel, which is Bishop Hill Road. After a little more than 1 mile, Bishop Hill Road begins diving. This is WFD #1. The top of this descent has a few curves and a tight right-hander, followed by a wide-open run to the bottom. Then you'll have a little less than 0.25 mile of flat to scrub off speed before you cross the slab bridge at Greasy Hollow. It's treacherous when wet (I have the scars to prove it). Even walking this slab could put you on your can if conditions are right.

Continue on. Bishop Hill Road ends at a stop sign. Turn left over the bridge onto Brooksburg-Manville Road, which is paved. About 0.5 mile later, it's decision time. Bear left to continue on Brooksburg-Manville Road back to Manville if you want the short option (skip over the instructions for the Long Option), or go straight 50 feet and turn sharp right onto Upper Dry Fork Road (short, steep, paved climb) for the long option.

Long Option

Upper Dry Fork Road soon turns to gravel. About 1 mile after turning onto Upper Dry Fork Road, turn right across the bridge, then immediately right again onto Comley Hill Road. Within 2 miles, Comley Hill Road has a short, rocky downhill to its end. *Stop* before turning left onto Big Doe Run, which is paved.

Just over 1 mile later, turn left onto Fagg Hill Road; if you hit the Switzerland County line, you've gone too far. Fagg Hill Road is paved and only 0.8 mile long, but it's nearly vertical. When the road Ts into Vernon Ridge Road (which is gravel), turn left.

Less than a mile on Vernon Ridge Road brings you to WFD #2. It's fast and gets even faster on the bottom half. At the bottom is a small slab bridge which is usually dry, then another one that often isn't. (I have a different set of scars from this one.) After crossing the second slab, turn right over the bridge, then immediately left.

Retrace your route back to Greenbrier Road. Turn left then immediately right onto Brooksburg-Manville Road. Follow the Short Option instructions from there.

Short Option

Brooksburg-Manville Road turns to gravel, then back to pavement near the end. It roughly follows Indian-Kentuck Creek for about 4 miles, at which point there's a stop sign. Turn left over the bridge, then left again at the Manville store and over another bridge. When the road splits, bear left up Manville Hill.

After 2 miles of climbing, you'll cross Pleasant Ridge and begin descending WFD #3, Bee Camp Road. The top is steep and rocky, with a sharp left at the bottom. From there it's a slightly downhill romp through creek crossings, past old stone homes, and back to IN 56, where you turn right and ride about 5 miles back to the courthouse.

RIDE 38 · Amish Amble

AT A GLANCE

Length/configuration: 40-mile loop, a little more than half of which is gravel.

IN

Aerobic difficulty: Moderate; lots of ups and downs on this one, but most of the climbs are long, gentle affairs. The exception is 1 granny-gear grinder roughly in the middle.

Technical difficulty: Easy. You'll have to pay attention on the downhills, but mostly this is a chance to gawk at the landscape.

Scenery: Amish folks and their homes, ridges, valleys, horses at pasture, and goats tied to fence posts—this is rural America at its best.

Special comments: You can have fun ripping this ride, but why? Slow down and smell the roses, or honeysuckle, or whatever. Pick up some fossils, shoot some pictures, pack a picnic.

Like all the rides in this section, this one's a mix of pavement and gravel roads. The gravel is the wild card. Some days it's hard-packed and fast, other days it's loose and sketchy. There's no way to predict conditions, so just go out and take your chances.

You're in the heart of southern Indiana's Amish country. No schmaltzy tourist ripoffs, no guided tours, no overpriced bed-and-breakfast shacks with Amish quilts from Honduras. This is the real deal. Humble people in dark clothes going about their business. Simple frame homes with white siding, and no electric lines. Their religion prevents them from being photo subjects—a biblical prohibition against graven images. Please respect their wishes.

If you want to shop where the Amish shop, go to the general store in Pleasant. It's in the southeast corner of IN 250 and IN 129. Check a map, or ask someone.

There are no guarantees you'll see any Amish people. This is their turf, but they're shy folks with work to do.

This area is also home to lots of Mennonites. You'll see truckloads of Mennonite men going to job sites; they're highly sought after for their remarkable carpentry skills. The Amish dress almost exclusively in black, but the Mennonites prefer a blue about the color of Yankee Civil War uniforms. Hardly garish, but a little flashier than their stricter brethren.

General location: The ride starts and stops where Ryker's Ridge Baptist

RIDE 38 · Amish Amble

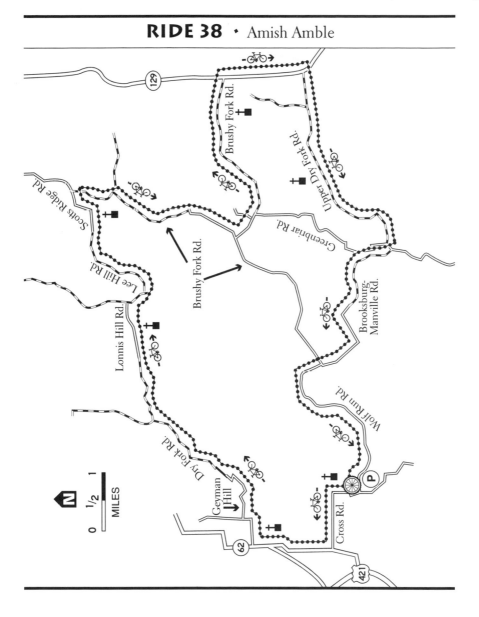

Church, Ryker's Ridge elementary school, and a small park are clustered on a corner about 5 miles northeast of downtown Madison.

Elevation change: Except for a few miles at the beginning and another few leading into Manville, there's almost no flat riding on this loop. Many of the climbs are gentle, rising only 50 or 100 feet before dipping down again. Some, however, clock in at 400 feet.

Season: Year-round, although spring and fall are best. May and early June offer spring wildflowers, and the creeks you ride beside will be running well. Mid-

September through the end of October are dry, and the fall foliage is incredible.

Services: There's a store in Moorefield, about 25 miles into the ride, and the Manville store is about 5 miles from the end. These places have only the basics; for all else, look in Madison where there's everything you need including hotels, restaurants, groceries, and 2 bike shops.

Hazards: This is a pretty benign ride, although there are a couple of fairly fast downhills. The big risk is getting so caught up in the scenery that you ride off into the landscape.

Rescue index: Madison is always fairly close, but these are remote roads. Once you're into the meat of the ride, you may see only a couple of cars all day—or none. Homes are similarly scarce.

Land status: Stay on the roads. Everything else is private property.

Maps: The county highway map, available from the highway garage on Clifty Drive/IN 62 or from the courthouse, is large, clear, and distinguishes between gravel and pavement. This loop makes a short foray into Switzerland County, of which a (poor) map is available from their courthouse or visitor's center in

Vevay. (It's pronounced "Vee-vee." Everyone already knows you're not from 'round here, but no sense in emphasizing the point by saying "Vee-vay.") You probably won't need that map unless you intend to explore beyond this route.

Finding the trail: From the Jefferson County courthouse at the corner of Jefferson and Main Streets in downtown Madison, drive north on Jefferson Street to Aulenbach Avenue. (It's the last right turn before you begin heading up the hill.) Aulenbach Avenue becomes Dugan Hollow. Follow it to the top; turn left at the T. This puts you on Ryker's Ridge Road (Telegraph Hill Road goes to the right from that intersection). Follow Ryker's Ridge Road to the corner where the Baptist church and elementary school are located.

Parking is available at the school, church, and park. Try the park first. It's the tiny patch of open land on your right as you come to this corner; there's a small picnic shelter at the far side. You can also ride here from downtown, if you wish.

Sources of additional information:

Madison Area Convention and Visitors' Bureau
(800) 559-2956

Jefferson County Historical Society
(812) 265-2335

Madison Area Bicycle Club
(812) 265-3620, ext. 7006

Madison Schwinn
2034 Lanier Drive
Madison, IN 47250
(812) 273-4278

Fizz'z Bike Shop
311 West Street
Madison, IN 47250
(812) 273-3499

Notes on the trail: Head north on County Road 300E, which runs along the west edge of the school. In about 0.5 mile, turn left at the T onto CR 300N/Cross Road. Just over 1 mile later is another T, which is Old State Road 62. Turn right. Just over 1 mile later, you'll again turn right onto eastbound IN 62. A half mile beyond that, turn right onto Olive Branch. Within about 0.5 mile, the road goes left; almost immediately after that, you'll turn right onto Geyman Hill Road.

A mile later, Geyman Hill Road turns to gravel and drops sharply. At the bottom is a slab bridge over a wide creek. That creek bed is a good place to pick fossils. Just remember, anything you find you'll have to carry for another 30 miles.

Follow Geyman Hill Road to where it Ts into (paved) China-Manville Road. Turn left over the bridge, then immediately right onto Dry Fork Road, which becomes gravel almost right away.

Stay on Dry Fork Road about 3.5 miles. The first half is nearly flat; the second half is a long, gentle climb. At the top, cross over Hall's Ridge Road onto Lonnis Hill Road, which is a fast, paved descent. At the bottom, turn right at the T onto (gravel) East Prong Road. Within 0.5 mile there's a Y; East Prong Road goes right, and you go left onto Lee Hill Road. Here's the toughest climb of the ride.

After 2 miles, turn onto Lee Hill Road and go straight onto Scott's Ridge Road, which is paved. A mile later, turn right onto Shaw Hollow Road, which is a happy little 1-mile, gravel descent.

Two miles after you turn onto Lee Hill Road, you'll come to Scott's Ridge Road. It goes both to the right and straight ahead. Go right at the T onto Brushy Fork Road. Within 1 mile, you're at another T, which is Tate Ridge Road. Turn right to remain on Brushy Fork Road, which is paved here. Take your first left, about 1 mile down the road, which is Little Brushy Fork Road, also paved. A half mile later, veer right at the Y to remain on Little Brushy Fork Road (Dow Ridge Road goes left and up the hill). Almost immediately after that, the pavement goes right. You go left to stay on Little Brushy Fork Road, which becomes gravel. (CR 850E, which is paved, goes to the right and up the hill.)

Little Brushy Fork is almost 4 miles of gentle, scenic climbing. At the top, turn right at the T onto IN 129. A mile later, you're at the corner of IN 129 and Greenbriar Road, which is pretty much the center of Moorefield. There's little more than a country store here, and not much on the shelves at that. But if you do need something, it's your last chance to stock up for a while.

Turn right (west) onto Greenbriar Road. (Smith Ridge Road goes east from this intersection.) Take your first left, which comes up in about 1 mile and is gravel. This is Dry Fork Road. A half mile after this turn is a Y; bear right. A half mile later there is another Y, and again you should bear right. This begins a fast, fun descent.

After 4 miles, the bridge of the Comley-Fagg option of Ride 37 will be on your left. Continue straight on Dry Fork until it dead-ends into Greenbrier Road, which is about another mile past the bridge. Turn left onto Greenbrier Road (not right and up a killer hill), then immediately right onto Brooksburg-Manville Road. The road turns to gravel within 100 yards.

Stay on Brooksburg-Manville Road for 4 miles until you reach the stop sign. Turn left over the bridge. (The Manville store is about 300 yards on the right if you need to stop.)

The last 5 miles have been on the same route as Ride 37; here's where the 2 routes diverge. Just past the bridge, Ride 37 goes up Manville Hill Road, while today's route goes right onto Wolf Run Road.

Wolf Run Road has a hump in it near the beginning. Otherwise, it's 5 miles of gentle, paved climbing back to Ryker's Ridge School and the church and that little park. Enjoy Wolf Run. You're probably tired from all that climbing, and this piece of road is really pretty. There are several cabins along the creek; look for the cluster of log structures reassembled on property to your right just before you begin the final climb. From Ryker's Ridge Corner (where you parked), retrace your steps down Ryker's Ridge and Dugan Hollow Roads to get back to Madison.

RIDE 39 · Freefall

AT A GLANCE

Length/configuration: 17-mile loop, a little more than half of which is paved.

Aerobic difficulty: Easy, except 1 moderate (paved) climb early on and 1 tough (gravel) climb about halfway through.

Technical difficulty: Easy, except a pair of white-knuckle descents and 1 tough (steep and loose) climb.

Scenery: Splendid ridge-top views, babbling country brooks, and a few friendly horses in a corral.

Special comments: It would be better if this were all gravel road, but the scenery is so nice, you won't mind being on pavement. As an aside, the pavement on some sections is so rough, we had to reroute our bike club's annual invitational ride (the Madison Meander). Too many complaints. You'll be fine on a mountain bike, though.

IN

Of the four Madison rides, this one has the toughest climb and two of the fastest descents. At the bottom of both descents are slab bridges. The first drop has two; the second drop has one. You'll be approaching them at speed, so heed all the warnings about these slippery devils. If the slab is anything but dry and whitish-gray, use extreme caution. Water or algae can bring you down and when they're both present, they're worse than ice.

There are several spots along this route with great overlooks of the Ohio River valley. Take your time riding, and pause to look over your shoulder occasionally.

The time you spend in the bottomlands is just as rewarding. Riding China-Manville Road is wonderfully scenic. But watch for cars. There's little traffic here, so the locals tend to drive fast. No real risk, as long as you stay right and keep your eyes open.

General location: This ride starts in China, about 5 miles northeast of Madison on IN 62.

Elevation change: The 2 drops are both good for about 400 feet of vertical, otherwise this one's fairly flat whether you're on the ridge or in the bottoms.

RIDE 39 · Freefall

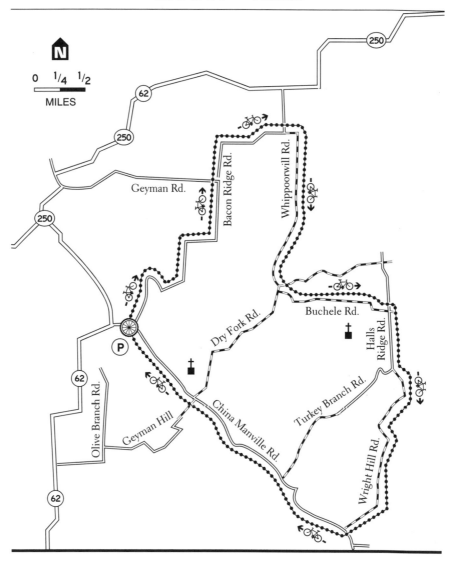

Season: Like all the Madison rides, this one's good year-round. Spring is pretty; fall is equally beautiful and drier.

Services: Madison has everything you need including hotels, restaurants, groceries, and 2 bike shops. If you need something while on this ride, you'll have to detour to Canaan or Manville.

Hazards: Those slab bridges

Rescue index: Emergency services are available in Madison; there's not much on these remote roads.

Land status: Stay on the roads—everything else is private property.

Maps: The county highway map, available from the highway garage on Clifty Drive/IN 62 or from the courthouse, is large, clear, and distinguishes between gravel and pavement.

Finding the trail: Take IN 62 east from Madison's hilltop. After the 4-way stop at US 421, IN 62 becomes 2 lanes. In a couple of miles, it begins a steep descent. At the bottom there's a curve to the right. In 0.5 mile, there's a sharp left onto a bridge over Razor Fork. Just over the bridge is an old stone church. Park along the road there.

Sources of additional information:

Madison Area Convention and Visitors' Bureau
(800) 559-2956

Jefferson County Historical Society
(812) 265-2335

Madison Area Bicycle Club
(812) 265-3620, ext. 7006

Madison Schwinn
2034 Lanier Drive
Madison, IN 47250
(812) 273-4278

Fizz'z Bike Shop
311 West Street
Madison, IN 47250
(812) 273-3499

Notes on the trail: From your parking spot, ride back across the bridge over Razor Fork. Instead of turning right to remain on IN 62, turn left onto China-Manville Road. Cross the bridge over the West Fork of Indian-Kentuck Creek, and take an immediate left onto Bacon Ridge Road. You'll begin climbing right away.

About 1 mile after Geyman Road comes in from the left, Bacon Ridge Road curves hard to the left, while (gravel) Whippoorwill Road goes straight ahead. Take Whippoorwill Road. (Veering left will take you to IN 62/250, where a right will put you into Canaan within 1 mile.) Within 20 yards, the Whippoorwill Road turns to the right.

Whippoorwill Road runs along the ridge for 1 mile or so, then descends suddenly. At the bottom of the descent are 2 slab bridges. Use caution crossing them. After crossing the second one, the road Ts into Dry Fork Road. Turn right. After 0.2 mile, turn left onto Buchele Road. This is one tough climb, but the worst of it is over soon.

You'll crest the hill and cruise along for about 1 mile to Hall's Ridge Road, which is paved. Turn right. Just under 2 miles farther along, turn left onto Wright Hill Road, which is gravel. If you begin to descend, you've gone too far and are on Turkey Branch Road.

Wright Hill Road is a study in opposites. There's at least 1 ugly little hillbilly homestead, some illegal dumping sites, and rotting autos up on blocks. There are also immaculate country homes, a wildlife preserve, and some of the most breathtaking ridge-top views to be found.

Wright Hill Road lopes along casually for almost 2 miles before it begins to descend its namesake hill. This drop is less than 0.75 mile long, but it's a thrilling descent. It can also be rough; I lost both water bottles coming down this once. At the bottom is a slab bridge; cross carefully.

When Wright Hill Road Ts into (paved) China Manville Road, turn right. (A left here will bring you to Manville in about 1 mile.) Follow China-Manville Road for about 3 miles back to IN 62. Turn right over Razor Branch and you're back to the start.

HOOSIER NATIONAL FOREST

The Hoosier National Forest presents the best riding opportunities in the state. Not that HNF is brimming with wonderful rides—it's not. It's just that there's so little else to ride, the forest goes to the head of the list by default.

Here are the numbers. Less than 3% of the land in Indiana is public land. (Compare that to 80% for some Western states.) Of that 3%, much of it is state land. The state, in its infinite wisdom, has decreed that mountain bikes are off-limits off-road on all its holdings, except for the 11-mile Kekionga trail around Huntington reservoir. (Perhaps this will have changed by the time you read this, but I doubt it.)

This is not to say HNF is small. The forest covers 194,000 acres from just south of Bloomington all the way to the Ohio River. But lots of the land within those boundaries is private land. Some is the Deam Wilderness. Both the private holdings and the wilderness are closed to mountain biking.

Sometimes there's disconnected chunks of land that would make great riding, if only you could get from one to another.

Even when you're on open trails, you're often competing with horses and hikers for space. There's lots of demand in this populous state, and little infrastructure to meet that demand. Oh, and don't forget the logging operations.

That's all external stuff. The forest has had its share of internal problems, too. Most of them center around severe budget cutbacks, which means there are fewer dollars, tools, people, maps, and everything else while the demand for recreational opportunities goes up.

Nature hasn't always been kind to the Hoosier, either. The year after the forest put its trail plan into effect, a massive late season wet snowfall popped trees throughout the forest. Before that got cleaned up, a wicked wind storm came through. Some trails had blowdowns every 50 feet.

And as if that weren't enough, much of what would be prime trail locations are off-limits because of archaeological sites, endangered plants, karst, or some other feature worthy of preservation.

Is there any good news in all this?

Yup. Several bits of it. The biggest is that the people at the forest offices, notably recreation manager Les Wadzinski, are dedicated, down-to-earth folks who insist on prevailing against all odds. They've done a lot with a little, and when mere mortals would have thrown in the towel, this crew found ways not only to maintain their property but even improve it.

The other piece of good news is that there's some really enjoyable riding in the Hoosier. I doubt anyone ever woke up one morning in Crested Butte or Moab and said, "Hey, I got an idea. Let's go where the riding is really great— Indiana." But there are about 200 miles of trails for different competency levels. And despite the congestion on some popular trails, others are virtually vacant, even on weekends.

Most of the riding is typical Eastern woods stuff. There's plenty of single track interspersed with old logging roads, short (often steep) climbs but little overall change in elevation, some streams, some rocks, lots of trees and an abundance of smallish critters.

So here's the summary: if you're looking for a place to spend your vacation doing fabulous trails, skip the Hoosier. On the other hand, if you're in Indiana anyway and have a bike with you, don't leave it parked thinking there's nothing to ride here. You'd be missing some riding that while not spectacular, is at the very least a lot of fun.

Final notes: as this is being written, the forest is testing a permit system. Call the forest office ((812) 275-5987) before you ride to see if it's in effect. Remember that most of the Hoosier permits hunting. I wear a fluorescent orange vest and helmet cover during hunting season as a minimum. And remember that trails are blazed for equestrians, too, which means many blazes are much higher in the trees than you might expect. Look up or get lost. Blazes for mountain biking are blue or yellow, often a blue dot in the middle of a white diamond (the white diamond is for hiking trails).

The forest office offers recreational opportunity guides. These ROGs are free and give general information and a trail map. In the past they've been marginally helpful, but they're now being updated with GPS information and topographic lines. The best bet if you plan on riding several trails is the Trails Illustrated map (#770). It shows all the trails in the forest on one map. They're available from the forest office, local retailers (such as J.L. Waters in Bloomington), and Trails Illustrated in Evergreen, Colorado ((800) 962-1643).

The Hoosier trail engineers have been spreading gravel on trails to harden them. In some places, this is appropriate. In most places, it's ugly and rough. Worse, the trails get widened to eight feet to allow passage of gravel trucks and spreaders. Several of us are working with forest officials to find alternate methods of hardening, but you can expect to encounter remnants of this eyesore on several trails.

And a final thought about safety: if you're relying on your cell phone to save you in an emergency, don't. The valleys in the Hoosier prevent reliable cell communication. Bring it if you want to, but don't think of it as your failsafe device. Not here.

For more information on the Hoosier National Forest, contact forest offices at 811 Constitution Avenue, Bedford, IN 47421 ((812) 279-3423) or 248 15th Street, Tell City, IN 47586 ((812) 547-7051).

RIDE 40 · Lick Creek

AT A GLANCE

Length/configuration: Combination of a 7-mile loop with a 1.7-mile spur to and from the parking area (about 10.5 miles total). Mostly wide single-track.

Aerobic difficulty: Easy. If your beginner has tired of circling Tipsaw Lake, here's another option.

Technical difficulty: Easy. The only challenges are a start than can be muddy and a short section of rock about halfway through.

Scenery: Typical eastern woods.

Special comments: An excellent trail for beginners, Lick Creek has a different feel and offers a different experience from Tipsaw. This trail is wide, rolls a bit, and is almost entirely wooded.

This wonderful little loop avoids being too easy by throwing in a few really short hills and a section of rocks. At times the entrance can be muddy.

This trail has it all: a chance for air right at the beginning, some hardwoods, some pines, some wide trails, and some narrow single-track. There are rocks and hills. But none of this shows up in daunting form. Just an easy little ride, sort of an off-road sampler for someone who's not sure what kind of riding is most appealing.

You can ride this as a warm-up, then hop back in the car and drive 20 minutes to the much more demanding Young's Creek. Or you can just do several laps here.

The Forest Service has planned a trail at Springs Valley for several years. At the request of the Forest Service, I've walked that trail with their trails engineer and other employees to give my view on it from a mountain biker's perspective. I came away excited. It's a great trail. Once built, it will offer an intermediate ride somewhere between the ease of Lick Creek and the high effort of Young's Creek. Best of all, a rider could put in 40-plus miles of single-track in this area with just a few road connections. Will Springs Valley get built? Eventually. When? Who knows. Call the Bedford office and check on progress.

In the meantime, enjoy Lick Creek. It's a unique trail that is neither boring nor daunting. It somehow packs in a lot of fun without any real fireworks.

General location: About 5 miles south of Paoli on State Highway 37

Elevation change: Minimal, maybe 50 feet in several stretches of gentle rollers, except that the rock section is a bit steeper and the in/out spur has a few steeper parts.

RIDE 40 • Lick Creek

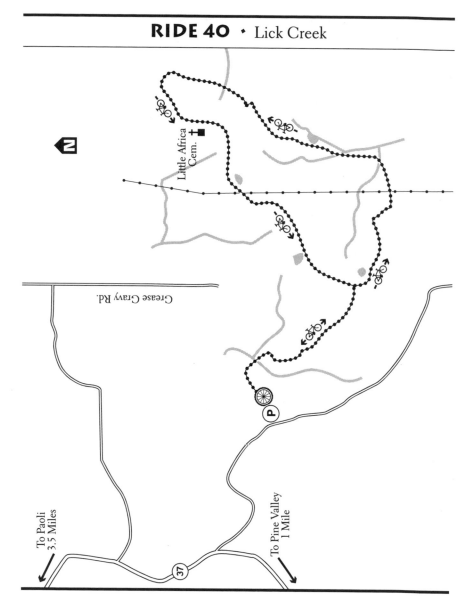

Season: Pretty much year-round, depending on precipitation. This one remains rideable even when nearby Young's Creek is swimming in mud. See the general introduction for more information.

Services: Paoli has a hospital, a couple of restaurants, and some lodging as well as groceries and other amenities. There's a bike shop in Salem, about 20 miles east of Paoli, but it doesn't have much. The nearest good shops are Louisville and Columbus.

Hazards: Virtually none

Rescue index: Because this trail is new, it isn't yet getting lots of use. It's probably prudent to ride with a buddy, especially in the off-season (October through early May).

Land status: National forest

Maps: The Trails Illustrated map or the ROG from the Forest Service, although it's unlikely you'd need either for this friendly little trail.

Finding the trail: Head south out of Paoli on IN 37. About 5 miles from town, IN 37 curves right and a county road goes left. There are Forest Service signs and a sign for Marengo Cave. Follow that county road for about 1 mile and you'll find the parking area on your left. The trailhead is apparent on the back side of the parking lot.

Sources of additional information:

Bicycles Etc. bike shop
1101 12th Street
Tell City, IN 47586
(812) 547-7161

Hoosier National Forest
811 Constitution Avenue
Bedford, IN 47421
(812) 279-3423
or
248 15th Street
Tell City, IN 47586
(812) 547-7051

Notes on the trail: Leaving the parking lot, the trail heads downhill. There are a number of earthen-berm water bars here, which make for good air. Just watch for return riders, as this same piece of trail is the way back out. Use caution if the trail is muddy.

Continue on this wide single-track as it rolls along. Less than 2 miles into the ride, the trail Ts. Go right; you'll be riding the trail counter-clockwise.

This trail is a snap to follow. There are no intersecting trails or old roads to confuse you. There's a natural gas pipeline that makes a handy reference point. You'll cross it about a mile from the **T**, and again about 6 miles into the ride.

Changes in scenery come fast, so the ride never becomes boring. About halfway through, there's a short uphill section over rocks. Otherwise, this is as easy as mountain biking gets.

Shortly after you cross the pipeline for the second time, the trail splits. The right fork dead-ends at a gate at Grease Gravy Road. Unless you're intrigued by the name, there's no reason to go there. Continue on to the left.

A half mile past that split, you'll be back at the **T** where you originally went right. Go right this time, too, and you'll return to the parking lot.

RIDE 41 · Young's Creek

AT A GLANCE

Length/configuration: 12-mile loop; mostly single-track.

Aerobic difficulty: Challenging. Hardly a flat 50 feet to be found; bring your best lungs, biggest legs, and lowest gears.

Technical difficulty: Challenging. Roots, rocks, steep hills, and lots of 'em. There are occasional stretches of deep standing water. In most cases there are alternative trails bushwhacked around the edges.

Scenery: Typical Eastern woods with a few nice ridge-top views.

Special comments: This is a tough little mother, made worse by blazes that are sometimes unclear, vandalized, or missing. It's also a lot of fun and made bearable by stretches of cruising between the lung-busting climbs.

The most enduring impression of this trail is that it's a lot of work. Some sections aren't bad. Some even border on easy. But the frequent steeps leave an overall impression of a trail that never really lets up.

Young's Creek trail is a testimony to the work of the Forest Service personnel. The first time I attempted to ride here in the early 1990s, I tried to access the trail from a half-dozen locations. In some places, I couldn't find the trail. In others, I could find the trail, but I couldn't ride it. It was overgrown with sticker bushes. After driving an hour and a half to get here, I turned back in frustration. I returned later, and found the trail blocked by blow-downs from the previous winter.

Now the trail is clear (although the condition of the blazes varies). The sticker bushes are gone, as are the blowdowns. The parking areas are well maintained.

The other lasting impression, besides that of tough riding, is loneliness. I've ridden this trail maybe a dozen times and have yet to see another human out here, not even at the main parking area. It's eerie.

General location: 4 miles south of Paoli, just off IN 37

Elevation change: There are lots of 350-foot climbs. In most cases you'll get some comparatively easy riding for recovery time between grunts.

Season: Pretty much year-round, depending on precipitation. The best time is fall. See the general introduction for more information.

RIDE 41 • Young's Creek

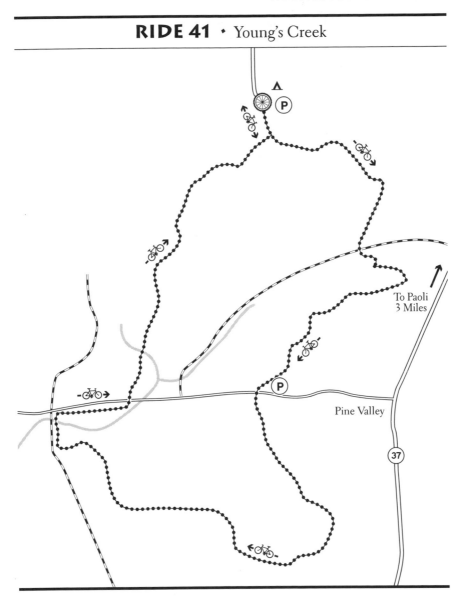

To Paoli
3 Miles

P

Pine Valley

37

Services: Paoli has a hospital, a couple of restaurants, and some lodging as well as groceries and other amenities. There's a bike shop in Salem, about 20 miles east of Paoli, but he doesn't have much. The nearest good shops are Louisville and Columbus.

Hazards: The rocks, roots, and remoteness deserve your careful consideration.

Rescue index: Probably wise to bring a buddy

Land status: National forest

Maps: The Trails Illustrated map and the ROG are available from the Forest Service, and it's probably a good idea to have one or both here.

Finding the trail: The roads to Young's Creek Horse Camp are clearly marked. Head south from Paoli on IN 37. About 3 miles out is a county road (if it were numbered, it would be County Road 250S). Turn right. A mile in is a gravel road to the left. (If it were numbered, it would be CR 50W.) A mile down this road is the parking area on the left near the top of a hill.

In the southeast corner of the parking area, near the picnic shelter and pit toilets, is a sign directing you to the trailhead. Follow the double-track 0.1 mile and watch for the signs when it runs out.

Sources of additional information:

Bicycles Etc. bike shop
1101 12th Street
Tell City, IN 47586
(812) 547-7161

Hoosier National Forest
248 15th Street
Tell City, IN 47586
(812) 547-7051

Notes on the trail: I took the left trailhead when I first rode here, only because someone's raggedy old trailer blocked my view of the other trail sign. I wound up doing the trail clockwise, and although it probably doesn't matter, now I always ride it that way.

About 2 miles of single-track brings you to a gravel road. Jog left for 20 feet and the trail dives back into the woods. In less than 2 miles, you'll come to a paved road. This is the road you came in on, the one that would be CR 250S, if it was signed. Go right for 20 feet and then left back into the woods.

Continue on this single-track until you hit a paved road. (Watch the blazes, as there are a few social trails coming in from private land.) At the road, turn right. A half mile down, turn right again on another paved road. A half mile later, turn left back into the woods. (Watch for the blazes and Carsonite markers. The trail goes into the woods on the near edge of a field.) You'll soon begin climbing. Maybe it's because it's late in the ride, but this climb always knocks the wind out of me. Just as the trail levels out, an illegal ATV trail comes in from the left. When it goes left again, the official trail goes to the right.

The trail comes briefly onto a gravel road near the end. On your left will be a really unusual, owner-built house. Just past the driveway, the trail angles off to the right into the woods again. Be watching for this, as it's not readily apparent despite the blazes.

In a matter of minutes you're back at the start. You'll come in on the opposite side of where you started. Turn left and follow the double-track back to where you parked.

RIDE 42 · Shirley Creek Trail, East Loop

AT A GLANCE

Length/configuration: Length varies, as a number of loops are possible; options from 4 to 25 miles or more are available. Most are single-track.

IN

Aerobic difficulty: Moderate to extremely challenging, depending on how much you're willing to climb.

Technical difficulty: Moderate to challenging as the climbs can be demanding. I have also found a lot of logs and other obstacles on this trail at times.

Scenery: Typical eastern woods.

Special comments: Hit the hills and this is the toughest ride in the state. At the time I rode this, the East Loop was poorly marked and intertwined with lots of social trails. It might not be worth going here if the East Loop were all that was available, but with the West Loop just across the road, this is a good destination.

Whether on the East or West Loop, the defining characteristic of this trail network is elevation. There are three places you'll be riding here: on the ridge tops, in the creek bottoms, or on one of the hills connecting them.

The East Loop is a workout. Tough hills, obstacles across the trail, missing blazes—at times I was wishing I could find a shortcut back to the truck.

This is a popular area with hunters and horse riders, so you may want to avoid it during hunting season. On the other hand, I've ridden here in the middle of deer season and seen hunters only in the parking area. Use your judgment.

General location: About 10 miles east of Orleans in northwestern Orange County

Elevation change: Major hills of about 400 feet with frequent smaller rises. You can avoid some of these with careful planning, but unless you're willing to spend all day riding back and forth on one leg of this route, figure on some serious climbing. The worst comes as you climb up out of the creek bottom, but even the middle of the ride can be demanding with frequent short, steep climbs.

Season: Year-round, depending on precipitation. Both east and west loops have frequent creek bed crossings. Refer to the general introduction for more information.

Services: Orleans has most of what you'll need—food, gas, and such. But the nearest bike shop is in Bloomington, and that's more than an hour to the north. Come prepared.

Hazards: Nothing unusual

Rescue index: There are phones in Orleans; the nearest hospital is in Paoli, about 20 miles to the southeast.

Land status: National forest, although you can detour onto public roads in spots if you wish.

Maps: The Trails Illustrated map and the ROG are available from the Forest Service, and it's probably a good idea to have one or both here.

Finding the trail: From downtown Orleans, go south on IN 37/Maple from IN 337/Washington for 2 blocks. Turn west onto Vincennes. This road changes to CR 700N outside the Orleans town limits, then to a variety of different numbers as it winds through the countryside. No matter. Just don't turn from the road you started on.

About 10 miles west of town, you'll come to CR 775W; turn left. (This intersection is Hindostan, or Hindustan, and appears on some old maps.) There's a Forest Service sign for Shirley Creek here.

It's just over 1 mile to the gravel road to the horse camp. Turn left onto this road. Go to the end and park in the horse camp. The trail leaves from that parking loop.

RIDE 42 • Shirley Creek Trail, East Loop

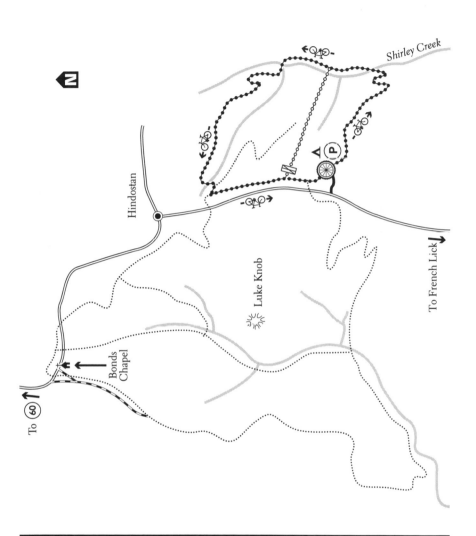

Source of additional information:

Hoosier National Forest
811 Constitution Avenue
Bedford, IN 47421
(812) 279-3423

Notes on the trail: The trail leaves from the parking area. Start by going east (the trail at the end, not the side, of the parking loop). Soon after you start on the trail, you'll begin descending to Shirley Creek.

Sometimes the trail stays down low along the creek. Other times it goes up, then comes back down. Watch the blazes so you don't get sidetracked onto a social trail.

There are 2 points at which you can ride back up. Taking the first will give a short loop of under 4 miles. The second uphill return will give you about 5 miles. Either return brings you to a piece of trail that parallels the road you came in on from Hindostan. Follow the trail back to the parking area, or cross the road to enter the Shirley Creek West Loops.

RIDE 43 · Shirley Creek Trail, West Loop

AT A GLANCE

Length/configuration: Length varies, as a number of loops exist; options from 4 to 25 miles or more are possible. Most are single-track; some have short sections of public roads. What I've described is about 17 miles, all either single-track or creek bed except 1 brief stretch of county road.

IN

Aerobic difficulty: Moderate to extremely challenging, depending on how many times you're willing to climb up out of the creek bottoms. I limited my climbing to 1 really steep ascent (and several smaller ones) by taking the outer perimeter of this system.

Technical difficulty: Moderate to challenging. In addition to the tough ascents, there are some steep, rocky downhills with switchbacks, and rocky creek beds.

Scenery: Typical eastern forest; mostly hardwoods.

Special comments: Hit the hills and this is the toughest ride in the state. It's also one of the prettiest, with the trail running along creek channels and under dense woods. The steepest climbs have produced some erosion problems, so those trail sections are slated for relocation.

The West Loops were much better blazed than the East, had less dead wood, and the climbs were farther apart. Even so, I spent plenty of time hike-a-biking due to logs, erosion gullies, and hills that were simply too steep.

Whether on the East or West Loop, the defining characteristic of this trail network is elevation. There are three places you'll be riding here: on the ridge tops, in the creek bottoms, or on one of the hills connecting them.

RIDE 43 · Shirley Creek Trail, West Loop

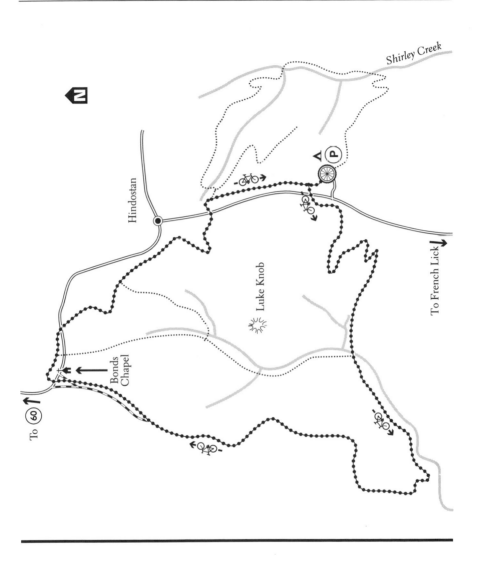

I like the West Loops. They offer more variety than the East Loop, which is to be expected since there are more miles of trail here. Even so, the variety and general nature of the West Loops was fun. And because they're farther from the parking area, you're less likely to encounter other users. Probably a moot point, as no part of this trail system is overrun with people.

Since there's a stretch where you're riding in a creek bed, it's best to avoid this trail after a heavy rain or when there's snowmelt. On the other hand, the creek makes a nice cool ride in the heat of summer.

General location: About 10 miles east of Orleans in northwestern Orange County

Elevation change: Major hills of about 400 feet with frequent smaller rises. There is only one time where you'll be powering up the full 400 feet. Between the pitch of the hill, the loose surface, and the deep erosion gullies, I wound up walking this part.

Season: All year, depending on precipitation (both East and West Loops have frequent creek bed crossings). Refer to the general introduction for more information.

Services: Orleans has most of what you'll need—food, gas, and such. But the nearest bike shop is in Bloomington, and that's more than an hour to the north. Come prepared.

Hazards: Rocky sections, some of them in creek beds

Rescue index: There are phones in Orleans; the nearest hospital is in Paoli, about 20 miles to the southeast.

Land status: National forest, with short sections of public roads

Maps: The Trails Illustrated map or the ROG from the Forest Service, and it's probably a good idea to have one or both here. The trail is easy to follow, but you may find yourself looking for a shortcut back, for which you'll need a map.

Finding the trail: From downtown Orleans, go south on IN 37/Maple from IN 337/Washington for 2 blocks. Turn west onto Vincennes. This road changes to CR 700N outside the Orleans town limits, then to a variety of different numbers as it winds through the countryside. No matter. Just don't turn from the road you started on.

About 10 miles west of town, you'll come to CR 775W; turn left. (This intersection is Hindostan, or Hindustan, and appears on some old maps.) There's a Forest Service sign for Shirley Creek here.

It's just over a mile to the gravel road to the horse camp. Turn left onto this road. You can follow it all the way to the end if you wish, or park near the gate if there's room. (The gate is on the right, just 50 feet from the county road, where the entrance road takes a left.) Ride back to CR 775W, turn right, and the trail goes left into the woods about 100 yards up.

Source of additional information:

Hoosier National Forest
811 Constitution Avenue
Bedford, IN 47421
(812) 279-3123

Notes on the trail: After a short time on the ridge, the trail drops rather abruptly down into a creek bottom. About 1.5 miles into the ride, the trail splits in a creek bed. Going through the creek and angling to the right yields a short option. For the long option, go left in the creek bed for 30 feet and back up the bank. (I chose the long option.)

The long loop runs along the creek bed at times; at other times, it runs in the bed. Follow the blazes.

About 1 mile down from the split, the trail pops up out of the creek bed and meets a dirt road. Turn right, and the trail quickly splits off from the road and goes left. Almost immediately you'll begin climbing. This area is badly eroded, so expect to carry or push your bike for much of the uphill. (This part of the trail may be relocated by the time you read this.)

Once you hit the ridge top, you can mostly cruise along. You're still climbing, but gradually. In time, you'll come to a spot where the ridge is open and the trail climbs to a gravel road. Take the road; the land on either side is private.

Follow that gravel road to a paved road. Turn right. You have a choice: if you're tired, follow the pavement back to Hindostan, turn right on CR 775W, and ride back to the parking area. Otherwise, you can pick up the trail again within 100 yards or so of making your right turn. The trail goes to the right from the road. At the first **Y**, bear left. There are some short climbs in this section. Bear left again at the second **Y**. When the trail crosses CR 775W, bear right. The trail stays fairly flat as it runs along CR 775W and back to the parking area.

RIDE 44 · Ogala Trail

AT A GLANCE

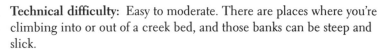

Length/configuration: A couple of loops totaling 10 miles or so, as of this writing. Mostly single-track.

Aerobic difficulty: Easy, except that low usage has allowed brush to grow up and make the trail indistinct in many spots.

Technical difficulty: Easy to moderate. There are places where you're climbing into or out of a creek bed, and those banks can be steep and slick.

Scenery: Typical Eastern woods, with a Native American ceremonial site thrown in.

Special comments: This trail is scheduled for a complete overhaul. However, the Forest Service is considering closing this trail rather than rebuilding. Be sure to get current information before riding here.

This is a user-friendly trail. The terrain is gentle, with rolling hills and a few tiny streams that stay dry most of the time. Once the trail system is expanded and refined, this should be a great place for beginners and intermediates to spend a day. Of course, if the decision is made to close it instead, too bad. The sentiment in the office as of this writing is that the Ogala Trail has enough going for it to warrant some work, if only the resources can be found.

The most intriguing reason to ride here is to see the site where the Lakota Sioux hold their purification ceremony every August. Outsiders are welcomed, although there are restrictions. Call the Forest Service office for more information. (One standing rule deserves noting here and now: *no cameras!*)

Three of us rode here one autumn afternoon and had a good time, despite the fact the trail was nearly invisible to us much of the time. We found some nice single-track and a few county road connectors. Best of all, trail conditions were excellent. The same could not be said of nearby Hickory Ridge, which we rode the same day and which was hopelessly muddy.

As an added bonus, there's Sundance Lake here. It's small, but offers plenty of spots for some lazy bank fishing.

General location: About 20 miles southeast of Nashville in the extreme southeastern corner of Brown County

Elevation change: Mostly flat with a few rollers. There might be 200 feet of change over the whole area.

RIDE 44 · Ogala Trail

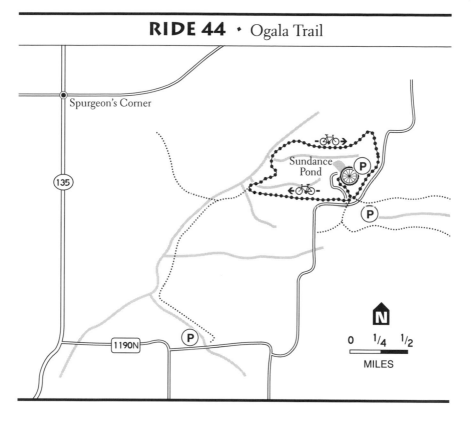

Season: Mostly year-round, although winters are snowier here than in the southern parts of the Hoosier. You can check trail conditions by calling the Bedford office of the Forest Service.

Services: Food, lodging, and gas in Nashville; all that and a hospital in Seymour. Both Seymour and Columbus have bike shops.

Hazards: Nothing unusual

Rescue index: This is a pretty lonely place most of the year; ride with a friend or at least tell someone where you're going.

Land status: National forest

Maps: The Trails Illustrated map and the ROG are available from the Forest Service, and it's probably a good idea to have one or both here. As it is now, the trail is a patchwork of single-track, creek bed, and county road. The map helps, although you'll still experience some confusion.

Finding the trail: From IN 135, follow the signs for Sundance Pond. You'll go west on CR 1190N, which is the first county road south of the Jackson/Brown County line. You can turn right off the access road and park in the lot by the pond, or go straight back to the gate and ride to the ceremony site.

Source of additional information:

Hoosier National Forest
811 Constitution Avenue
Bedford, IN 47421
(812) 279-3423

Notes on the trail: The day we rode this we ran into lots of dead-ends and disconnected trail segments. The trails were poorly marked and little used, so it was tough to pick them out against a carpet of fallen leaves. What we discovered, however, was that the trails we could find were a joy to ride. Occasionally we'd hit an old erosion gully, but otherwise everything visible was rideable. Would I go back? Yes. The area holds plenty of promise. If you come here, bring a sense of adventure and ride what you can find. When that thrill is gone, head to Hickory Ridge or the Nebo Ridge segment of the Knobstone Trail. They're both within 0.5 hour by car.

RIDE 45 · Hickory Ridge

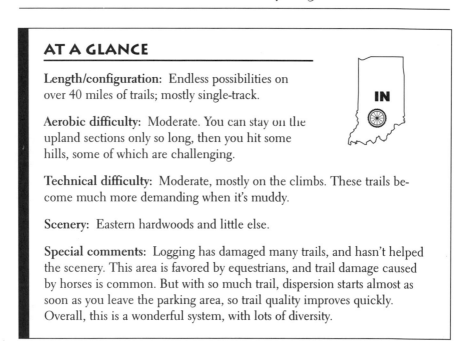

AT A GLANCE

Length/configuration: Endless possibilities on over 40 miles of trails; mostly single-track.

IN

Aerobic difficulty: Moderate. You can stay on the upland sections only so long, then you hit some hills, some of which are challenging.

Technical difficulty: Moderate, mostly on the climbs. These trails become much more demanding when it's muddy.

Scenery: Eastern hardwoods and little else.

Special comments: Logging has damaged many trails, and hasn't helped the scenery. This area is favored by equestrians, and trail damage caused by horses is common. But with so much trail, dispersion starts almost as soon as you leave the parking area, so trail quality improves quickly. Overall, this is a wonderful system, with lots of diversity.

General location: On IN 58 about 25 miles west of Seymour

Elevation change: Most of the ups and downs were fairly easy to ride and offered maybe 300 feet of elevation change. Some, especially those north of Forest Service Road 1619, were too steep to ride up or down.

RIDE 45 • Hickory Ridge

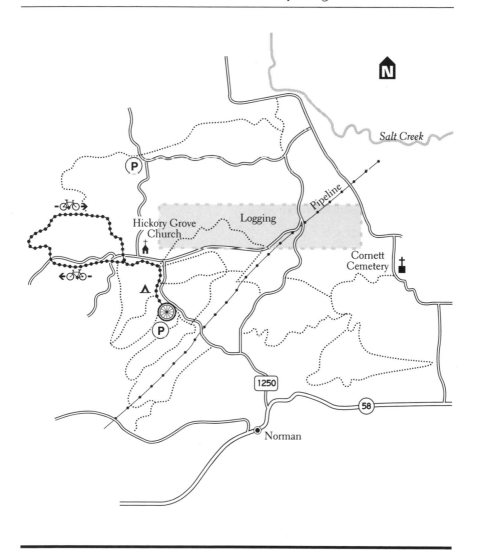

Season: Year-round, weather permitting. Best in fall because it's dry. If there's the slightest residual water, the horses will pound the trail into muck.

Services: Everything (including bike shops) in Columbus and Bloomington. Most services (including a bike shop) in Seymour. Most services (including Hoosier National Forest headquarters, but no bike shop) in Bedford.

Hazards: Nothing unusual, but you should call first to see if there's active logging in the area.

Rescue index: Lots of users, but they fan out widely so it's best to ride with a buddy.

Land status: National forest

Maps: The Trails Illustrated map and the ROG are available from the Forest Service, and it's probably a good idea to have one or both here. There's too many miles of trails, and too many options to trust to luck in finding your way around. The local horseback riders club has signed the trails and assigned numbers to them, but those numbers don't show up on the map. Still, the signing is an immense improvement over the simple Carsonite markers that were there.

Finding the trail: Less than 0.5 mile east of Norman on IN 58 are signs to the trailhead. Park in the horse camp area.

Source of additional information:

Hoosier National Forest
811 Constitution Avenue
Bedford, IN 47421
(812) 279-3423

Notes on the trail: There are too many options here to list, so I'll give some generalizations. Horse people tend to go north, so those trail segments are generally rougher, but wider. The best single-track runs to the southwest of the horse camp area. Terrain is similar either direction, with lots of small hills and a few longer, tougher climbs. The north side has more challenging hills, and more of them. If you feel you haven't gotten your money's worth unless I recommend a specific ride, here it is. Take the trail that parallels FS 1618. It starts by running northwest from the parking area along the road. About 3 miles from the horse camp, the trail crosses FS 1618, loops north before cutting east, then returns south, crossing the road again. From there you can take a left and retrace your route to the start.

RIDE 46 · Nebo Ridge

AT A GLANCE

Length/configuration: 17-mile combination. The trail in and out adds up to under 2 miles; the rest is in a loop. Nebo Ridge is mostly single-track with some county road.

IN

Aerobic difficulty: Moderate. There are few really difficult climbs, but lots of small to medium-sized ones.

Technical difficulty: Moderate. This trail gets quite a bit of mountain bike use, so it's nicely buffed. The worst technical challenge is the old flapper-style water bars, with a rubber lip poking up above the dirt. They're little threat on the downhills, but can stop you cold on the climbs.

Scenery: Eastern hardwoods, sections of pines, very pretty overall.

Special comments: This trail gets lots of use, yet is holding up well. It's a lot of fun for any rider of intermediate ability.

I think this was my first ride in the Hoosier National Forest. A group of us came here and rode around before there even was a trail plan. It changed my thinking. I had believed there was no decent single-track in the state of Indiana. Now I believed there was, I just resented driving two hours to get to it.

This is a wonderful trail with plenty of variety. Although there are some demanding climbs, there's nothing overwhelming. There are two sections I really like. One goes through a pine woods. The other is a roller-coaster ride that undulates along firm trail that's banked just right.

One note of caution: don't stray from the trail. Though there have been no incidents on the trail or in the forest, adjacent landowners have been openly hostile, even to the point of threatening riders and hikers with guns. The odds of it happening to you on the trail are virtually zero. Even if you get lost, it's unlikely you'll have trouble. Just be aware that such confrontations have occurred in the past.

If you want to make a weekend of it, stay overnight in Nashville. The town is packed with craftspeople and antiques shops.

General location: Just south of Story, which is about 30 miles southwest of Columbus or 20 miles south of Nashville

Elevation change: Several 250-foot climbs and descents. Most of the hills are less than that. Some of the climbs are steep, but there are also several gentle, sustained ascents.

RIDE 46 • Nebo Ridge

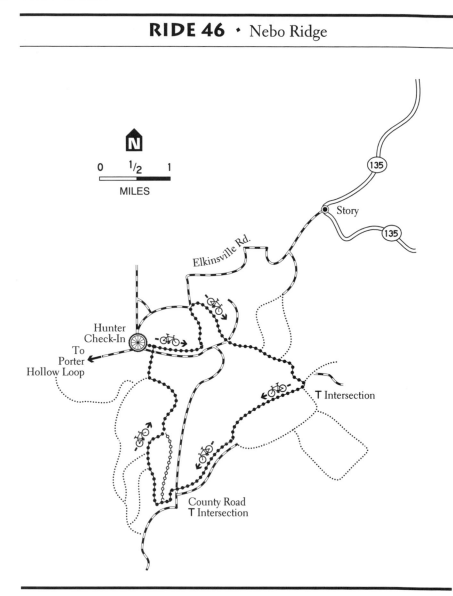

Season: Year-round, weather permitting; best in fall when it's dry. See the general introduction for more information.

Services: Most services (groceries, gas, places to stay, great gobs of shopping) in Nashville; everything (including bike shops) in Columbus and Bloomington.

Hazards: This is an old trail, with old-style waterbars, both flapper type and treated timber. Use caution riding over exposed wood, particularly if it's wet. Please do not ride around waterbars, which causes trail damage.

The old wagon road provides modern-day fun with its rocky descent.

Rescue index: Usually a lot of people out here, especially in the summer and on nice weekends any time of year. In the off-season, it's best to ride with someone.

Land status: National forest with a few public roads

Maps: You could get the Trails Illustrated map or the ROG from the Forest Service, but the trail is clearly marked and well used, so a map is not a necessity here.

Finding the trail: Take IN 135 south from Nashville. At Story, IN 135 goes hard left; you go straight onto the paved county road (Elkinsville Road). Follow this road as it twists and turns. It will change to gravel. Soon after, the road makes a sharp right and goes up a steep hill. There is parking on the left where the road goes right. Note: this parking area is slated to be moved and will at some point be closer in on Elkinsville Road, before the turn to the right.

Source of additional information:

Hoosier National Forest
811 Constitution Avenue
Bedford, IN 47421
(812) 279-3423

Notes on the trail: The trail leaves only one direction from the parking area. You're immediately in wooded single-track and climbing gently. In less than 1 mile, the single-track goes left into the woods. Go straight on the abandoned roadbed. Within 10 yards, you'll come to a gate. Go around it, then turn left onto the county road. (This short section isn't on the Trails Illustrated map, but will be open to use by the time you read this.) The county road is rough, wet, and fast. It gets smoother as it goes along. When you come to paved road, continue straight. (Turning right would bring you to the north end of Hickory Ridge.) In about 1 mile the trail goes up the hill to your left; look for a series of treated wood waterbars like steps. From there, follow the clearly blazed trail through rolling hills and some very fast single-track back to the split. This is where you went straight and around the gate. Now you turn right and retrace your path to the parking area.

RIDE 47 · Tipsaw Lake

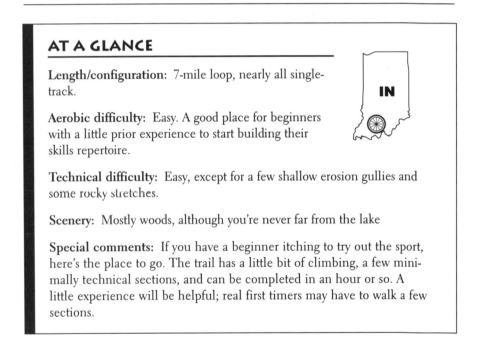

AT A GLANCE

Length/configuration: 7-mile loop, nearly all single-track.

IN

Aerobic difficulty: Easy. A good place for beginners with a little prior experience to start building their skills repertoire.

Technical difficulty: Easy, except for a few shallow erosion gullies and some rocky stretches.

Scenery: Mostly woods, although you're never far from the lake

Special comments: If you have a beginner itching to try out the sport, here's the place to go. The trail has a little bit of climbing, a few minimally technical sections, and can be completed in an hour or so. A little experience will be helpful; real first timers may have to walk a few sections.

Tipsaw Trail is one of my favorites in the Hoosier National Forest. Taken slowly, it's a gentle romp through the woods, with just enough technical challenge to keep it from being mundane. Taken at speed, it's a challenging little loop with rocks, roots, ravines, and other wheel-turners.

The trail alone would be worth coming here for. Another reason to come down is that there's plenty of other stuff to do. There's camping (including group sites), a clean beach with a modern bathhouse and concessions, picnic shelters and, of course, the lake. Tipsaw would be a great place to blow an afternoon in a canoe or sailboat, or fishing (electric motors only).

RIDE 47 · Tipsaw Lake

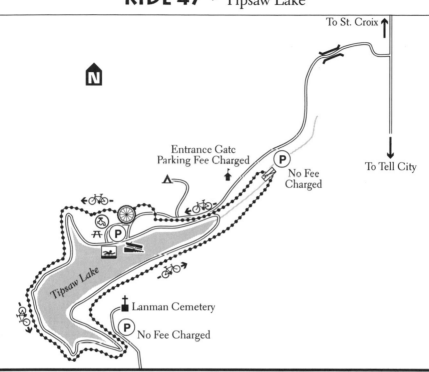

Best of all, while you're here, you have plenty of other options. Birdseye, Mogan Ridge, and both Oriole Trails are all within a half-hour drive.

General location: About 45 miles west of Louisville, Kentucky

Elevation change: Not much, just a few short hills at the beginning and end

Season: Year-round. You'll need to pay a parking fee ($2 as of this writing) from May 15 to October 15.

Services: Water is available at the picnic and camping areas; plan on stopping in Louisville or Tell City (about 30 miles farther south) for everything else. Both of those cities have medical facilities, bike shops, grocery stores, places to stay, shopping, and so on.

Hazards: Pretty innocuous trail

Rescue index: The nearest hospital is in Tell City. Off-season, this place is desolate. In-season, someone will find you before gangrene sets in.

Land status: National forest

Maps: Trails Illustrated map #770 from the Forest Service and area retailers, or the ROG from the Forest Service office.

Finding the trail: The entrance is from IN 37 about 7 miles south of I-64. Once you're past the gatehouse, you can pick up the trail in a couple of places. The easiest and most obvious is where the road curves left to go to the beach and the trail goes right, past a pit toilet and into the woods.

Sources of additional information:

Bicycles Etc. bike shop
1101 12th Street
Tell City, IN 47586
(812) 547-7161

Hoosier National Forest
811 Constitution Avenue
Bedford, IN 47421
(812) 279-3423
or
248 15th Street
Tell City, IN 47586
(812) 547-7051

Notes on the trail: Park at the beach or, if that's full, the boat ramp. (The ramp comes up before the beach, so you'll have to double back.) As you approach the beach, watch to the right as the road curves to the left. At this point, the trail crosses the road and goes into the woods. This is your starting point.

The first mile or so has a few short climbs and some shallow gullies to cross. Nothing too demanding, just a nice warmup.

The single-track comes out into an open area along the lake. Soon after, you'll cross the dam. The trail then follows an old double-track. This comes to an end at a gravel logging road; the trail is gated at this point. Turn left onto the logging road. When it goes right, follow the other old road to the left. Soon you're back in the woods on single-track again.

Near the end of the trail, you can dump out onto the parking lot for the boat ramp. Don't. Instead, follow the markers and cross the entrance road. You'll have a climb and a little more single-track before you return to your starting point.

This trail is a snap to follow, another reason it's perfect for beginners. They can concentrate on riding technique and not worry about scouting for obscure trail blazes.

RIDE 48 · Birdseye Trail

AT A GLANCE

Length/configuration: 11-mile main loop with a
spur that adds 6 or 7 miles, for a total of about 18
miles. It's a mix of single- and double-track with
some gravel and dirt roads.

Aerobic difficulty: Easy to moderate. Most of the
climbs are gradual.

Technical difficulty: Easy to moderate. It would all be easy except that
some of the single-track is tight and twisty, and there are some sections of
rock.

Scenery: Beautiful woods, a tiny lake, plus evidence of past settlements.

Special comments: A great ride for the beginner who has graduated beyond the most basic trails, Birdseye will give you a taste of everything
nice about mountain biking. Some single-track, some chances to catch
air off rolling dip water bars, and places where you're just coasting along
through the woods on cruise control.

I'm reluctant to share this trail. It's so much fun and so under-used that I'm
afraid it will lose its character if word gets out.

Birdseye has it all. There are fast descents on county roads where the berms
seemed to have been designed for catching air. There are miles of tight single-
track. Pine trees and hardwoods, streams and a lake, it's all here.

The only downside is that at times it's tough to follow the trail. Getting on
and off county roads, going into and out of the woods—the transitions make for
some head-scratching moments. Then there are a few trail junctions where
what's old and illegal isn't always distinct from what's new and legal.

Despite the minor—very minor—problems, this is my favorite trail in the
Hoosier National Forest, narrowly edging out the Nebo Ridge segment of the
Knobstone Trail and Young's Creek for that honor.

General location: About 20 miles southeast of Jasper near the Crawford
County line

Elevation change: Minimal; maybe 200 feet on a few of the hills, usually
stretched over 0.75 mile. There is, however, one tough uphill about a third of
the way into the ride. It's still only 200 feet of gain, but it comes in less than
0.25 mile.

RIDE 48 · Birdseye Trail

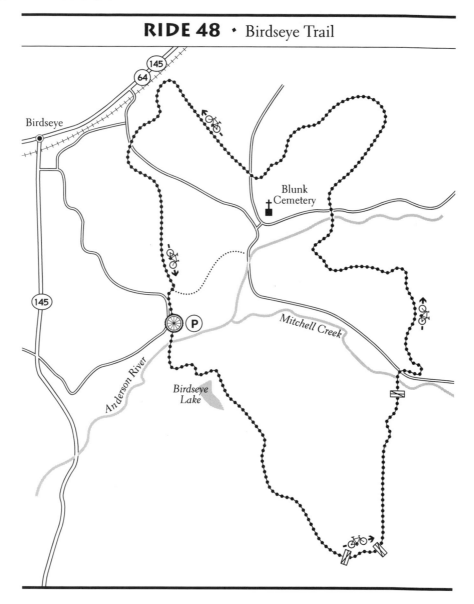

Season: Year-round; fall is best because it's dry, although Birdseye would only be too muddy to ride after a monsoon.

Services: There's a convenience store—and little else—in Birdseye; the nearest hospital, hotels, grocery stores, are in Jasper. The nearest bike shops are in Jasper and Tell City.

Hazards: Hunters in spring and (especially) fall

Rescue index: This is unspoiled because no one's out here. Even the sections that run on county roads get little use. Ride with someone.

Land status: National forest

Maps: Get the Trails Illustrated map or the ROG from the Forest Service. It's easier to follow the trail with the map; it's also easier to find shortcuts on county roads if you want to go back and repeat favorite sections.

Finding the trail: Go north on IN 145 from I-64 toward the town of Birdseye. To get to the Forest Service parking, turn right on the road that runs along the south side of the railroad tracks in town. At the **T**, turn right. Parking is up on the right in about 0.25 mile (watch for trail crossing signs). Because that area can be muddy and crowded, I park elsewhere. About 1.5 miles south of town off IN 145 is Birdseye Loop Road. Turn east. In 1.5 miles, there's a small parking area on the right. The trail starts at the gate there.

Sources of additional information:

Bicycles Etc. bike shop
1101 12th Street
Tell City, IN 47586
(812) 547-7161

Hoosier National Forest
248 15th Street
Tell City, IN 47586
(812) 547-7051

Notes on the trail: Ride around the gate, along the edge of the field. After the trail turns left, watch for it to veer right into the woods. (It looks like the trail goes straight ahead; it doesn't.) Ride across the dam, then skirt the east edge of U-38 Lake. When you come to the gate, turn left, then follow the blazes. When the old road meets the county road, turn right, then left back into the woods for a tough climb. It's after this climb that you're most likely to see evidence of past habitation: old cars, a cemetery, and other such items. This is also where you'll find the best single-track.

After you cross the second road (where the main parking area is), you'll go another mile or so and come to a **T** in the trail. Turn right and you're back on Birdseye Loop Road, where you can turn left, go up over the hill, and return to the parking area. A better bet is to turn left at the **T** and climb. You'll soon come to a descent with lots of earthen waterbars that are good for catching air. Follow this trail to the county road. You can then turn around and go back to Birdseye Loop Road, or turn right and follow the county road. If you do the county road, watch for the trail to come in from the right. Turn onto it and you'll retrace the first 4 miles backward past the lake.

RIDE 49 · Mogan Ridge West

AT A GLANCE

Length/configuration: Several loop options, the longest being about 13 miles, the shortest being 7 miles. Mix of single- and double-track and gravel roads. The long option is where the sweetest single-track lurks.

Aerobic difficulty: Mostly easy to moderate, except for a few extended climbs.

Technical difficulty: Mostly easy, except for spots of loose soil on hills and muddy spots resulting from ATV damage.

Scenery: Like most Hoosier National Forest trails, Mogan Ridge has a mix of creek bottoms, hills, hardwoods, and pines. Unlike others, Mogan has few ridge-top views.

Special comments: Mogan Ridge offers a splendid mix of single-tracks and fire roads that interconnect for lots of riding options. The downside is rampant illegal ATV use that has all but ruined what would otherwise be the best single-track in the Hoosier.

There's nothing too tough about Mogan. Mud is rarely a problem (except as noted below). The hills are gradual (although long). The creek crossing midway through the eastern loop has rocky approaches, but the angle is shallow and the water placid in normal times. The single-track is medium tight in spots, but never overly technical, and just about the time you're getting fuzzy-headed from concentrating on the trail, boom, you're back to a fire road.

Mogan Ridge West is a sweet, inviting trail that will build skill in beginners and keep intermediate riders on their toes.

The bad news is that illegal ATV use is ruining this trail. Maybe it will be fixed by the time you read this. I hope so. The descent to Ash House Branch of Oil Creek is a muddy mess because of this, and the bottomlands once you cross the creek are unrideable at times. The Forest Service knows of the problem, but enforcement of the ATV ban is neither cheap nor effective.

General location: Hoosier National Forest, approximately 10 miles south of I-64 on IN 37

Elevation change: Change totals about 400 feet. You'll start the ride by descending, then climbing a gentle grade to the top. There's some easy climbing

RIDE 49 • Mogan Ridge West

in the middle. The tough climb comes after the creek, when it seems you're going up forever. There's also a steep gravel road climb near the end.

Season: Year-round, best in late fall when it's dry, but avoid hunting season

Services: There's a convenience store on the west side of IN 37 between I-64 and IN 70. Otherwise, Tell City has everything, including a hospital and a bike shop. Bring your own water.

Hazards: None beyond those listed in the HNF introduction

Rescue index: The nearest hospital is in Tell City. This is another piece of the Hoosier where I've never encountered another trail user, despite the dozen or so times I've been here. Ride with someone.

Land status: National forest

Maps: Pick up the Trails Illustrated map or the ROG from the Forest Service. It's easier to follow the trail with the map; it's also easier to find shortcuts on fire roads if you want to go back and repeat favorite sections.

Finding the trail: Take IN 37 south of I-64 about 9 miles to Old Highway 37. Turn left onto Old 37. The trailhead is less than 1 mile down the road. Watch for signs. If you miss Old 37, turn left onto IN 70, then an immediate left onto the south end of Old 37; go north to the trailhead.

Sources of additional information:

Bicycles Etc. bike shop
1101 12th Street
Tell City, IN 47586
(812) 547-7161

Hoosier National Forest
248 15th Street
Tell City, IN 47586
(812) 547-7051

Notes on the trail: Park at the base of the state police radio relay tower. Ride past the gate on the gravel road. In less than 0.5 mile the trail cuts into the woods past a gate on the right. This is a wonderful 3-mile single-track that runs mostly downhill to a parking area on IN 70. At the gate for that parking area, turn sharply left and start up the hill. This section can be mucky. Within 2 miles, you'll come to a gravel road. For reference, let's call this Point B. If you turn left to cut the ride short, you'll be back at the parking area in about 2 miles. This makes up the short, 7-mile loop. For the longer loop, turn right. Within a half mile, you'll go past a gate, continue on the gravel road.

About 1.5 miles past that gate, the road goes straight to another parking area, while the trail turns left into the woods. Take the trail. Within 50 yards the trail turns hard left; watch the blazes so you don't inadvertently continue straight onto an old trail. From here the trail runs mostly downhill to a creek bottom. (There's another left with a fake straight section that sneaks up on you less than 1 mile into this single-track. Again, watch the blazes.) This downhill and the bottomland section of trail may be the best part of this ride, but you pay the price with an extended uphill coming out again. The climb isn't very steep, but it goes on and on like the night howl of a lonely dog. It's fairly technical; the scenery's great; so sit and grind and enjoy life.

At the top of this climb (about 10 or 11 miles into the ride), you'll pop back out onto the gravel road. Several options exist here. The easiest is to turn right and head back to the parking area, which is about 1.5 miles (and 1 near-vertical climb) down the road. This gives you the 13-mile loop. Or you can turn left, which will bring you back to Point B in 0.5 mile. From here, you can turn right, dive into the woods and repeat the first section of trail backward, or continue straight and repeat the downhill-bottomlands-uphill piece and return to this point.

RIDE 50 · Oriole Trail West

AT A GLANCE

Length/configuration: A 1.2-mile spur to and from a 6.1-mile loop, for a total of 8.5 miles; all single-track, some of it quite wide.

Aerobic difficulty: Mostly easy except for 2 moderate climbs.

Technical difficulty: Mostly easy, depending on how fast you want to go. Pick up the pace on the descent and you'll catch air, then have to twist your way through some tight single-track.

Scenery: Oriole West packs everything any HNF trail offers into 1 compact little package: hills, technical sections, rip-roaring descents, pines, hardwoods, creek crossings. You name it, it's here.

Special comments: The crushed stone trail surface means Oriole West stays rideable when other trails are a ribbon of mud. The bad news: they're wide and not very aesthetically pleasing for the rider seeking single-track. The good news: the best single-track remains unmolested by the gravel truck.

I've ridden this trail clockwise and counterclockwise. It's much more fun counterclockwise. Then it's almost too much fun. The amount of effort put into the climbing doesn't seem like much of a price to pay for the big fun on the descent. The single-track along and through the creek is wonderful. And the technical weaving through tight trees near the end is great.

The sister to this trail, Oriole East, is a lot of fun in its own right, but if you have time for only one ride, follow Horace Greely's advice and go west.

The only freaky thing about this trail is the parking. It's at the end of what looks like someone's private lane. It isn't private, but it still seems like an odd place to park. The Forest Service knows this, and is trying to find a way to connect parking at Oriole Pond with the trail. (They don't want people on the road, so they're trying to discover trail options.) So far, private property has blocked their attempts. Too bad. It would be nice to ride both West and East without having to drive from one to the other.

General location: Hoosier National Forest, about 4 miles south of I-64 on IN 66

Elevation change: Two climbs of about 400 feet each.

Season: Year-round, best in late fall when it's drier, but avoid hunting season.

RIDE 50 · Oriole Trail West

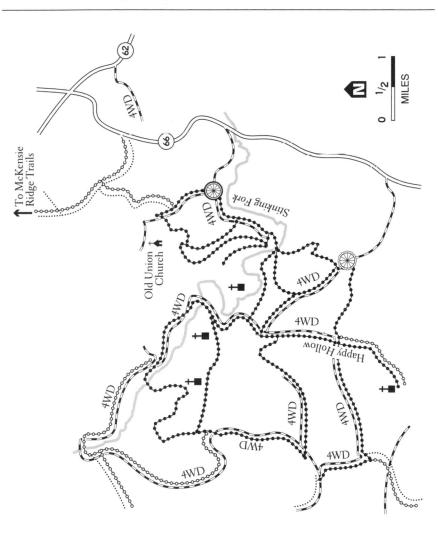

Services: Sulphur has a convenience store, as does Derby, to the south. Everything else, including a bike shop, is in Tell City. Bring your own water.

Hazards: None beyond those listed in the HNF introduction

Rescue index: This remote trail actually sees quite a few riders, but don't count on someone showing up in your hour of direst need. The nearest hospital is in Tell City.

Land status: National forest

Maps: The Trails Illustrated map and the ROG are available from the Forest Service, although you probably won't need them once you find the parking area. The 7.5 minute USGS quads for this area are Beechwood and Branchville.

Finding the trail: Follow IN 66 south from its split with IN 62 in Sulphur for exactly 3 miles; the access road (CR 52/Orange Grove) angles off to the right. The road is rough. Follow it to the end, where there's parking on the right.

Source of additional information:

Hoosier National Forest
248 15th Street
Tell City, IN 47586
(812) 547-7051

Notes on the trail: From the parking area, ride around the gate. The trail generally runs downhill here, and there's plenty of opportunity for air off the earthen berm water bars.

Once you hit the creek bed, turn right. Follow the creek bed for some distance. At times it's not clear whether the trail is beside the creek or in it; generally you'll want to stay out of the creek and on the adjacent trail. Watch for the trail to turn sharply left and start climbing about 1 mile into the ride.

After the climb, you'll come to a point where the trail goes left or right (about 5 miles into the ride). The right merely goes to another out-of-the-way parking spot. You go left and begin descending. You'll have 1 mile or more of downhill, the first part of which has another chance for catching air off of rolling dip water bars. That's followed by some tight, technical descending through small trees. The trail levels out, then heads back to where the spur comes down from the parking area. Ride up the hill to return to your car, or repeat your earlier route for more thrills.

RIDE 51 · Oriole Trail East

AT A GLANCE

IN

Length/configuration: 10.5-mile loop; mostly wide single-track with some gravel road.

Aerobic difficulty: Mostly moderate with a few tough climbs.

Technical difficulty: Moderate with some sketchy ups and downs, one of which I have yet to ride all the way up.

Scenery: Mostly typical Eastern hardwoods with one stretch of county road through farmland.

Special comments: Ride this one and Oriole West in a day and you've had a good workout. Compared to Oriole West, East sees more horse traffic because there's space to park horse trailers. I see horses about half the time I come out here, and the riders have been unfailingly friendly.

Ride this trail as I did and there's a county road section just 2 miles in. The road is steep and fast, a good chance to fling some mud out of your knobbies and into your gaping mouth. As a bonus, the road runs through some nice farmland.

If you're beat, if your bike's broken, or if you just don't like what Oriole East has to offer, there's a shortcut about four miles into the ride. It'll spare you some miles and some technical up and down. That's only good news if you don't like comfortably demanding hills.

My suggestion is to do the whole route. The single-track at the northeastern end is wonderful.

General location: Hoosier National Forest, 4.5 miles south of I-64 on IN 66

Elevation change: There's really only 1 difficult climb. It comes early in the ride when you grind up a quarter-mile ascent with 200 feet of elevation gain. The extreme northeast leg also has a good climb, but it's more gradual.

Season: Year-round; best in fall when it's drier, but stay clear of hunting season. One of my favorite trips on this trail was the day after Christmas.

Services: Sulphur has a convenience store, as does Derby, to the south. Everything else, including a bike shop, is in Tell City.

Hazards: None beyond those listed in the HNF introduction

Rescue index: A fair amount of activity out here, since the horse folks like this trail, too. But don't count on someone coming by. There are a few homes on the county road portion. The nearest hospital is in Tell City.

RIDE 51 • Oriole Trail East

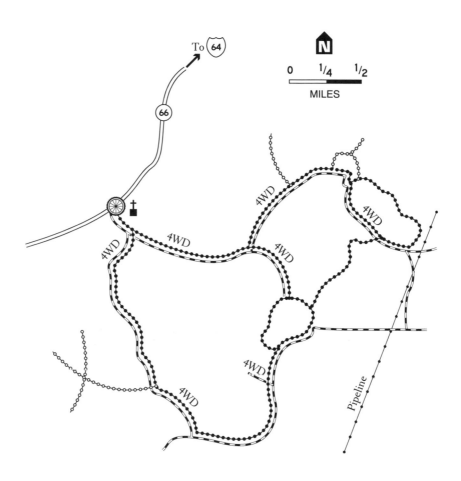

Land status: National forest or public road

Maps: The Trails Illustrated map or the ROG from the Forest Service would be nice to have, but unnecessary. The USGS 7.5 minute quad is Beechwood.

Finding the trail: It's 0.3 mile past Oriole West when coming south from Sulphur on IN 66. Pass CR 52/Orange Grove, go up the hill. At the top is Jeffries Cemetery. Park there or across the road at Oriole Pond.

Source of additional information:

Hoosier National Forest
248 15th Street
Tell City, IN 47586
(812) 547-7051

Notes on the trail: Ride around the gate at the parking area next to the cemetery. Within 0.1 mile, the trail splits. Bear right. This sweet strip of fat single-
track goes for about 2 miles before it pops out onto a county road. In that 2
miles are a fun descent and a brutal climb.

Turn left on the road and you drop like a rock. Be careful; there are a couple
of turns at the bottom. In less than 2 miles, the trail jumps back into the woods.
It's easy to spot: there's a big gate to the left when the road makes a sharp right.

Within 0.2 mile, the trail splits again. Bear left for the short ride, which is
fun in itself. Better yet, go right, strap in, and hang on.

For about 1.5 miles you'll be switchbacking your way down an increasingly
technical descent. At the bottom, you come onto a gravel road. Turn right for
about 50 feet, then left onto the trail and back into the woods. (Keep a sharp
eye out; it's easy to miss this left turn.)

Now you're faced with an uphill that, while less technical than the descent
you just braved, is demanding nonetheless. At the top, you come out onto a
pipeline. Turn left for 50 feet, then left again into the woods.

There's some more down-and-up fun before you come onto the little connector trail about 8 miles into the ride. You can turn left here and left again before the gate at the other end to repeat the down-and-up part, or continue straight back to the parking area, which lies just under 1.5 miles ahead.

RIDE 52 · German Ridge Trail

AT A GLANCE

IN

Length/configuration: This system is laid out like a ladder, with sides connected by rungs. The result is multiple loop options to over 40 miles; the loop described here is just under 5 miles. Most of the trail is as wide as a country lane and covered in gravel; a little single-track remains on the north end.

Aerobic difficulty: Moderate at 1 climb. Otherwise pretty easy.

Technical difficulty: If you hit the single-track fast, things happen in a hurry. It's easy to get in over your head, especially when going downhill. On the other hand, the sections that have had gravel applied to them offer boredom as their biggest threat.

Scenery: More woods, hills, and streams.

Special comments: In their attempt to harden this trail for the extensive equestrian use it gets, the Forest Service has spread crushed stone on much of it. The result is a gravel boulevard through the woods. Hit the single-track on the north end for happier riding.

German Ridge is popular with the equestrians, especially on the southern end, where the campgrounds are located. This loop takes you to the northern end, away from most of the horses.

Should you absolutely avoid the southern end? No. The scenery is pretty, and if you're with someone who isn't ready or able to hammer technical single-track, the gravel parts offer an alternative.

The first time I rode here, the ascent on the north end was murder. Since then, the Forest Service has relocated the trail and the climb is pretty tame. It's also gravel. But there's only a short stretch of gravel in several miles of good single-track, so that's not too bad.

General location: About 45 miles west of Louisville, or 15 miles north of Tell City

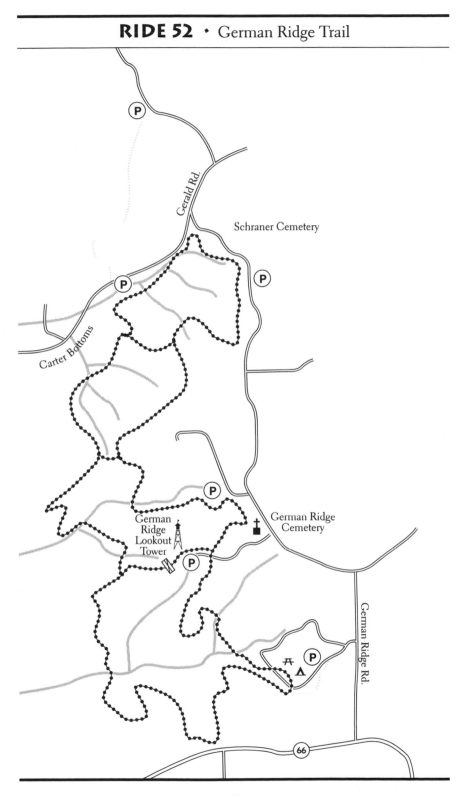

Elevation change: One rollicking descent and several lesser ups-and-downs. Because the trail is being relocated in several areas, the climbs are fairly gentle.

Season: All year, best in late fall. Heavy horse use occurs in summer, especially on the southern end.

Services: Everything you need, including a bike shop, in Tell City

Hazards: All the regular HNF stuff, plus a lot of horses on nice days

Rescue index: The equestrians don't often get this far north, so don't count on getting found if you snap a collarbone. The nearest hospital is in Tell City.

Land status: National forest (the forest lies west of German Ridge Road, and private land lies east)

Maps: The Trails Illustrated map or the ROG from the Forest Service would be nice to have so you can see how to put together options from this unique layout.

Finding the trail: Take IN 66 east from Tell City, through Cannellton, then watch for the Forest Service signs. This will get you to the campground. From there, go north on German Ridge Road. The only tricky part is 0.5 mile out, where another county road comes in from the right; bear left here. Stay on German Ridge Road for 3.2 miles and the parking area will be on your left.

If you come in from the north from IN 37, turn east on IN 70. In less than 1 mile, turn right where the big "German Ridge Recreation Area" sign indicates. When that road Ts into another, turn right. You're now on Gerald Road. Watch for German Ridge Road on your left. Turn there, and the parking area is 0.9 mile south.

Sources of additional information:

Bicycles Etc. bike shop
1101 12th Street
Tell City, IN 47586
(812) 547-7161

Hoosier National Forest
248 15th Street
Tell City, IN 47586
(812) 547-7051

Notes on the trail: The parking area lies smack in the middle of the trail. Take the trail from the north end of the parking area. From here it follows the road for a short time and is mostly flat, lulling you into a false sense of safety.

Soon, the trail drops to the bottom lands. You don't get much of a break, though. There's a short stretch that should be flat, except that the horses have pounded divots into the soil so you'll be bouncing around like a hula doll in the back window of a '57 Chevy.

The trail smoothes out once the climbing begins. The first day I rode this, someone on an ATV had (illegally) been through, drifting the corners and roosting the hills. All the ground cover was gone, and I was left riding on a slimy surface with the traction of phlegm. I'd ride 20 feet into a climb, spin out, and walk. On later trips, the trail had been moved. This ascent was much gentler, and covered in gravel.

About 2.5 miles into the ride, it was decision time. Going essentially straight would have brought me to the next rung on the ladder. I chose instead to turn left and head back, staying on the single-track and descending almost immediately, then climbing again.

There are some rollers, then suddenly the trails pops out into the parking area.

BLOOMINGTON/NASHVILLE AREA

Indiana's motto is "The Crossroads of America." If you look at a road map, you will conclude that Indianapolis must be the crossroad point, since many major interstates meet there. However, I'd like to make the case that, as far as mountain biking is concerned, Bloomington takes the crossroads honors. For those interested in outdoor activities, this is the place to be. The Brownstown district of Hoosier National Forest is nearby, as is Yellowstone State Forest and the state's largest park, Brown County State Park. While the latter two do not permit mountain biking, they add to the beauty of this rugged area. There are many scenic drives in this region. In fact, slong some roads near the forests and parks, expect to find heavy traffic in the fall as motorists ramble along, viewing the fall colors.

You will not be disappointed by Gnaw Bone. While it's not as technically challenging as the Hoosier trails, this area has a flavor all its own, with its rustic cabins and dining hall and the wide, clean trails suitable for all riders. And if the Bloomington/Nashville area seems like a mountain bike-friendly place, let Wapehani Mountain Bike Park serve as a testament. Although small in size, this city park is one of the few areas in this guide officially designated for mountain bike use. If that isn't progressive, what is?

Special thanks to Charlie McClary, who helped supply information for the rides to this area.

RIDE 53 · Gnaw Bone Camp

AT A GLANCE

Length/configuration: There are about 20 miles of well-designed and spread-out interconnected trails through the woods. The trails are a mixture of single-track and old logging roads.

IN

Aerobic difficulty: Moderate

Technical difficulty: Easy to moderate since the owners maintain the trails

Scenery: Streams, ridges, some scenic vistas along the trails. Also a pond with a rope swing at the camp.

Special comments: There's more to do here than ride. If you can, make this an overnighter—you won't be bored.

I knew I would love Gnaw Bone from the moment I entered the camp and was greeted by a host of golden retrievers. If you're looking for that self-contained area of mountain bike challenges and charming services, this is by far one of the best in the state.

Most of the trails aren't too technical; you won't find any obstacles to jump. The owners keep the trails clean, which makes them fun for people of all abilities to ride. You'll need stamina and endurance more than anything else.

You'll encounter a few scenic vistas and several stream crossings. The stretch by Lake Road is flat and easy, as is the stretch called Mulcahy. One section near the Grouse Trail is affectionately known by local riders as "Return of the Jedi" because, just like Luke Skywalker in the namesake movie, you dodge pine trees on a narrow trail. Some of the trails follow ridges where you'll find streams at the bottom. In short, the riding here is good for experts and novices alike: the experts can push it for a good workout and tackle the few technical spots, and the novices can travel at a relaxing pace, sticking to less exhausting sections.

You would be remiss, though, if you came to Gnaw Bone only to ride. When you pull in, you'll notice immediately that the place has the feel of the Old West. There are several cabins, a big dining hall, and a lodge with a fireplace, all built with a rustic feel. You can rent a cabin or stay at the hotel. You'll even find a museum containing natural wonders, like animal skeletons, rocks, snake skins, and hornet nests. When you're done riding and checking out the museum, head down to the pond and play on the swing. Bring the spouse, kids, and whoever else knows how to have a good time.

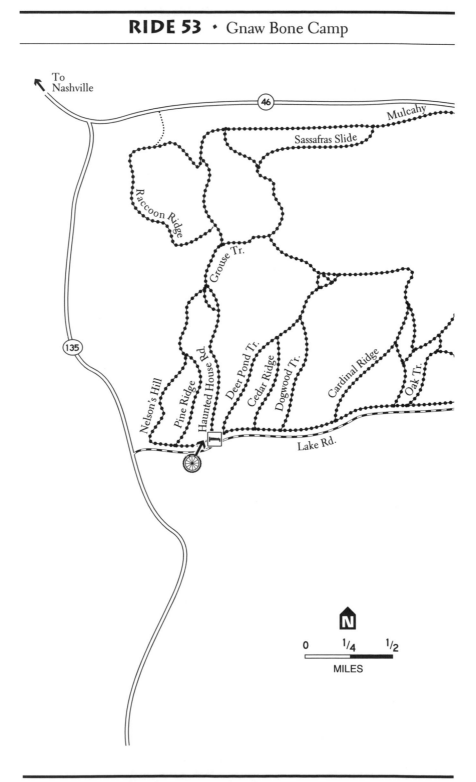

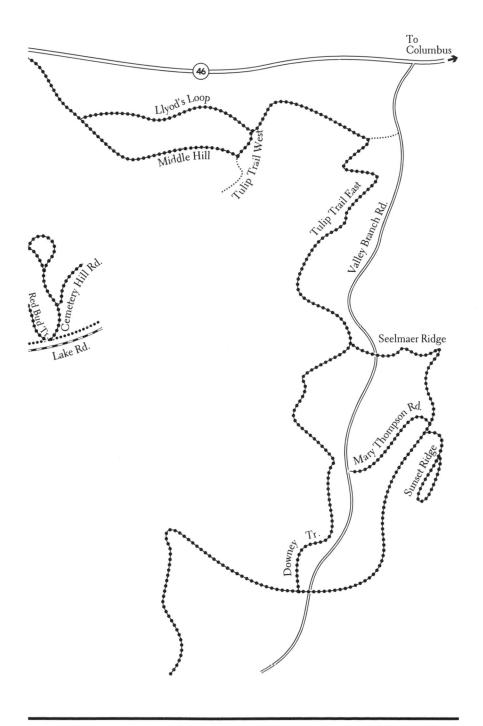

To
Columbus

46

Llyod's Loop

Middle Hill

Tulip Trail West

Tulip Trail East

Valley Branch Rd.

Cemetery Hill Rd.

Red Bud Tr.

Lake Rd.

Seelmaer Ridge

Mary Thompson Rd.

Sunset Ridge

Downey Tr.

Return to the past at Gnaw Bone Camp.

General location: Twenty-two miles east of Bloomington on State Highway 135.

Elevation change: The overall gain is around 350 feet.

Season: You'll be able to ride here whenever the camp is open. There are 4 weeks in the summer when Gnaw Bone is rented out as a girls' camp. The area might also be unavailable if other groups rent it. The trails are used by cross-country skiers when there's snow on the ground. Bikes are not allowed on the trails when they are wet. Check first at the address below before coming.

Services: Lodging is available at Gnaw Bone. All services are available in Bloomington or Columbus. For bike service, check out The Bicycle Garage in Bloomington.

Hazards: You won't find many hazards. A few trails have rugged and rocky downhill sections, but you'll be able to see them coming.

Rescue index: If you need assistance, make your way back to the main lodge area.

Land status: Private property. The day-use fee is $2.50, but it's your loss if you only come out for a day. Also, you ride at your own risk.

Maps: The main lodge area has a map showing the different trails on the property. The USGS 7.5 minute quad is Nashville.

Finding the trail: In Nashville, take IN 135 south for 2 miles. You'll see the sign for Gnaw Bone Camp for Boys and Girls on your left.

The trails at Gnaw Bone are suitable for all riders.

Sources of additional information:

Gnaw Bone Camp
R.R. 2, Box 91
Nashville, IN 47448-9698
(812) 988-4852

The Bicycle Garage
507 East Kirkwood
Bloomington, IN 47408
(812) 339-3457

Notes on the trail: You'll see where to begin the ride from the main lodge. The trails are marked with signs indicating which trail you're on. Make sure you stay off any trail that isn't on Gnaw Bone property.

RIDE 54 · Wapehani Mountain Bike Park

AT A GLANCE

Length/configuration: The main trail is only a mile long single-track, but there are alternate trails that tack on a couple more miles.

Aerobic difficulty: There are a few hills, but on so short a ride, it can't rate more than a moderate aerobic workout.

Technical difficulty: You'll come across some obstructions along the trail, but again, nothing terribly challenging: a solid moderate.

Scenery: The main trail loops around Lake Wapehani, and the park consists of both woods and fields.

Special comments: Support trails like this one that are designated for mountain bike use, and just maybe we'll get some more. Don't support them, and we won't. Period.

Why include a mountain bike ride where the main trail is only a mile long? Advocacy. Trail access is a volatile issue in many areas, but Wapehani, located near an urban area, is one public site designed specifically for mountain bikes. And in actuality, it's not a bad place to ride, especially for enthusiasts who don't have a lot of time to devote to long workouts. You will need technical skills on this mostly dirt single-track as you tackle ruts, stumps, and rocks. You'll also climb some hills. The trails go through woods and fields, and the main trail circles Lake Wapehani.

Wapehani Mountain Bike Park is only two miles from downtown Bloomington and is close to the Indiana University campus, so after the Fighting Illini beat the Hoosiers (sorry, Indiana fans), this is a great place to come to burn off the hot dogs. Charlie McClary, a local mountain bike advocate, sums up Wapehani best when he says, "It's small and compact, but it has everything."

General location: In Bloomington

Elevation change: The elevation change is about 150 feet, and you will need to climb a few hills.

Season: It's open all year, but it gets crowded when the weather is nice.

Services: All services are available in Bloomington. For bike service, check out The Bicycle Garage.

Hazards: Your major concern will be the other bikes using the park. Wapehani also open to joggers and hikers.

Rescue index: From any point on the trail, you're never far from busy IN 37.

Land status: Bloomington Parks and Recreation Office. You will need to wear

RIDE 54 · Wapehani Mountain Bike Park

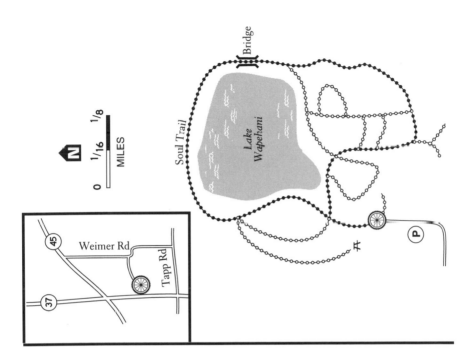

a helmet and have a bike waiver on file at the Bloomington Parks and Recreation Office or any local bike shop. Refer to the addresses below.

Maps: Bloomington Parks and Recreation can send you a map of the area. The USGS 7.5 minute quad for this area is Bloomington.

Finding the trail: From IN 48, take IN 37 south just over 1 mile and turn left at IN 45. Take IN 45 about 0.5 mile to Weimer Road. Turn right and go another 0.5 mile to a sign pointing you into the park. You'll be able to spot the trailhead easily enough from the parking lot.

Sources of additional information:

Bloomington Parks and Recreation Office
349 South Walnut
Bloomington, IN 47401
(812) 332-9668

The Bicycle Garage
507 East Kirkwood
Bloomington, IN 47408
(812) 339-3457

Notes on the trail: Stay on the legal trails. If we bikers follow the rules, perhaps we'll see more mountain bike facilities available in the Midwest.

OTHER INDIANA RIDES

M iscellaneous trails exist on private land. There are also several city and county parks throughout Indiana that offer mountain biking. Most urban areas have some trails, which may or may not be legally open. If you're wondering about what's available in a particular area, call a local bike shop and ask.

It's hard to ferret out information on these small trails, and their minimal mileage and questionable legal status make them inappropriate for a regional guide book. Instead, Dave and I each offer an example of the lesser-known trails that can be uncovered with a bit of investigative work.

RIDE 55 · Crane/Lake Greenwood

AT A GLANCE

IN

Length/configuration: 17-mile loop; nearly all tight single-track.

Aerobic difficulty: Easy; fairly flat with a few short climbs.

Technical difficulty: Challenging; very narrow trails, often little more than a handlebar width between trees. There are some rocky sections, as well.

Scenery: Rolling hills and frequent views of the lake.

Special comments: The Crane Division of the Naval Surface Warfare Center is a military facility, and there are rules to be followed.

R ule number one: you must, must, *must* call ahead for a gate pass. They only need 24 hours' notice, and the process is simple. But *you must call ahead*

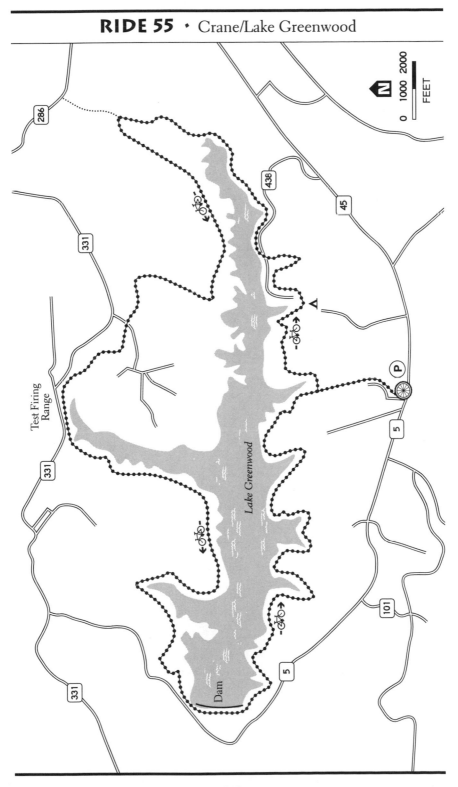

Lake Greenwood

Test Firing Range

Dam

to arrange access. Is that clear? The number is (812) 854-1165; hours are 6:30 a.m. to 3 p.m. (or 0630 to 1500, if you really want to get into the spirit of things).

This trail provided me an interesting first in my life: I was contacted by a land manager to ask for help in recruiting mountain bikers *onto* a hiking trail. Seems this 17-mile loop doesn't get enough foot traffic to keep the brush beat back, so they were hoping we'd come and help out.

Because this trail was built for hiking, it presents some challenges for mountain bikers. Not all of it is rideable, though the hike-a-bike sections are few and short. The worst part is finding your way. Due to low usage, the trail is not always distinct. Compounding the problem are markers that are good at walking pace, but marginal at riding speed. When in doubt, I dismounted, backed up, and approached the trail as a hiker. Suddenly the route became obvious.

The map provided at the Natural Resources building was helpful. It has mileages printed on it, and dots for every tenth of a mile. There are also blue Carsonite markers every tenth of a mile along the trail.

Also because this trail was built for hiking, the treadway is narrow. Often the width was one handlebar plus one inch. It wasn't all like this, but more than you'd seen on most shared-use trails.

Most of the trail is typical eastern hardwoods forest. There are a few shallow ravines. These fill after a heavy rain, but drain within a half hour after the rain stops.

General location: Just east of Bedford, and southeast of Bloomington

Elevation change: Minimal, probably not 100 feet in any one spot on the whole trail

Season: Can be ridden year-round, although spring and fall are best

Services: Bloomington has everything, including bike shops. Bedford has most things, but no bike shop. Don't expect to find anything but water on base.

Hazards: None that are noteworthy

Rescue index: Crane has full medical facilities, as does Bloomington.

Land status: Stay on the trail or the roads and you won't risk running into restricted areas.

Maps: The Natural Resources office at Crane offers a free, fairly complete map. As a bonus, the flip side contains a trail description.

Finding the trail: IN 37 is the main highway between Bloomington and Bedford. Near the Bedford end, IN 58 heads west to Avoca. Take this road, continue on past Avoca until you get to the entrance to Crane. It's on your left (south side of the road). To the right of the guard's gate is a small building. You'll pick up your pass there (bring your ID). Ask them how to get to the Natural Resources Center. The trail starts from behind the center.

Source of additional information:

Crane Lake Naval Surface Warfare Center
Natural Resources Center
(812) 854-1165

The Natural Resources office can tell you anything you need to know about riding here.

Notes on the trail: Start from the back of the Natural Resources Center. About 0.1 mile in, you'll come to a wooden marker. Bear left, toward the lake. In another 0.5 mile you'll cross a long foot bridge; turn right. This turn isn't obvious; you'll know you've gone too far if you come to the lake, or if the Carsonite markers are suddenly facing away from you.

Stay on the trail and you'll soon be at the lake and then the campgrounds. Follow the paved road that bisects the campgrounds as it begins to ascend. Veer off onto the gravel, then past the picnic shelter. The trail picks up again on the other side of the shelter.

The trail remains fairly distinct until you reach the access road from H-290. You'll know you're approaching this point when you cross a small suspension bridge. This is about 4.5 miles into the ride. The access road goes more or less straight ahead; you turn left to continue on the trail.

The trail can be obscure here on the back side of Lake Greenwood. Be patient, use your common sense—look for marker posts, blazes, and traces of the trail, however faint. Keep your orientation to the lake—and you'll be fine.

In just under 12 miles, you'll encounter a road that leads to the dam. Virtually everyone is forbidden to cross the dam, but a tiny sign lists the exceptions: hikers and bikers may continue.

If you're tired, now's your chance to bail. Follow the road up to II-5 (which has a nice shoulder), turn left, and you'll be back at the Natural Resources Center in less than 2 miles. Otherwise, after crossing the dam, turn left on the trail back into the woods and follow it back in.

You won't get lost as long as you follow the map, watch for blazes, and pay attention to your surroundings. You're never far from the lake. In a worst-case scenario, ride to a road and wait for a military vehicle to arrive. Ask the driver to orient you on the map. Once you find that point, you can be on your way again.

This can be an intense ride. But it's also a fun ride. The scenery is great. It's technically demanding, but not overwhelming. Except for a few short sections, it's not that tough physically. And it has the appeal of riding with special privileges on government property. All you have to do is *call ahead*.

RIDE 56 · Yellowbanks

AT A GLANCE

Length/configuration: The dirt single-track depicted on the map shows the 4-mile main loop that is used for races, but there are many other trails on the property. If you choose, you can also tack on about 8 miles of gravel road.

Aerobic difficulty: The total elevation change is minimal, but with so many climbs and quite a few of them steep, you'll find this trail is a workout.

Technical difficulty: Oh, you'll be challenged here. There are some difficult stream crossings, and among all the sharp curves, there will be at least one you'll never forget.

Scenery: You'll pass a few lakes on the way into the hardwood and pine forest, and in spring the dogwoods bloom.

Special comments: In short, you should find this an enjoyable, competitive ride in a rough remote area.

When I was researching this guide, one name kept coming up: Yellowbanks. Now I know why. A site for NORBA races, this is "the greatest trail—one of the best," according to expert racers. Beginning racers simply call it "tough." There are many climbs and descents on steep hills along this narrow dirt single-track. The trail goes through heavy woods and contains several muddy creek crossings, some of which you'll be able to ride through; others, maybe not.

The ride begins on the south side of the campground and passes a few lakes before heading into the woods. You'll find several sharp curves on the trail, passing through the trees. In fact, there's one rutted, muddy curve that might grab your front tire, and you could end up finishing the curve before your bike does. The trail passes near the edge of a coal mine, but you won't see much of it. You may, though, see deer, wild turkey, and coyote among the hardwood and pine forest.

Come for the riding, but stay for the extras. Those who ride here enjoy the facilities as much as the trail. There are many full-service campsites at Yellowbanks, and several rustic cabins available, too. When you're done riding, relax down at the beach. Hand-turned pottery from clay found right on the grounds is also made at Yellowbanks. Other nearby recreational opportunities include an amusement park and a visit to small town called Santa Claus. How can you beat that?

RIDE 56 · Yellowbanks

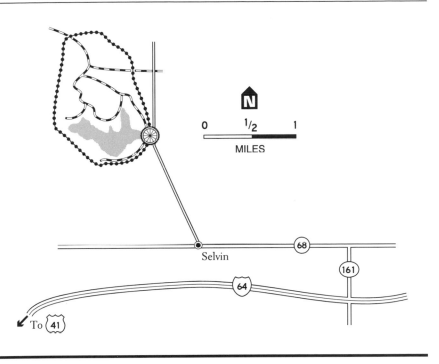

General location: About 35 miles northeast of Evansville

Elevation change: The elevation changes only about 40 feet, but you will find climbs both gradual and steep.

Season: It gets hot in the summer, so spring and fall are best. The dogwood is in bloom in the spring, and rumor has it that good mushroom hunting can be done then, too.

Services: Water and lodging are available at Yellowbanks. Bike service can be found in Evansville or Jasper.

Hazards: Deadfall isn't much of a problem. Stay alert on the turns, especially on the hills.

Rescue index: There's a phone in the campground. On the trail, you're never too far from the back of the campground.

Land status: Private property. The day-use fee is $1.50. You may need to sign in and out if you ride.

Maps: The USGS 7.5 minute quad for this area is Holland.

Finding the trail: Coming from the east: From Interstate 64 and IN 161, go north on IN 161 for 0.25 mile. You will come to a T. Turn left and drive approximately 1 mile until you get to Selvin. In Selvin, turn north on the county blacktop (you'll see a sign for Yellowbanks). Follow the blacktop for 0.75 mile; then follow the signs.

Coming from the west: From I-64 and IN 61, go north on IN 61 about 1,000 feet to a caution light, and turn right onto old IN 68. Go 10 miles into Selvin and turn left on the county blacktop. Follow the signs from there.

Source of additional information:

Yellowbanks
R.R. 2 Dale
Selvin, IN 47523
(812) 567-4703

Notes on the trail: The folks at the campground will direct you to the trail-head. The 4-mile course is marked for the races, but it may vary from the map as race officials change the route for each race.

CHICAGO AREA OUT-AND-BACKS

A t one time, most of Illinois was covered by expansive prairies, but that soon gave way to agricultural development. Then especially in the northeast corner of the state, in an area commonly known as Chicago and the Collar Counties, agriculture gave away to industry, commercial development, and housing. Prairies are almost a memory. However, you can still find vestiges of this state from a bygone era. In several of the trails listed in this section, you'll see restored prairies.

The trails described here all have one thing in common—they're out-and-backs. The Chicago area has arguably one of the highest concentrations of rails-to-trails conversions. Two are listed here—the Prairie Path and the Great Western Trail. In addition, you'll find one towpath trail, the I & M Canal, as well as one nature trail, the Des Plaines River Trail. All of these trails are easy to ride and suitable for all ages and abilities. Being an eclectic trail guide with a "something for everyone" approach, I've put these popular multipurpose trails in one section for the benefit of those who want a relaxing ride. Hard-core mountain bikers should skip ahead.

Choosing which out-and-backs to include was a challenge. There are many fine trails in the area, but several are mostly paved and so are not included in this guide. The four trails in this section are located in each of the areas surrounding Chicago. You should have something easy to ride in any direction you choose. If you want to ride the out-and-back trails east of Chicago, get yourself a boat.

RIDE 57 · Des Plaines River Trail South

AT A GLANCE

Length/configuration: A 26-mile (13 each way) out-and-back multipurpose trail.

Aerobic difficulty: Easy

Technical difficulty: Easy

Scenery: The trail runs along the Des Plaines River, through marshes, fields, and the MacArthur Woods Perserve. Along the river, look for beavers, turtles, and herons.

Special comments: Though not an advanced ride, this trail has two major points going for it: it's conveniently located in a suburb of Chicago, and it's got more than just the trail to recommend it. Try the fishing, take a picnic, bring the kids.

Running parallel to the Des Plaines River for most of the route, this trail will give you an easy ride along its crushed gravel surface. You'll pass through woods, fields, and marshes with many views of the lazy Des Plaines River, as well as through MacArthur Woods Forest Preserve, a dedicated preserve that can only be accessed via the trail. Take the family and enjoy a relaxing day of riding. Go fishing, ice skate in the winter, barbecue at the picnic shelters, and let the kids bird-watch—but above all, try this bike ride in the northern suburbs of Chicago.

General location: Off State Highway 22 in Lincolnshire

Elevation change: Mostly flat

Season: Ride here all year long, but the fall colors along the river are especially pleasing.

Services: Water is available at the trailhead.

Hazards: Since the trail is popular, look out for other bicyclists, hikers, or equestrians. Major road intersections have bridges and underpasses, so traffic is not a major concern.

Rescue index: The trail is well traveled and regularly patrolled by rangers and volunteers. There is a phone at the trailhead.

Land status: Lake County Forest Preserves

Maps: You can get a trail map from the forest preserve district at the address below.

RIDE 57 · Des Plaines River Trail South

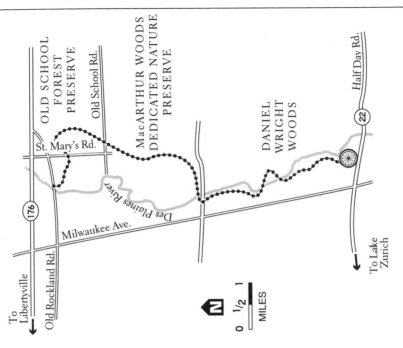

Finding the trail: From Interstate 94 and IL 22 (Half Day Road), go west on IL 22 for 2 miles to Milwaukee Avenue. Turn right on Milwaukee Avenue and go 1 mile to Half Day Preserve. Follow the directional signs to the trailhead.

Contact Lake County Forest Preserves for additional places to pick up the trail.

Source of additional information:

Lake County Forest Preserves
2000 North Milwaukee Avenue
Libertyville, IL 60048
(847) 367-6640

Notes on the trail: There is also a Des Plaines River Trail North, covering another 11-mile route. The north section has fewer woodlands and more open prairies and savannas. However, the 2 trails do not connect and are 2 miles apart. Eventually, the 2 sections will connect for a trail distance of 33 miles one-way.

Geese and cyclists, side by side.

RIDE 58 · Illinois Prarie Path

AT A GLANCE

Length/configuration: 122-mile out-and-back, primarily limestone, along a railway. The trail divides into two major branches, one nortwest toward Elgin and one southwest toward Aurora.

Aerobic difficulty: Easy

Technical difficulty: Again, easy.

Scenery: The main trail winds through suburban areas and there are also some street crossings and congestion, but you'll find more wooded areas on either of the two branches.

Special comments: This tree-lined trail is especially pleasant in fall when the leaves begin to turn.

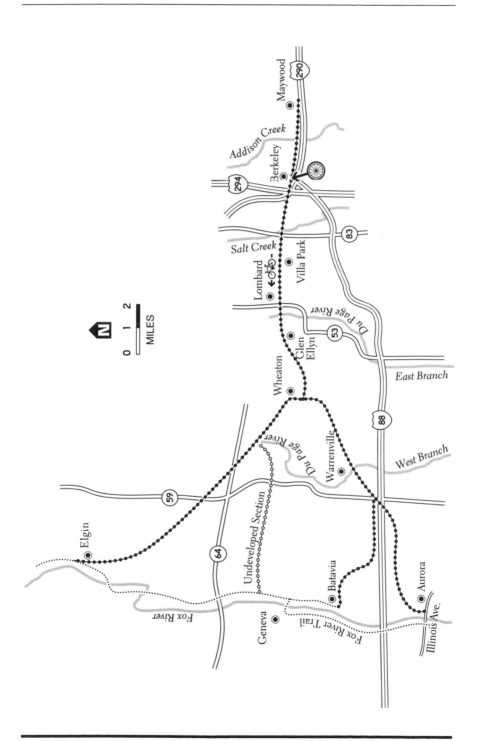

You can't write a guide that includes any rails-to-trails conversions in Illinois and not mention the Illinois Prairie Path. This 61-mile one-way (122 miles total) out-and-back—following the route of the former Chicago, Aurora, and Elgin Railway—was the country's first major rail-to-trail conversion and the first nationally designated trail in Illinois. This trail was first established in 1966, with various extensions added throughout the years. Most of the path is limestone screenings (agricultural limestone); only a handful of spots contain asphalt to prevent erosion. The ride is easy and popular with bicyclists, hikers, joggers, and nature enthusiasts.

The ride begins in Maywood (in Cook County), but in the town of Wheaton (in Dupage County) it branches off in two directions. One branch heads northwest to Elgin, and the other goes southwest to Aurora (both in Kane County). A spur off the Aurora branch heads toward Batavia. The main stem out of Maywood, through Bellwood, Hillside, and Berkeley was blacktopped and landscaped in 1998. Much of the main stem travels through suburban areas and, if nothing else, will give you a flavor of the communities in the western suburbs of Chicago. The right-of-way is mostly tree-lined, making for a pleasant ride. Also, there are frequent street crossings in this area. You'll pass through the downtown districts of Glen Ellyn and Wheaton. In Wheaton, be sure to admire the three spans of Volunteer Bridge, built by Prairie Path volunteers and welded by trade school students, at the Wheaton junction. If you take the southwest branch toward Aurora, the congestion lessens. You'll pass through some wooded areas and agricultural lands. On the Northwest branch, you'll pass a few more wooded areas, including the Pratt's Wayne Woods Forest Preserve, where you'll find egrets, blue heron, and other wildlife.

General location: The eastern trailhead is at 1st Avenue in Maywood. The Wheaton intersection point, the middle, is often considered the starting point. The trail's branches take you to Aurora, Batavia, Geneva, and Elgin.

Elevation change: Negligible

Season: Ride the Illinois Prairie Path any time of year. In the autumn, the colors are beautiful. The trail is used most during the warmer summer months. It's less crowded on weekdays. Cross-country skiing is popular in winter.

Services: Services can be found in many of the towns along the route, including Elmhurst, Wheaton, Aurora, Batavia, Geneva, and Elgin.

Hazards: Look out for other trail users when the weather is nice and be careful at the numerous street crossings.

Rescue index: The area is well populated, so finding help should be no problem. In case of emergency, call 911.

Land status: Various organizations manage the Illinois Prairie Path. In Dupage County, the Division of Transportation maintains the trails. In Kane County, the forest preserve district and the Fox Valley Park District are responsible. In Cook County, an association of the several municipalities as well as the Illinois Department of Natural Resources are responsible.

The first rails-trails conversion, the Illinois Prairie Path tours the western suburbs of Chicago.

Maps: The Illinois Prairie Path office, at the address below, can send you a map of the trail.

Finding the trail: People often pick up the trail at various points along the route. If you want to begin at the eastern end of the trail, you can pick it up at First Avenue in Maywood (Cook County). If you want to begin in Berkeley which is closer to Dupage County line, from I-290 and St. Charles Road, take St. Charles Road east for 0.5 mile to Taft. At Taft, turn right and go 0.5 mile to the 4-way stop at Electric Avenue. Turn right at Electric Avenue and park in the lot half a block on your right, across the street from the fire station/police department/town hall. You'll see the trailhead easily enough on the west side of the parking lot. Contact the Illinois Prairie Path for additional places to pick up the trail.

Source of additional information:

The Illinois Prairie Path
P.O. Box 1086
Wheaton, IL 60189
(630) 752-0120

Notes on the trail: The route is marked and easy to follow. You can find information about the trail at various kiosks along the way.

RIDE 59 · Great Western Trail

AT A GLANCE

Length/configuration: 36-mile rail-to-trail conversion, primarily limestone gravel, through the outskirts of Chicago.

IL

Aerobic difficulty: Easy

Technical difficulty: Easy

Scenery: This trail has a bit of everything, from commercial and manufacturing to agricultural and natural areas. It feels less developed than it is, and the natural areas include a nice spectrum of local scenery, from wetlands to fields.

Special comments: Heavy rains have been known to cause washouts along this trail.

This 18-mile one-way (36 miles total) rail-to-trail conversion runs through the rural areas on the outskirts of the Chicago suburbs. Ninety percent of the trail is limestone gravel and about 10% is blacktop. You'll pass through agricultural, housing, commercial, and manufacturing areas. Even though you'll ride through these developed areas, this trail will give you a nice flavor of fields, marshes, and wetlands the further west you go. In fact, you'll pass seven designated natural areas on the trail. You'll see several natural species of grass as well as abundant white-tailed deer, fox, and beaver. The trail runs from St. Charles in Kane County to Sycamore in DeKalb County. You'll pass through several old farming towns that you might want to explore: Wasco, Lily Lake, Virgil, and Richardson. Come see why Illinois is called the Prairie State.

General location: The ride begins on the western edge of St. Charles, west of Randall Road on Dean Street.

Elevation change: Negligible

Season: All seasons are good, but you might want to head out here in the spring to break cabin fever. Of course, the fall colors in the Midwest are noteworthy.

Services: There is water at the trailhead and at the various communities along the way. All services are available in St. Charles.

Hazards: Washouts after a heavy rain could cause problems. Also, look for mud patches at farm vehicle crossings.

RIDE 59 · Great Western Trail

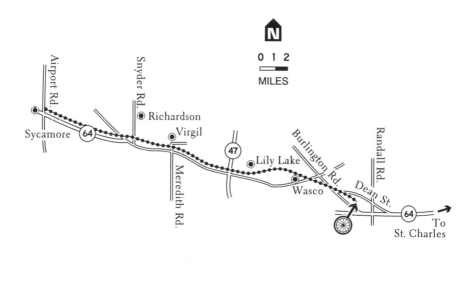

Rescue index: You're usually not far from an intersection where you can flag down help. There are mile-marker posts along the route so you will know your location.

Land status: Kane County Forest Preserve District

Maps: The Kane County Forest Preserve District (address below) can send you a map of the trail. The USGS 7.5 minute quads for the Great Western Trail are Geneva, Elburn, Maple Park, and Sycamore.

Finding the trail: From IL 59 and North Avenue (IL 64), go west 7 miles to Randall Road at the other side of St. Charles. Turn right on Randall Road and go north for 0.5 mile. At the next traffic light, go west on Dean Street for another 0.5 mile. You'll see the entrance on the left side of the road. Contact Kane County Forest Preserve District for additional places to pick up the trail.

Source of additional information:

Kane County Forest Preserve District
719 Batavia Avenue
Geneva, IL 60134
(630) 232-1242

The Great Western Trail spotlights Illinois's Prairie State status.

Notes on the trail: The trailhead is apparent from the parking area, and the route is well marked and easy to follow.

RIDE 60 · Illinois and Michigan Canal State Trail

AT A GLANCE

Length/configuration: 122-mile out-and-back along a former towpath. The trail runs along a canal, and it's surface is base gravel and limestone.

IL

Aerobic difficulty: Easy

Technical difficulty: Easy

Scenery: It's simply outstanding. The waterway is home to countless turtles, and the surrounding area supports a great variety of bird life. Also of note is the view from Starved Rock—well worth the climb.

Special comments: I can't think of a time when I wouldn't want to ride here.

Steeped in historical significance, this 61-mile one-way (122 miles total) former towpath makes for a beautiful, relaxing ride along the I & M Canal. Riders of all ages will enjoy the serenity of this out-and-back trail, disturbed only occasionally by a "plop" as one of the countless turtles sunning on logs dives into the water—or by the occasional boat and barge traffic from either the Des Plaines River or the Illinois River. Even though there is intermittent industry on the other side of the waterways, you'll be able to overlook that as you admire the variety of bird life along the canal. I've seen bluebirds, goldfinches, herons, kingfishers, woodpeckers, egrets, and scarlet tanagers. It's a bird-watcher's paradise.

Aside from the turtles and birds, there are historical and natural sites to see. Where the Des Plaines, Kankakee, and Illinois Rivers meet, you'll see Dresden Nuclear Power Station across the way, the first nuclear power-generating station in the world. If you wish to go back in time, check out the various exhibits and relics from the era when the mule-boat teams used the canal to pull barges— old lock tender houses, locks, and aqueducts.

Near the canal in Utica is Starved Rock State Park, where you can climb to the top of Starved Rock for a breathtaking view of the Illinois River and the surrounding countryside. The town of Ottawa was the first site for the famous Lincoln-Douglas debates. A visitor's center in Utica and an information center in Gebhard Woods in Morris can provide much more of the history. There are also information centers at Buffalo Rock and at the Channahon access. Living so close to the I & M Canal, I may be biased, but when it comes to riding along old towpaths or abandoned railways, this trail is my personal favorite.

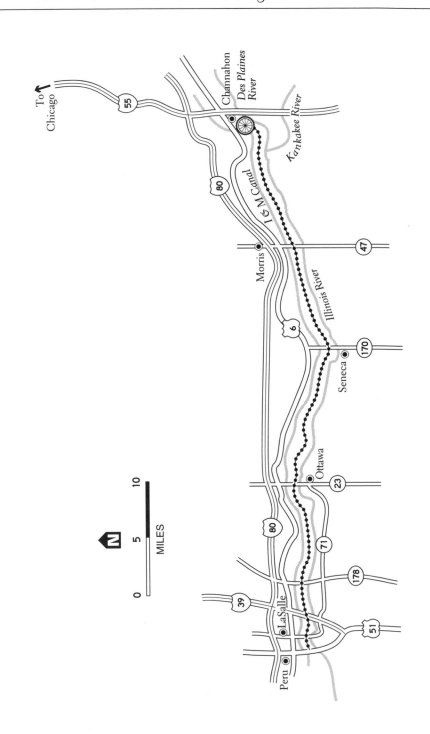

Ron and son, Craig, enjoy the historic towpath trail.

General location: The trail begins in Rockdale and makes its way through Channahon, Morris, Seneca, Marseilles, Ottawa, and Utica before finishing in LaSalle.

Elevation change: Negligible

Season: Any time.

Services: Water is available at Channahon Access, AuxSable Access, McKinley Woods, and Buffalo Rock. Primitive camping is available at Channahon Access, AuxSable Access, McKinley Woods, and Gebhard Woods. Good bike shops can be found in Joliet and Morris. Seneca, Marseilles, and Ottawa all have fantastic mom-and-pop restaurants if you get tired and decide to rest in one of these authentic canal towns.

Hazards: Occasionally you'll pass other cyclists and hikers, but this trail is less crowded than others of its kind.

Rescue index: There are usually enough people around if you run into a problem. You can also find help in the various towns you pass along the way.

Land status: State trail

Maps: You can get a map of the trail from the information center, Visitor Center, and ranger stations. The Heritage Corridor also has trail information. Write to the address below. The USGS 7.5 minute quads for this trail are Channahon, Minooka, Coal City, Morris, Seneca, Marseilles, and Ottawa.

Finding the trail: Take I-55 to Exit 248, Highway 6, which is 2 miles south of I-80. Go west on US 6 into Channahon, and 4.5 miles from I-55, on US 6, you'll see a sign for the I & M Canal on Canal Street. Turn left and go down to the second stop sign. Turn right on Bridge Street. In another block, after you cross the first bridge, turn left into the parking area. If you cross the second bridge, you've gone too far. You'll see the starting point at the other end of the parking area. There are other access points to the trail. Contact the Heritage Corridor Visitors Bureau for additional sites.

Sources of additional information:

Illinois and Michigan Canal State Trail
P.O. Box 272
Morris, IL 60450
(815) 942-0796

Heritage Corridor Visitors Bureau
81 North Chicago Street
Joliet, IL 60431
(815) 727-2323

Notes on the trail: The trailhead described above is a good place to begin your ride. The services at Channahon Access are on the other side of Bridge Street, down the trail about 0.25 mile.

CHICAGO AREA: FOREST PRESERVES AND PARKS

Chicago is the third largest metropolitan area in the United States, and, as you may imagine, is not perceived as a mountain biking mecca. While there are a few nice paved bicycle paths in the city of Chicago, there isn't much in the way of unpaved trails. However, you don't have to get too far out of the city to find areas where you can do some serious riding, even though several of the rides listed in this section are surrounded by fairly well-populated areas.

Urban sprawl has created an interesting situation in the Chicago area. Cook County (where Chicago is located) and the surrounding collar counties all have county forest preserve districts. Scattered throughout this urban and suburban area, you'll find little pockets of wilderness where people in the city flock on weekends. Unlike in expansive national forests, it's difficult to get seriously lost in a forest preserve. However, that doesn't mean you can't find dense woodlands. In fact, many of the forest preserves and parks here offer a variety of terrain, including woods, fields, prairies, and marshes.

As far as mountain biking goes, some of these preserves offer easy riding, while others make up in technical demands what they lack in elevation. But don't be fooled. Areas like Swallow Cliffs and Deer Grove can have elevation changes ranging around 100 feet. It's not Colorado, but, in an area where people think the tallest thing around is the Sears Tower, they're often surprised at what they find here. Some of these trails, like the Regional Trail, and the trails in Waterfall Glen and Moraine Hills State Park have neither technical challenges nor serious elevation changes, but they do provide a nice option if you are interested in the course prerequisite for Mountain Biking 101.

The trail descriptions that follow were written with the help of several people. Thanks to Bart Dahlstrom for providing information about Deer Grove, Duane Anderson and Mike Palezzetti for the Regional Trail and Elsen's Hill, Andy Pilska for Swallow Cliffs and Maple Lake, and Mark Karner for Hammel Woods.

RIDE 61 · Moraine Hills State Park

AT A GLANCE

Length/configuration: 10 miles of trails comprised of three connecting loops, Fox River, Lake Defiance, and Leather Leaf Bog.

Aerobic difficulty: Moderate

Technical difficulty: Easy

Scenery: This trail covers the majority of terrain you'll find in the Chicago area: lakes, woods, marshes, and praries.

Special comments: The Fox River Trail is the flattest, and the Lake Defiance Trail and Leather Leaf Bog are hillier.

IL

Moraine Hills State Park is a good place to ride if you're looking for a non-technical trail, but still want a workout. The crushed limestone surface is wide and well maintained, but the area is fairly hilly.

You'll pass through a variety of terrains—lakes, woods, marshes, and prairies. By the marshes, get off your bike and spend a few minutes at one of the two viewing platforms observing the variety of waterfowl, including blue and green herons, mallards, teals, and wood ducks. The trails are also home to fox, deer, mink, and beaver. In the vegetation department, look for marsh marigold, Saint John's wort, hoary willow, and other rare species. If you like to see battles between the plant and animal worlds, Pike Marsh, southeast of the Lake Defiance Trail, is home to one of the state's largest known colonies of pitcher plants, a rare species that traps and eats insects. If that makes you hungry, there are two concession stands in the park. Also, fishing and boat rentals are available. In short, Moraine Hills State Park is a great getaway not far from the Chicago area.

General location: Three miles south of McHenry, on River Road

Elevation change: Elevation change is minimal; look for gently rolling hills.

Season: You can ride all year long, but the spring and fall are busier. I happen to like the smell of the lilacs and other wildflowers in the spring. The fall colors are pleasant, too.

Services: Water is available at the trailhead. All services are available in McHenry and Crystal Lake.

Hazards: Your main concern will be other trail users on pleasant days.

Rescue index: You're never too far from a parking lot. You'll find a phone at the park office and at McHenry Dam.

RIDE 61 • Moraine Hills State Park

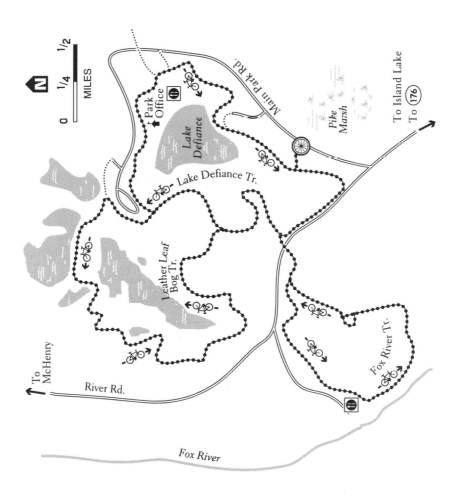

Land status: State park

Maps: You can pick up a map at the park office or you can write Moraine Hills State Park for one at the address below. The USGS 7.5 minute quad is Wauconda, with a small portion of the park falling into the McHenry quad.

Finding the trail: From State Highway 53 and Highway 12 (Rand Road), go west on US 12 for 12.5 miles to IL 176 (Liberty Street). Turn left on IL 176 and take that for 3.5 miles to River Road. Turn right on River Road, and the entrance

You don't have to go far from Chicago to cherish the solitude of a state park.

will be 2 miles on your right. There are 10 day-use areas in the park, each with parking, picnicking, and a trail access point.

Source of additional information:

Moraine Hills State Park
914 South River Road
McHenry, IL 60050
(815) 385-1624

Notes on the trail: You'll see the trailhead from any of the day-use lots. The one-way trails are color coded and have distance markers along the way.

RIDE 62 · Deer Grove

AT A GLANCE

Length/configuration: Several paved bicycle trails.

Aerobic difficulty: Moderate

Technical difficulty: Easy

Scenery: Forest; most noticably, you'll be sharing the main trail with hikers and horses, so be cautious.

Special comments: The maps do not include the spurs off the main trail because these are closed to bikers per Cook County Preserve policy.

If you're north of Chicago, Deer Grove is where you should go to get some mountain bike action. There is a paved bicycle trail in the forest preserve.

With its variety of riding options, Deer Grove is good for the intermediate mountain biker looking for the moderate riding found along the paved areas. As local area mountain biker Bart Dahlstrom puts it, "It's long enough to work up a good sweat without going around in circles."

General location: In Palatine, off Dundee Road

Elevation change: The variation here is almost 100 feet.

Season: It's drier in the summer, so ride then if you don't mind the mosquitoes. The spring and fall can be wet and muddy. Cook County Forest Preserve prohibits riding the trails if they are the least bit soggy.

Services: Water is available at Deer Grove. All services are available in Palatine.

Hazards: The areas with the steep climbs are rocky and muddy.

Rescue index: The preserve gets a lot of use. The area is bounded by several busy roads as well.

Land status: Forest Preserve District of Cook County

Maps: You can write the Forest Preserve District of Cook County at the address below for a map. There are also trail signs posted at the various parking areas. The USGS 7.5 minute quad for Deer Grove is Lake Zurich.

Finding the trail: From Interstate 90 and IL 53, go north on IL 53 for 5.5 miles to Dundee Road (IL 68). Turn left (west) on Dundee Road and go for 3 miles to Quentin Road. Turn right on Quentin Road, and you'll see the entrance for Deer Grove 0.5 mile on your left.

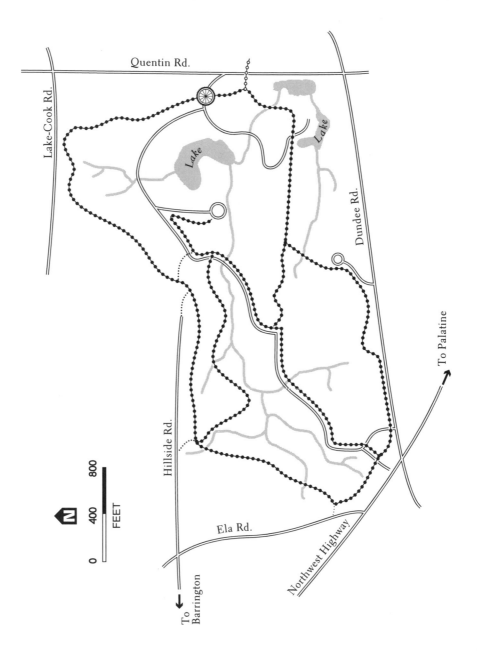

Quentin Rd.

Lake-Cook Rd.

Lake

Lake

Dundee Rd.

To Palatine

Hillside Rd.

800

400

FEET

0

Ela Rd.

Northwest Highway

To Barrington

Source of additional information:

Forest Preserve District of Cook County
536 North Harlem
River Forest, IL 60305
(312) 261-8400 (city)
(708) 366-9420 (suburbs)

Notes on the trail: You can park at any lot you come to, but you might want to park at the first parking area and ride back a few yards to pick up the main trail where the trail map sign is.

RIDE 63 · Elsen's Hill—West DuPage Woods

AT A GLANCE

Length/configuration: 4 miles of grass and gravel loops.

Aerobic difficulty: Easy to moderate; some steep grades, especially toward the river.

Technical difficulty: Easy to moderate, depending on horse traffic.

Scenery: Upland oak woods with trails following the DuPage river and curling around ponds.

Special comments: Elsen's Hill is a good place to ride if you're interested in mountain biking but haven't had a lot of experience.

Though there are only about four miles of trails through this upland oak woods, the area presents a few more challenges than the Regional Trail (see Ride 64). Located at one of the few fens in DuPage County, this trail has steeper grades especially toward the river. Elsen's Hill consists of three mowed grass loops, and occasionally you'll find gravel sections. The orange loop takes you along the meandering west branch of the DuPage River. If ponds are more your speed, stick to the green loop. The trail is easy since the forest preserve district keeps it clear and the trail wide. If horse use is heavy, the trails will have severe divots.

General location: Twenty-eight miles west of Chicago, near Winfield

Elevation change: Total elevation change hovers around 60 feet.

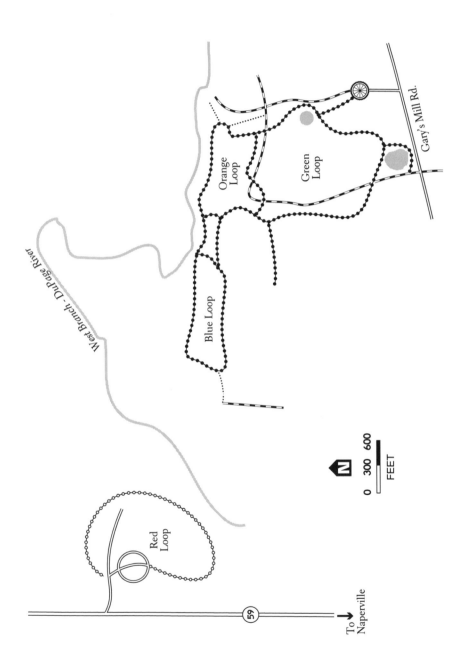

Pedaling down the wide double-track at the end of the Elsen's Hill trail.

Season: Ride here year-round, but in the late fall and early spring the rain can muddy the trail.

Services: Water is available at the forest preserve. All services are available in Warrenville, Wheaton, Naperville, and Lisle.

Hazards: There is a lot of horse traffic in the area, so remember your trail etiquette, should you pass an equestrian.

Rescue index: The area is fairly populated. You'll find a gas station at the corner of Winfield and Roosevelt Roads.

Land status: Forest Preserve District of DuPage County.

Maps: Maps are available at the Visitor Information signs located at the entrance to the trail. You can also write the Forest Preserve District at the address below.

Finding the trail: From I-88 and IL 59, go north on IL 59 for 4 miles to Gary's Mill Road. The road itself is not marked, but there's a yellow intersection sign just before it. Turn right on Gary's Mill Road and you'll find the entrance just over 1 mile on your left.

Source of additional information:

Forest Preserve District of DuPage County
P.O. Box 2339
Glen Ellyn, IL 60138
(630) 933-7300

Notes on the trail: The trail begins on the north end of the Elsen's Hill parking lot. Go up the service road from the lot past the rest rooms and turn left at the water pump. You can begin your ride there, or to the left of the pond. The trails are signed. As always, please show respect if the trails are closed during wet weather.

RIDE 64 · Regional Trail

AT A GLANCE

Length/configuration: 16 miles of limestone gravel trails.

Aerobic difficulty: Easy

Technical difficulty: Easy

Scenery: You'll have a quiet ride through praries, meadows, woodlands, marshes, and wetlands. Many areas are scattered with wildflowers, and there is an impressive variety of animal life.

Special comments: This trail winds through the Blackwell, Herrick Lake, and Danada Forest Preserves. It's well maintained, and while not a difficult ride, it is an excellent diversion from the stresses of the city.

Jaunt—that's the perfect word to describe the Regional Trail. Neither technical nor taxing, this ride carries you along a wide, multipurpose, limestone gravel path. The Regional Trail itself is about 7.5 miles one-way (15 miles total), but when you add in the spur loops in the three forest preserves it crosses, your total ride comes to a little over 16 miles. The Forest Preserve District of DuPage County does an excellent job maintaining its trails and takes great pride in them. As I rode with one of the sector managers, Mike Palazzetti, he enthusiastically pointed out to me where edges of the trail had been cleared and diversion ditches had been dug. In fact, he even stopped to give an erosion explanation to a group of riders who had strayed off the trail. He has a lot to be proud of: on the fringes of the suburban Chicago area, this trail passes through oak woodlands, open meadows, marshes, rivers, lakes, wetlands, and prairies in the Blackwell, Herrick Lake, and Danada Forest Preserves.

In the Blackwell Forest Preserve on the northernmost section of the Regional Trail, you can branch off and ride the intersecting loops of the Catbird, Nighthawk, and Bob-O-Link Trails. These three trails circle McKee

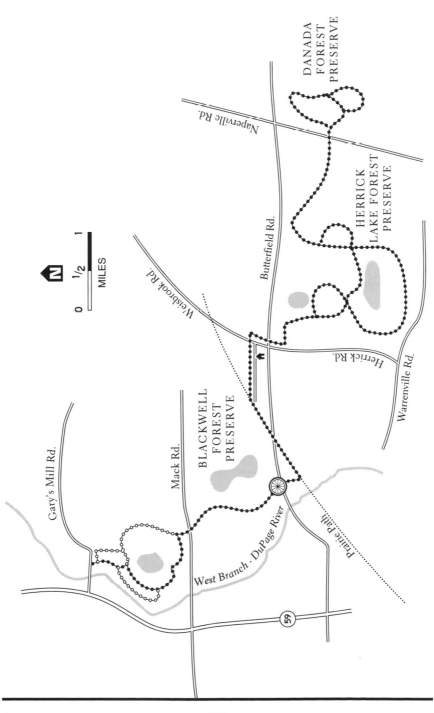

Marsh. The Nighthawk and Bob-O-Link trails are gravel and limestone. The Catbird is a grass trail, which will give you a bumpier ride than the Regional Trail. If you're a casual rider taking the family out for a stroll, you might wish to bypass these trails, but most mountain bikers will find this easy. McKee Marsh, by the way, was the site where the skeleton of a woolly mammoth was excavated.

As the Regional Trail makes its way into the Herrick Forest Preserve, it becomes part of three intersecting limestone gravel loops: Meadowlark Trail, Green Heron Trail, and Bluebird Trail. Perhaps you'll spot egrets munching on tadpoles in the cattail marsh in the middle of the Green Heron Trail loop.

The final leg of the Regional Trail goes through Danada Forest Preserve and passes by a Kentucky-style equestrian center. At the eastern end of the Regional Trail, the one-mile, double-loop Nature Trail gives you a slightly different feel than the main trail. Still crushed limestone, the Nature Trail is a little narrower and does not have mowed borders. Curving through an open savanna, you'll pass many beautiful wildflowers in the summer—columbine, spring beauty, shooting stars, and toothwort among them.

Even though you're in the Chicago suburbs, the area doesn't lack for variety of animals: coyotes, fox, weasels, painted turtles, leopard frogs, owls, hawks, bob-o-links, meadowlarks, orioles, egrets, and great blue herons. All in all, this easy ride is fun for the entire family and makes for a pleasant diversion from the commotion of our busy lives.

General location: Twenty-nine miles west of Chicago near Warrenville, off IL 59 and IL 56

Elevation change: Negligible

Season: Ride the Regional Trail year-round. Late fall and early spring can produce a lot of rain, so you might want to avoid the grass trails at Blackwell then.

Services: Water can be found by Silver Lake in Blackwell, by Herrick Lake, and near Danada Mansion in Danada. There are telephones by the entrance to Blackwell and in a few spots by Herrick Lake and Danada. There are even concession stands open during the summer in Blackwell and Herrick Lake. All services are available in Warrenville, Wheaton, Naperville, and Lisle.

Hazards: The only hazards present on this trail are other cyclists, hikers, and equestrians.

Rescue index: The trails are heavily used and bounded by several major roads. You can also find help at the guard residence, the concession area, and the shop complexes at Blackwell; at the concession stand at Herrick Lake; and at the 2 guard residences at Danada.

Land status: Forest Preserve District of DuPage County

Maps: You can pick up maps of the forest preserves at the Visitor Information signs in the various parking areas. You can also write to the Forest Preserve District of DuPage County to get copies. The USGS 7.5 minute quads for this

Duane and Mike glide easily down the well-maintained Regional Trail.

area are Naperville and Wheaton, but the maps from the Forest Preserve District will be sufficient.

Finding the trail: From I-88, go north on IL 59 for 1.2 miles to Butterfield Road. Turn right (east), and in 1.5 miles, you'll see the entrance for Blackwell on your left. As you pull in, the parking area is just off to your right.

Source of additional information:

Forest Preserve District of DuPage County
P.O. Box 2339
Glen Ellyn, IL 60138
(933) 790-7200

Notes on the trail: The Blackwell Forest Preserve trailhead isn't at the beginning of the trail, but this provides a good place to park. (You can park, if you wish, at Herrick or Danada and begin your ride from there.) From the parking area, you can access the Herrick and Danada portions of the trail by riding out the way you came in and crossing to the new ISTEA section of the Regional Trail, which runs parallel to Route 56 (Butterfly Road) and goes east to Winfield Road. This is the preferred crossing to the Prairie Path as opposed to the single-track at the Blackmill entrance. The Prairie Path will take you directly to Weisbrook Road. Turn right on Weisbrook and go 1 block to Butterfield Road. (South of Butterfield Road, Weisbrook Road turns into Herrick Road.) At the southeast corner of the intersection, you'll see where the trail picks up in Herrick Lake Forest Preserve. As you follow the trail through Herrick, you'll come to several intersections where you can turn off on Meadowlark Trail, Green Heron Trail, or Bluebird Trail. Take whatever options you fancy, or ride straight through into Danada Forest Preserve. Once in Danada, you'll pass by the exercise track before riding under Naperville Road. If you ride through the parking area and past the barns, you'll come to the last 0.25 mile of the Regional Trail and the 1-mile Nature Trail.

After you return to the Blackwell Forest Preserve parking lot, you'll see where the Regional Trail picks up on the west side of the parking area. As you ride that portion, you'll cross Mack Road. About 0.25 mile later, you'll come to the trails of Nighthawk, Catbird, and Bob-O-Link. Branch off on these trails or continue on the Regional Trail. When you hit Gary's Mill Road on the north, you've reached the end of the ride.

This trail also connects up with Prairie Path.

RIDE 65 · Waterfall Glen

AT A GLANCE

Length/configuration: An 8-and-a-half-mile loop of wide, gravel trails.

Aerobic difficulty: Easy

Technical difficulty: Easy

Scenery: You'll find several scenic views and interesting sites along this pleasant trail that winds through a number of terrains: meadows, praries, woodlands, and wetlands.

Special comments: Although the entire forest preserve surrounds the Argonne National Laboratory, a major scientific installation, you never really see it.

You'll love this scenic, eight-and-a-half-mile loop. Period. One of the most popular multipurpose trails in the western Chicago suburbs, it passes through a variety of terrains, including meadows, praries, woodlands, and wetlands. The eight-foot-wide gravel trail is suitable for all ages and abilities. This is the perfect place to get away from the flurry of your daily life and spend some time on a leisurely ride. Few technical skills are required, so you could fly down the trail—but why would you want to? Relax.

RIDE 65 · Waterfall Glen

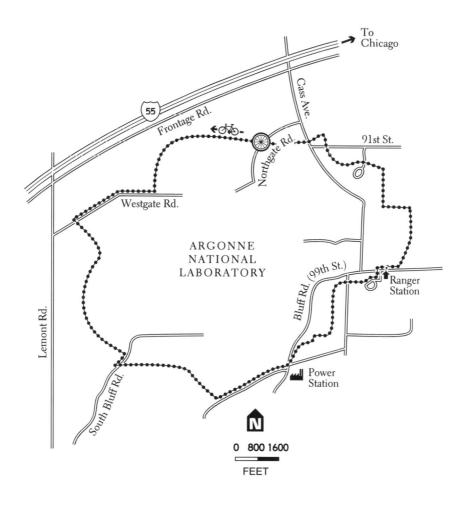

The forest preserve contains several sites of note. The county's only artesian well is at the south end of the preserve. You'll pass through the "leaning forest," an area where a 1976 tornado bowed the trees. For a scenic view, look across the Des Plaines River at the town of Lemont nestled in the hills. You may spot many species of animals, including coyotes, beaver, bluebirds, herons, and cranes. But the animal you want to keep your eyes peeled for is the deer. I don't mean your average, everyday, brown-colored deer, but a species of white deer. Not a genetic mutation caused by Argonne National Laboratory, these white

Savoring a quiet ride down the popular Waterfall Glen trail.

fallow deer were actually imported here from Asia at the turn of the century. Oh, and one more thing. With a name like Waterfall Glen, you'd expect to see a waterfall—and there is one. Oddly enough, though, the waterfall has nothing to do with the name of the preserve. The area was named after Seymour "Bud" Waterfall, an early forest preserve district president.

General location: Off Cass Avenue, south of I-55 in Darien

Elevation change: Negligible. The only small hill is by Saw Mill Creek.

Season: Enjoy the changes year-round. The autumn colors are especially vivid.

Services: Water and restrooms are available at the trailhead. All services can be found in Downers Grove or Willow Springs.

Hazards: Since this is a popular multipurpose trail, you'll be sharing the path with both pedestrians and equestrians. Especially watch the traffic crossing Cass Avenue.

Rescue index: The ranger station often isn't staffed, but Lemont Road to the west of the preserve and Cass Avenue to the east are quite busy. Also, there's a guard booth for Argonne National Laboratory near the trailhead. You proba-bably don't want to bother the lab, but in an emergency, would they turn you away?

Land status: Forest Preserve District of DuPage County

Maps: The Forest Preserve District has a great color map, which is sufficient for your needs. You can write for one at the address below. Also, maps are available at the information sign at the trailhead. The USGS 7.5 minute quad is mostly Sag Bridge with a portion in the Romeoville quad.

Finding the trail: From I-55, take the Cass Avenue south exit. Go south on Cass Avenue 0.25 mile and turn right on Northgate Road. Go to the second entrance labeled "Waterfall Glen — Ski Equestrian Trailhead Area." The trail begins at the south end of the parking lot to the left of the restrooms.

Sources of additional information:

Forest Preserve District of DuPage County
P.O. Box 2339
Glen Ellyn, IL 60138
(630) 790-4900

Notes on the trail: Since the area has had trail usage conflicts in the past, please stay on the main trail marked by brown Carsonite posts with a white circle. Don't take any user-made, single-track spurs you might find. Following the trail is easy, except in a few spots: by Westgate Road, you'll need to ride down the road a little, and the trail will continue again off to your left. Later, when you get to the power station, turn left down the road; the trail will pick up on your right in a few yards. Finally, you'll enter a clearing. The markings aren't clear here, so look carefully for another clearing on your left, heading west, where you will want to turn. This stretch is a little rough from horse use, but it will be well worth it when you come to a majestic wetland area, where I've even seen a sparrow chasing a 6-foot crane. Only in the Chicago area!

RIDE 66 · Swallow Cliff Woods

AT A GLANCE

Length/configuration: A wide, seven-mile, gravel loop.

Aerobic difficulty: Easy

Technical difficulty: Easy

Scenery: Woods and meadows, with some water crossings.

Special comments: If you ride this trail in the winter, bring a sled for the toboggan slide, the longest and highest in the Chicago region.

IL

If you follow the main gravel loop, about a seven-mile trip, you'll ride along a wide, quiet trail used by joggers, hikers, and equestrians. The woods along the trail contain sycamores, large ironwood trees, and white pines, as well as blackberry, dewberry, and raspberry patches in meadow areas. Without a doubt, riders of all abilities will flock to this area. Sunday riders will enjoy following the main trail, tested occasionally by a few small hills and short water crossings. Forest Preserve District has been ticketing those who do not adhere to the posted trail markers.

General location: At the Palos Forest Preserve off IL 83, 0.5 mile west of US 45

Elevation change: The overall elevation gain is about 150 feet.

Season: Ride all year long. In the winter, bring that toboggan. In the fall, head out to the Great Pumpkin Smash Off-Road Rally, sponsored by Wheel Thing.

Services: Water is available at the trailhead. Many of the surrounding suburbs have all services, including LaGrange and Orland Park.

Hazards: On the main trail, be prepared to contend with horses and hikers. Also, be careful when crossing the 2 major intersections.

Rescue index: You're never far from a major road if you need help.

Land status: Forest Preserve District of Cook County

Maps: The Forest Preserve District can send you a map depicting the main trail and several of the picnic areas and sites along the way. Write to the address below. If you feel you need it, the USGS 7.5 minute quads for this area are Palos Park and Sag Bridge.

Finding the trail: From the north: from Interstate 55 and LaGrange Road (US 45), take LaGrange Road south for 5.5 miles to IL 83. Exit at IL 83 and turn left off the exit ramp. Go down IL 83 for 0.5 mile to the Swallow Cliff Toboggan Slide. You can park in this lot.

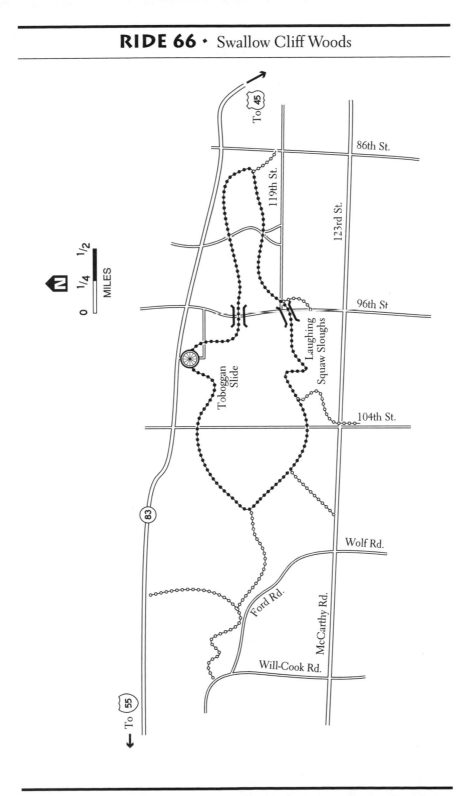

To 45

86th St.

119th St.

123rd St.

96th St

Laughing
Squaw Sloughs

N

0   1/4   1/2
MILES

Toboggan
Slide

104th St.

83

Wolf Rd.

Ford Rd.

McCarthy Rd.

Will-Cook Rd.

To 55

Riders of all abilities find a home at Swallow Cliff woods.

From the south: from I-55 and IL 83, take IL 83 south for 7.5 miles to the Swallow Cliff Toboggan Slide.

Sources of additional information:

Forest Preserve District of Cook County
536 North Harlem Avenue
River Forest, IL 60305
(312) 261-8400 (city)
(708) 366-9420 (suburban)

Wheel Thing
15 South LaGrange Road
LaGrange, IL 60525
(708) 352-3822

Notes on the trail: You can begin the ride at the parking area entrance where the trail crosses the access road. Start in whichever direction you like. The main trail is not difficult to follow. The map does not show any of the spurs because they are closed to mountain bikers.

The Maple Lake Trail is also accessible from the Swallow Cliff Trail by riding north on 104th Avenue.

RIDE 67 · Maple Lake

AT A GLANCE

Length/configuration: A gravelly 12-mile loop.

Aerobic difficulty: Easy

Technical difficulty: Easy

Scenery: You'll pass through wetlands, meadows, and woodlands; the trail skirts sloughs and a few lakes.

Special comments: This is one of the best family-oriented rides in the area, with several educational attractions along the trail and trail conditions suitable for kids.

One person's algae is another's slough. This 12-mile loop is a little longer and slightly more difficult than the Swallow Cliff loop. It passes around six sloughs and a couple of lakes. Several other sloughs dot this forest preserve. These wetland areas are home to numerous waterfowl, including ducks, geese, and egrets. Traveling through woods and meadows, this gravelly multipurpose trail features a wide path with few obstacles, making it a pleasant ride for the entire family.

Several attractions also make this an ideal family recreation spot. In addition to picnicking, you can fish at Bullfrog Lake and at Maple Lake. If the kids don't want to fish, they can scour the banks for bullfrogs and crawdads. Boat rentals are also available at Maple Lake. Another attraction is the Little Red Schoolhouse, a nature center near Longjohn Slough containing indoor exhibits and native animals. Also, on the southwest corner of the trail is the site of the first Argonne Laboratory, where nuclear fuel from the original Manhattan Project is buried. Spent fuel aside, this is a great spot to come if you want a simple, peaceful ride only minutes from one of the largest urban areas in the country.

General location: At Palos Forest Preserve off IL 83, 3 miles west of US 45

Elevation change: Surprisingly, you'll find 120 feet of elevation change here.

Season: Ride here year-round. Summer is crowded; the fall colors are pleasing in October.

Services: Water is available at the trailhead. All services are available in LaGrange and Orland Park.

Hazards: The trail is popular with horses and hikers. Be careful crossing the streets.

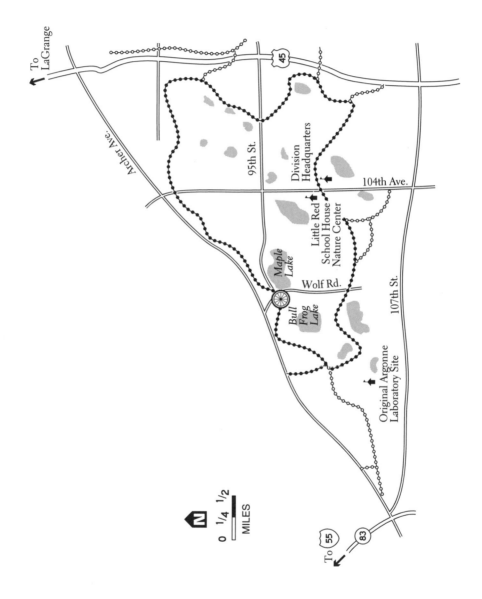

To LaGrange

Archer Ave.

45

95th St.

Division Headquarters

104th Ave.

Little Red School House Nature Center

Maple Lake

Wolf Rd.

Bull Frog Lake

107th St.

Original Argonne Laboratory Site

N

0 1/4 1/2
MILES

To 55

83

Dotted with several sloughs, Maple Lake provides riders a "nature break" not far from Chicago.

Rescue index: The trail is well traveled and crosses several major roads.

Land status: Forest Preserve District of Cook County

Maps: The Forest Preserve District can send you a map of the main trail and several of the attractions. Write to the address below. The USGS 7.5 minute quads for this area are Palos Park and Sag Bridge.

Finding the trail: From the north: from I-55 and LaGrange Road (US 45), take LaGrange Road south 1 mile to Archer Avenue (IL 171). Go south on Archer Avenue 3 miles to 95th Street. (Look for the Maple Lake sign.) Turn left and stay to the right, hooking up with Wolf Road in just 0.3 mile. The parking area is on your right for Maple Lake West and Bullfrog Lake.

From the south: from I-55 and IL 83, take IL 83 south for 3 miles to Archer Avenue (IL 171). Turn left and go 2.5 miles to 95th Street. (Look for 2 yellow intersection signs to help you locate 95th Street.) Turn right and stay to the right, hooking up with Wolf Road in just 0.2 mile. The parking area is on your right for Maple Lake West and Bullfrog Lake.

Sources of additional information:

Forest Preserve District of Cook County
536 North Harlem Avenue
River Forest, IL 60305
(312) 261-8400 (city)
(708) 366-9420 (suburban)

Wheel Thing
15 South LaGrange Road
LaGrange, IL 60525
(708) 352-3822

Notes on the trail: You can pick up the trail from the north side of the parking lot. Pass through the picnic area and you will run into the trail. You can go left or right.

The Swallow Cliff Trail is also accessible from Maple Lake Trail by riding south on 104th Avenue. The map does not show any of the spurs, as these are closed to bikers. This is new Cook County District Preserve policy.

RIDE 68 · Hammel Woods

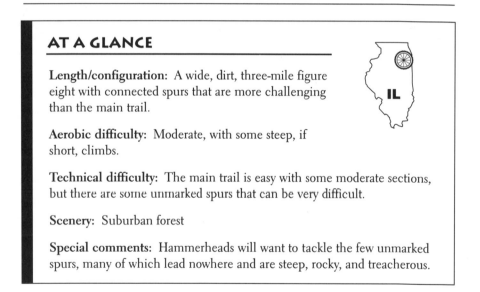

AT A GLANCE

Length/configuration: A wide, dirt, three-mile figure eight with connected spurs that are more challenging than the main trail.

Aerobic difficulty: Moderate, with some steep, if short, climbs.

Technical difficulty: The main trail is easy with some moderate sections, but there are some unmarked spurs that can be very difficult.

Scenery: Suburban forest

Special comments: Hammerheads will want to tackle the few unmarked spurs, many of which lead nowhere and are steep, rocky, and treacherous.

Hammel Woods is the quintessential suburban forest preserve: a small area used for recreational groups, popular with weekend and after-work joggers. Don't be deterred by the fact that this trail is a short three miles. This figure eight with a connecting spur is a great place for a quick aerobic workout—take as many laps as you like. In fact, I use Hammel Woods for my training rides. It's popular with the Joliet Bicycle Club because of the short but steep uphill and downhill at a bridged stream crossing.

The primarily dirt trail is wide, so you won't need a lot of technical skills. The eastern side of the northern loop does have some blind curves and the surface is rooted—a good place to practice bike handling techniques. As you pedal through the woods, keep an eye out for the occasional deer and the flit of a scarlet tanager.

RIDE 68 • Hammel Woods

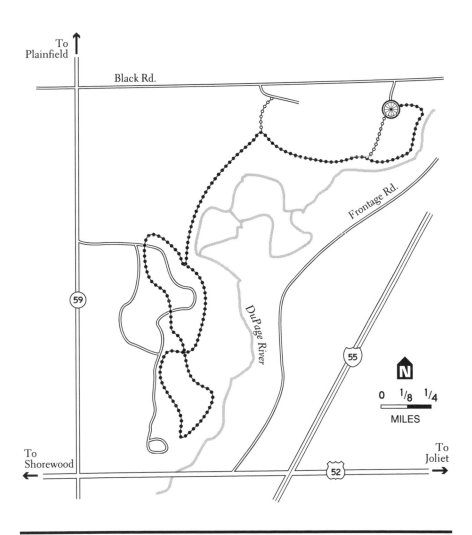

General location: In Joliet, northwest of I-55 and IL 52

Elevation change: The one steep hill doesn't significantly affect the elevation.

Season: Ride this one all year long, but carry mosquito repellent in the summer at dusk.

Services: Water and rest rooms can be found at the picnic groves. All services can be found in Joliet. For bike service, try Al's Bike Shop in Joliet.

Mark practices his climbing technique on Hammel Woods' uphill climb.

Hazards: Keep an eye out for pedestrians out for a jog or a leisurely stroll. You will need to pay attention on the one major hill as the steep trail runs alongside a metal stairway.

Rescue index: Since the area is small, you're never far from a major road. Black Road, IL 59, and IL 52 are all major thoroughfares.

Land status: Forest Preserve District of Will County

Maps: You can get a map from the Will County Forest Preserve District at the address below. The USGS 7.5 minute quad for this area is Plainfield.

Finding the trail: From I-55, take IL 52 west to the first stop light, IL 59 (Brook Forest Avenue). Turn right (north) on IL 59. Pass up the entrance on IL 59 and go to the next stop light, Black Road. Turn right on Black Road, heading east a short distance. Pass the first entrance to Hammel Woods and take the second entrance a few yards further. The brown Carsonite sign marking the trail entrance is east of the soccer field.

Sources of additional information:

Forest Preserve District of Will County
P.O. Box 1069
22606 South Cherry Hill Road
Joliet, IL 60434
(815) 727-8700

Al's Bicycle Shop
1418 West Jefferson Street
Joliet, IL 60435
(815) 741-8383

Notes on the trail: Beginning at the DuPage River Access spur will ensure that you hit the steep hill. As you start off, the grass portion of the trail will flank the fields along the DuPage River before heading into the forest. After you travel alongside the Crumby Recreation Area and over 2 small wooden crossways, you'll come to a point where you will see a small shelter ahead of you. The main trail will veer to the right. Soon, you'll come to the stairway heading down. Keep to the left of the stairs. At the top of the hill on the other side, go left or right to enter the figure-eight loops.

ROCKFORD

R ockford is the second largest city in the state, and the trail listed here represents the northernmost ride in this guide. The original prairies here have mostly disappeared, as have the forests, but reforestation, as well as prairie and wetland restoration efforts, have created a few pockets of natural areas similar to the original landscape.

Though not difficult, this ride will give you a chance to enjoy some mountain biking amidst beautiful scenery. Rockford may be well populated, but Rock Cut State Park is a great place to come for a little R&R.

Rest and relaxation is one way to look at it. You could make a case for the opposite—you can "take it hard" if you like and give yourself a workout, too. Though not a technical ride, Rock Cut State Park, with its wide, maintained trails, is a good place for a challenging aerobic ride.

Thanks to Tom Hutten, who helped supply information for Rock Cut State Park.

RIDE 69 · Rock Cut State Park

AT A GLANCE

Length/configuration: 10 miles of mostly dirt trails, 7 open to cross country skiers and bikers.

Aerobic difficulty: Easy or challenging if you push it.

Technical difficulty: Easy

Scenery: As you ride, keep an eye out for wild turkey, deer, fox, and beaver. The spring and summer showcase over 100 types of wildflowers.

Special comments: Remember to ride only on the trails posted with bicycle symbols or crosscountry ski signs. Park officials ask that you do not ride when trails are wet or covered with 2 or more inches of snow.

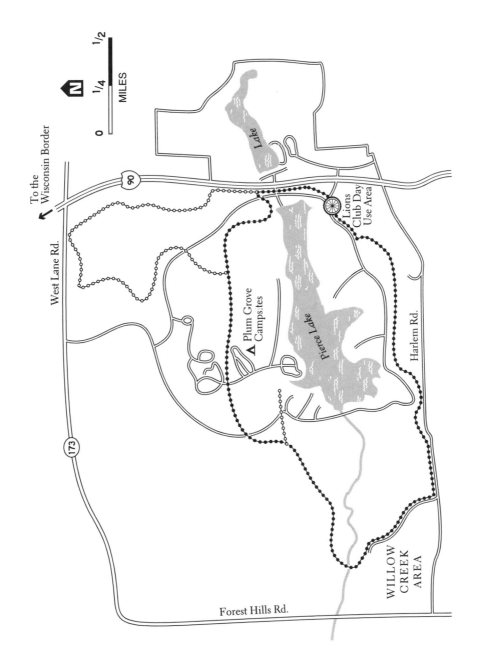

Tom hits a gradual hill on the cross-country ski trails at popular Rock Cut State Park.

Come to Rock Cut to cycle and stay for the swimming, boating, and fishing. There are ten miles of trails at Rock Cut, and seven cross-country ski trails open to mountain bikers. The mostly dirt trails are well maintained; in the winter months, park workers clear the trails for the cross-country skiers. Leave most of your technical skills at home, but bring along the ones that help you avoid hikers.

This loop trail offers a shorter connecting loop to the northeast. You're not likely to get lost on this ride, but often the trail runs parallel to some designated strictly for hikers, so pay attention. Your endurance won't be challenged here; the few climbs are neither hard nor steep, just long—and that's long by Illinois standards, so don't sweat it.

General location: In Love's Park, just north of Rockford

Elevation change: The climbs are slight.

Season: You may ride in the spring and summer, but the fall is nice when the colors are out, the trails are drier, and the air is less humid.

Services: Water, camping, and concessions are found in the park. For bike service, try Kegel's Bike Shop in Rockford.

Hazards: If you're picking up speed, be careful of roots on the trail and hikers or other cyclists.

Rescue index: The park is usually well populated. There are phones by the boat launch, campground, and the swimming lake.

Land status: State park

Maps: The map available at the park office or the main concession stand will suit your needs. You can also write the park at the address below. The main USGS 7.5 minute quad is Caledonia, with a small portion found on the Rockford North quad map.

Finding the trail: From Interstate 90, take the East Riverside Boulevard exit. Go left. At the first stop light, turn right at McFarland road. Go a short way to the end of the road where it Ts and turn right. Shortly after you cross back over I-90, you'll see the entrance on your left. Once you're in the park, turn left at the first stop sign. Go for just a bit and turn left again. Take this road to the Lions Club Day Use Area and park your vehicle.

Sources of additional information:

Rock Cut State Park
7318 Harlem Road
Loves Park, IL 61011
(815) 885-3311

Kegel's Bike Shop
2605 Charles Street
Rockford, IL 61108
(815) 229-5826

Notes on the trail: From the parking area, turn right onto the road; go a few yards down, and the entrance to the trail will be on your left (look for the crosswalk). When you get to the Willow Creek area, you'll come to a gravel stretch. Turn right onto the gravel; then you'll see a sign where the grass trail picks up on your left. Cross a quaint bridge, and soon you'll come to a Y intersection. Take the left trail. You'll pass through a valley, followed by a mild climb with a nice view of the tree ridge in the distance. After a fun little downhill section, you'll come to another uphill—not difficult, just long. At the top of the hill, you'll come to a road; turn left, and a few hundred feet further turn right onto the trail again. After you pass the Plum Grove campsites, you'll have the option of taking a loop to your left if you want to add a little more mileage to your ride; otherwise, keep going straight. After you cross a road, you'll see 2 parallel trails. Take the trail on your right, and soon you'll be riding parallel with I-90, followed by another fun downhill. When you come to the next road, turn left, and that road will take you back to your vehicle.

PEORIA

What happens when you combine the Illinois River with a rich agricultural basin? You get Peoria, Illinois. And you also get some wonderful areas to mountain bike. Early French settlers in the area probably didn't have mountain biking on their minds when they erected Fort Crevecoeur, the first foreign fort in Illinois, but those of us who followed can appreciate the unique terrain here.

That variety shows up in the trails. With the exception of the easy Rock Island Trail, the rest provide a mix of riding experiences. I would be remiss if I didn't make special mention of Jubilee College State Park, perhaps one of the best intermediate-level trails around. In all, Peoria is rich in mountain biking opportunities.

Mountain biking—will it play in Peoria? You bet.

Thanks to Troy Pritchard for supplying information on some of his favorite rides.

RIDE 70 · Rock Island Trail

AT A GLANCE

Length/configuration: 52-mile (26 each way) multi-purpose trail of crushed limestone.

Aerobic difficulty: Easy

Technical difficulty: Easy

Scenery: Farmland and prarie, with wildflowers scattered throughout.

Special comments: A nice ride for a family outing or weekend getaway.

This popular multipurpose trail follows the abandoned Rock Island Railroad line between Alta and Toulon. Spanning 26 miles one-way (52 miles total), this crushed limestone trail is the perfect place to take the family for an easy weekend ride. The tree-lined trail makes its way through farmlands, prairie grass, and wildflowers. The best spot to see the prairie as it was years ago is between the Peoria and Stark County lines. You'll also ride over a couple of nice bridges, the most interesting being a trestle bridge crossing the Spoon River between Wyoming and Toulon. Make sure you stop for refreshments in the five towns through which the trail passes: Alta, Dunlap, Princeville, Wyoming, and Toulon. After all, you won't want to rush this ride.

General location: The Rock Island Trail begins in the town of Alta and ends in Toulon.

Elevation change: Negligible

Season: This trail can be ridden year-round. You'll especially enjoy the changing colors in autumn; bring your cross-country skis in the winter.

Services: Services are available in the towns along the way. The folks at Russell's Cycle World in Washington will be most helpful with bike service.

Hazards: Watch for other trail users during nice weather. Also, use caution at street crossings.

Rescue index: The trail is widely used, and you'll cross many streets where you can flag down traffic.

Land status: Illinois state park

Maps: You can write Rock Island State Park for a brochure map at the address below. The USGS 7.5 minute quads for this area are Dunlap, Edelstein, Princeville, and Wyoming.

RIDE 70 • Rock Island Trail

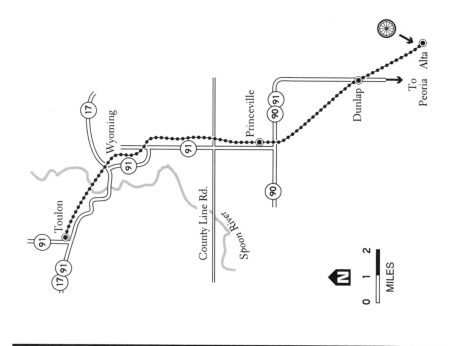

Finding the trail: In Peoria, Interstate 74 hooks up with State Highway 6 north. Take IL 6 north to Allen Road exit, turn north, and drive 1 mile to Alta. Continue west through Alta to the trail parking lot approximately 1 mile on the north side of Alta Lane. From the parking area, you'll see the trailhead. Contact Rock Island Trail State Park for additional places to pick up the trail.

Sources of additional information:

Rock Island Trail State Park
P.O. Box 64
Wyoming, IL 61491
(309) 695-2228

Russell's Cycle World
308 North Main
Washington, IL 61571
(309) 444-2098

Notes on the trail: The trail is easy to follow. When you pass through the towns, directional signs will point the way along streets and sidewalks.

RIDE 71 · Jubilee College State Park

AT A GLANCE

Length/configuration: 40 miles of dirt and grass loops.

Aerobic difficulty: Easy

Technical difficulty: Moderate, this trail manages to keep both seasoned and novice riders happy.

Scenery: Wooded state park, with streams and some gullies that will certainly get your attention.

Special comments: It's easy to get turned around here, so allow time to get lost. You can get your bearings from any of the signs posted along the trail. When all else fails, you can take one of the picnic area access trails back to the main road.

"Fun" is how Derrick Moscardelli, an International Mountain Bicycling Association IMBA/RIDE coordinator, describes this area. I agree. The day I rode here, we assembled an ad hoc group of riders from the local area, as well as Springfield, Joliet, Chicago, and even as far away as Iowa. Everyone had varying degrees of experience, but all concluded this was some of the best riding around. There are over 40 miles of dirt and grass loop trails at Jubilee, about 80% of which are open to mountain bikes. The area has the right mix of uphill and downhill riding, and best of all, gully crossings, some of which retain water. The gullies will challenge your bike handling skills, but if you're not feeling daring, you could walk around those.

The creek crossings have bridges without railings, so take care as you wind around the trails and come across one—especially in the winter, when the bridges might be slick. (Of course, it was summer when your humble author missed a bridge and ended up in the briars: "I'm okay! Really, I'm okay!") The trails are wide and well maintained, so you won't have to worry much about deadfall, rocks, and the like; it's those wonderful gullies that require your attention. Some of the grassy areas of the trail are a little rough, but not enough to cause you concern.

General location: Off I-74 in Brimfield, slightly northwest of Peoria

Elevation change: The hills roll along, but the overall elevation change is no more than about 100 feet.

Season: The autumn colors make a nice backdrop for this ride.

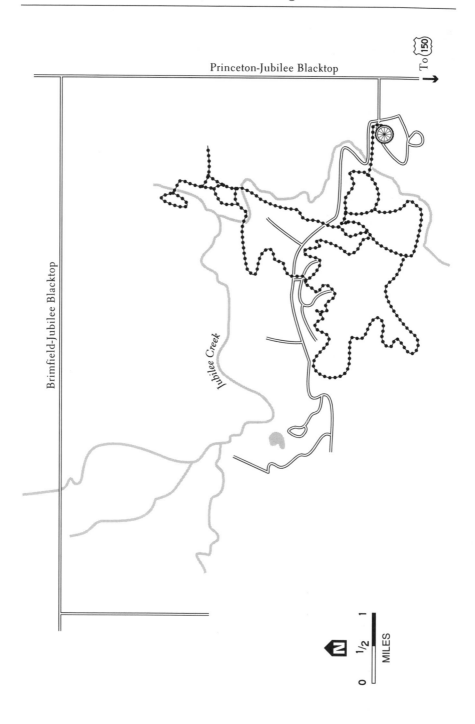

Princeton-Jubilee Blacktop

To 150

Brimfield-Jubilee Blacktop

Jubilee Creek

N

0   1/2   1

MILES

You'll find some of the best mountain biking in the state at Jubilee College State Park.

Services: The parking area has water. Food and lodging are available in Kickapoo. All services are available in Peoria. For bike service, visit Russell's Cycle World in Washington.

Hazards: Use your bike handling skills to navigate the gullies, of course, but also be careful about hammerheading too fast around a curve and encountering a hiker.

Rescue index: There is a phone in the parking area by the maintenance shop. From the picnic areas, you can follow the access roads out to the main road.

Land status: Illinois state park

Maps: A topographical map is available from Jubilee College State Park. Write for one at the address below. The USGS 7.5 minute quad is Oak Hill.

Finding the trail: From I-74, take Exit 82, Kickapoo/Edwards Road, north. A mile later, turn left at Highway 150. Another mile later, turn right at the Princeville-Jubilee blacktop. Go 2 miles and turn left on Jubilee College Road, which will take you into the entrance.

Sources of additional information:

Jubilee College State Park
13921 West Route 150
Brimfield, IL 61517
(309) 446-3758.

Russell's Cycle World
308 North Main
Washington, IL 61571
(309) 444-2098

Notes on the trail: From the parking area, go back up the road you came in. Just outside the entrance, turn left up the road. You'll see the entrance to the trail on your left just before a 15 mph speed limit sign. Look for the trail between the trees.

When you're on the trail, the first sign you come to will have an arrow pointing to the right, but keep going straight on a narrow single-track. When you come to an intersection with a cross-country ski sign, go left. You'll ride through a grassy area before you enter the woods again. At a trail-map sign, veer to your left. At the next cross-country ski signed intersection, go right. You'll go straight across 2 picnic areas. After the second one, take the trail to your right. You'll ride down a hill, across a bridge, and back uphill again. At the top, hang a right at the trail map. Soon you'll come to a wide clearing; turn left and ride up the clearing. Turn right at the next trail map. The next intersection has left, soft right, and hard right options. Take the soft right. And at the next intersection, follow the ski route trail to the left. After another grassy area, you'll enter the woods again. Take the trail to the right. You'll come to another intersecting trail. Turn left, and from here you should be able to retrace the way you came in.

RIDE 72 · Pimiteoui Trail

AT A GLANCE

Length/configuration: 5 miles on a wide path, followed by 7 miles through a suburb, then the more serious riding begins with 3 narrow, single-track trails.

Aerobic difficulty: Challenging

Technical difficulty: Moderate to challenging

Scenery: You'll come across everything here. The first part of the ride follows a river, then you find yourself in a residential section, then in dense woods.

Special comments: For you BMX bikers, there's a BMX course next to Detweiller Park.

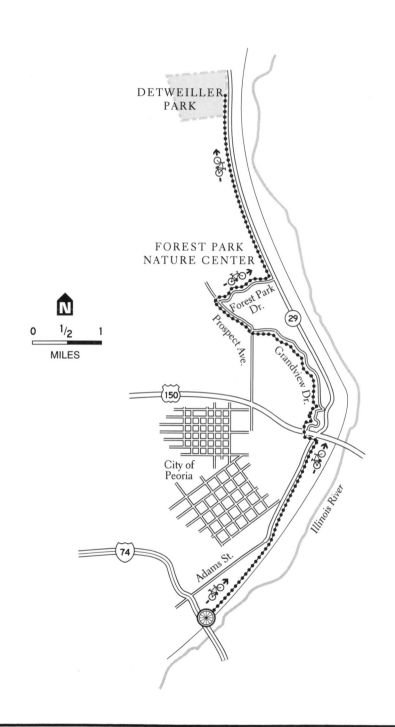

DETWEILLER
PARK

FOREST PARK
NATURE CENTER

Forest Park
Dr.

29

Prospect Ave.

Grandview Dr.

N

0   ½   1

MILES

150

City of
Peoria

Illinois River

74

Adams St.

Located on the outskirts of Peoria, the Pimiteoui Trail begins as a smooth, flat ride along the Illinois River. Despite the fact that it begins in an industrial area, the trail along the river is rather scenic. You'll travel about five miles one way on a wide path. After the first five miles, things get more interesting. You'll ride roughly seven miles through a paved residential area, where you'll get a taste of the hills you can expect when you get to Detweiller Park at the end. The ride up Grandview Drive, for instance, features a rough hill with a view of the surrounding area. This is a fashionable neighborhood, so feel free to admire the homes. In fact, you'll be near an older historic area with many quaint shops.

By the time you get to Detweiller Park, the trail picks up again and the real mountain biking begins. In Detweiller, there are actually three trails from which to choose: Pimiteoui, Ridge Top, and Dry Run. These loop trails are quite demanding because of their narrower single-track. You'll also have to contend with many obstacles in the dense woods—such as fallen trees—on these unmaintained trails. Of course, what will really get you are the hills. The climbs will be challenging by central Illinois standards, but the view of the Illinois River will be worth it. At the water crossings, be prepared to ride over logs. The area borders a major city, so you won't find a lot of wildlife, but you'll want to come here for the scenery and the hills.

General location: On the east side of Peoria

Elevation change: You'll find an elevation gain of roughly 300 feet.

Season: You can ride this trail year-round. Because of the tree cover, the trail doesn't get very muddy. In the fall, the Illinois River Valley is one of the prettiest areas in the state.

Services: Detweiller Park has water. All services are available in Peoria. If you need help with your bike, visit Russell's Cycle World in Washington.

Hazards: Look out for the obstacles on the single-track—expect to dismount.

Rescue index: Shelters are located throughout the park, so you're never more than 5 or 10 minutes from a phone. You'll find light traffic on the roads.

Land status: Peoria park district

Maps: The USGS 7.5 minute quads are Peoria East and Spring Bay.

Finding the trail: From downtown Peoria, take I-74 south and get off at the Adams exit. Go west on Adams for a couple of blocks to Hamilton. Turn left on Hamilton and take that a short way down to the river. Park by the metered parking by the Boat Works.

Sources of additional information:

Peoria Park District
Glen Oak Pavillion
2218 North Prospect Road
Peoria, IL 61603
(309) 682-1200

Russell's Cycle World
308 North Main
Washington, IL 61571
(309) 444-2098

Notes on the trail: The ride begins directly underneath I-74. Follow the trail for 5 miles until you get to US 150. At the war memorial, take US 150 about 3 miles to Grandview Drive. Enjoy the hill and the view, and take Grandview to Prospect Avenue. When you get to Prospect Avenue, take a right and go about 1 mile to Forest Park Drive. Turn right on Forest Park Drive. (If you go left on Forest Park Drive, you'll hit the shops in the historic area.) You'll pass the Forest Park Nature Center, where you can stop for a visit if you like. Forest Park Drive connects with Galena Road (IL 29). Take Galena Road 3 miles into Detweiller Park, where you can pick up the trail.

RIDE 73 · Farmdale Recreation Area

AT A GLANCE

Length/configuration: 10 miles of dirt roads and trails.

Aerobic difficulty: Easy on the dirt roads, moderate on the trails.

Technical difficulty: Easy on the dirt roads, moderate to challenging on the trails.

Scenery: A wooded area crisscrossed with quite a few creeks, which, regardless of whether you choose to follow the road or the trails, you will certainly notice.

Special comments: The creek and stream crossings can be demanding, so use a little extra caution, especially if you're riding the labyrinth of trails.

You can do two kinds of rides at Farmdale Recreation Area. For those of you looking for an easy ride, follow the dirt roads that cross through the low-lying areas. The roads make for good family riding. But for those of you looking for more adventure, turn onto any of the dirt trails you find branching off the roads. These trails will be narrower, more difficult to climb, and fraught with several challenging obstacles—not the least of which will be planning your own loops and out-and-backs from the maps available. There are simply too many trails for me to direct you to any one of them without confusion.

RIDE 73 · Farmdale Recreation Area

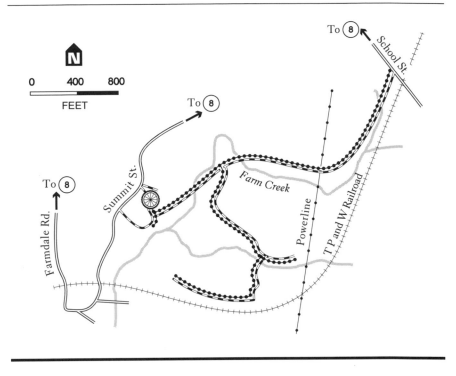

Between the easy and more difficult riding in Farmdale, you'll have about ten miles of trails to ride. Even the easier sections aren't without their taunts, as you'll encounter three major creek crossings. Plan to get your feet wet! On the more difficult spurs, the grade will test your climbing ability. It will be well worth it when you find a nice, smooth trail waiting for you at the summit. You'll also have to skirt around rocks, branches, and smaller, yet more difficult, stream crossings than the ones on the easier route. Deer and coyote can also be found in this wooded area. In essence, Farmdale Recreation Area has a variety of terrains and levels of difficulty—something for everyone.

General location: In East Peoria, 10 minutes from Peoria

Elevation change: The elevation gain is roughly 100 feet.

Season: Summer, fall, and winter are best. Avoid the spring, when it can get quite wet.

Services: There is a campground in Farmdale Recreation Area. Food and lodging are available in East Peoria. All services are available in Peoria. Russell's Cycle World in Washington offers bicycle service.

Hazards: Be careful at the water crossings. In the more demanding areas, the obstacles can present some difficulties.

Rescue index: From anywhere in Farmdale, you're only minutes from a road where you can flag down help.

Land status: U.S. Army Corps of Engineers—Rock Island District

Maps: The Army Corps of Engineers has a map listing the easier route without the spurs. Write for one at the address below. The USGS 7.5 minute quads for this area are Washington and Peoria East.

Finding the trail: Take I-74 south out of Peoria to IL 8. Take IL 8 east about 3 miles to Farmdale Road and turn right. Go 2 miles to Summit Street. Turn left on Summit Street and follow it a short way to the parking area.

Sources of additional information:

Park Ranger
U.S. Army Corps of Engineers
Foot of Grant Street
Peoria, IL 61603
(309) 676-4601

Russell's Cycle World
308 North Main
Washington, IL 61571
(309) 444-2098

Notes on the trail: Pick up the trail from the parking lot. It's a dirt road that travels throughout the park. The map included in this guide lists only the easier, dirt-road ride; the more challenging spurs are not shown.

RIDE 74 · McNaughton Park

AT A GLANCE

Length/configuration: Two connecting loops, totaling 12 miles of wide dirt trails.

Aerobic difficulty: Moderate

Technical difficulty: Easy to challenging

Scenery: Woodlands

Special comments: While these trails aren't marked, they're easy to follow.

RIDE 74 · McNaughton Park

Looking for a little challenge? You'll find both easy and difficult trail riding at McNaughton Park, but for the most part, this area can be challenging. McNaughton Park consists of two connecting loops—the Potawatomi Trail and the Running Deer Trail—for a total distance of about 12 miles. Primarily, both trails are wide, ranging from one to four bike widths. Potawatomi is wider than Running Deer, and its dirt trail gets a little sandier as you approach the creeks. You'll find many steep, short climbs and creek crossings, making this a moderate to challenging ride. Running Deer Trail is also dirt, but has a few more grassy sections than Potawatomi. The difficulty of this trail ranges from easy to challenging, and you'll find a few sections where the trail has narrow uphills and white-knuckle descents. It's easy to slip on these narrow hills, so no one will think less of you if you decide to walk your bike down. There are more roots and obstacles on Running Deer Trail than on the other, and it has creek crossings to test your "wetness quotient."

Those who want their wooded trails to give them the same emotional ups and downs as the terrain will like McNaughton Park. You'll appreciate the nice, rolling, smooth sections as well as the technical, endurance-testing ones.

General location: Just east of Pekin

Elevation change: The elevation changes range around 100 feet.

Season: Plan on riding here in the summer and the winter when the trails are drier than the spring.

Services: Water is available at the trailhead. Pekin has all services. For bike service, visit Russell's Cycle World in Washington.

Hazards: The water crossings and some of the narrower passages on the hills can be hazardous.

Rescue index: You're never far from a road where you can flag down help.

Land status: Pekin Park District

Maps: You can write the Pekin Park District at the address below for a map of the park. The USGS 7.5 minute quad for this area is Marquette Heights.

Finding the trail: Take IL 29 out of Peoria; when you get to Pekin, take IL 98 east (left). Go approximately 4 miles on IL 98 and you'll see the park on the right side of the road.

Sources of additional information:

Pekin Park District
1701 Court Street
Pekin, IL 61554
(309) 34R-PARK

Russell's Cycle World
308 North Main
Washington, IL 61571
(309) 444-2098

Notes on the trail: You'll see 3 trailheads from the parking area. Take whichever trail you desire because they all loop back to the start. The trails aren't marked, but can be followed easily. The intersection of the 2 trails isn't marked, but it's also easy to find.

EAST CENTRAL ILLINOIS

E ast central Illinois is not the mountain bike capitol of the world, but that doesn't mean you can't dig up a few high-quality rides in the area. For instance, as you ride down Intersate 74, it's all corn, but suddenly you come to a heavily forested area and you wonder, is this a good spot for mountain biking? The spot is Kickapoo State Park, and the answer is a resounding "Yes." You'll even find some sheer drop-offs and hill climbing to test both your endurance and your technical skills. Says Fritz Miericke of Champaign Cycle, "It's a good place to go to if you like to go off-road and not be surrounded by corn and beans."

Further south, you'll find the Chief Illini Trail and Newton Lake. The Chief Illini Trail is also surprisingly challenging for its location in the state. As you look down the ravines on this ride, you'll wonder where the corn is. Newton Lake is not as difficult as the other two, but it will provide a nice getaway ride in a not too densely populated part of the state.

Thanks to Fritz Miericke for information about Kickapoo State Park and Derrick Moscardelli for information about the Chief Illini Trail.

RIDE 75 · Kickapoo State Park

AT A GLANCE

Length/configuration: 6.5 miles of trails divided into three loops.

Aerobic difficulty: Moderate

Technical difficulty: Moderate to challenging

Scenery: Woods with several lakes and some great views if you ride up the ridges.

Special comments: Keep your eyes peeled for deer and eagles.

RIDE 75 · Kickapoo State Park

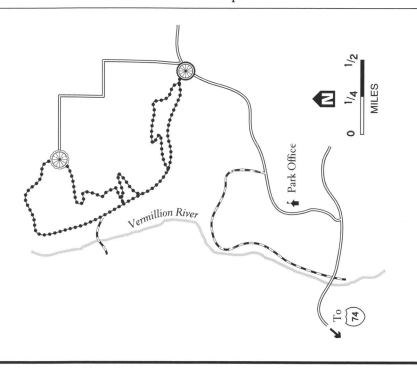

W ith most state parks, it's up to the site manager to determine whether mountain biking will be permitted. Kickapoo State Park is the first to get official approval through the Illinois Department of Natural Resources—and the mountain bikers of east central Illinois are grateful! In an area where you wouldn't expect to find mountain bike opportunities, there are 600 acres set aside for mountain bike use. Currently, six and a half miles of trails cut their way in three loops through a reclaimed strip mine area where tractors first plowed an eight-foot-wide path. Then the trail was cleared of stumps and other debris. At one time, this area was set aside for motorcycle use, but the trails have since been abandoned. Members of the Kickapoo Mountain Bike Club are in the process of "rediscovering" them.

"This is as close as we get to hills and rough stuff," says Fritz Miericke, a member of the Kickapoo Bike Club. And Fritz is right. You'll find moderate climbs, some of which can be technically challenging, that weave in and out of ridges and around creeks. At the top of one of the major ridges, you'll get a great view of the tree line below. At the bottom, you'll find a nice, quiet pond. In fact, you'll encounter several ponds in the area. For those who want to get their feet wet, there are several water crossings. Kickapoo is not without its difficulties. As you ride through the trees, you'll need to pay attention to the direction of the trail, as there are some sheer drop-offs. Kickapoo State Park, with its six and a half miles currently developed, is a great place to ride. This is truly a mountain bike oasis in the middle of corn country.

General location: Kickapoo State Park is in Oakwood, 10 miles west of Danville.

Elevation change: The elevation change ranges around 700 feet.

Season: The fall and early spring are best because it's drier, and you'll be able to see the landscape changes more easily. In the summer, you'll have to contend with heat and deer flies.

Services: Kickapoo State Park has camping, fishing, boating, and canoe rentals. All services are available in either Danville or Urbana-Champaign. I recommend Champaign Cycle in Champaign for bicycle service.

Hazards: You'll need to pay attention and look ahead where the trail dips down to avoid those cliffs.

Rescue index: You can get assistance from the ranger station at the park entrance.

Land status: State park

Maps: The USGS 7.5 minute quads for Kickapoo State Park are Danville NW and Collison.

Finding the trail: Follow I-74 west out of Danville about 10 miles and take the Oakwood exit. Go north 3.5 miles and follow the signs to Kickapoo State Park. Stop at the ranger station for directions to the trailhead.

Sources of additional information:

> Kickapoo State Park
> 10906 Kickapoo Park Road
> Oakwood, IL 61858
> (217) 442-4915
>
> Champaign Cycle
> 506 South Country Fair Drive
> Champaign, IL 61821
> (217) 352-7600
>
> Kickapoo Mountain Bike Club
> www.angelfire.com/il/kmbc

Notes on the trail: The 6 miles of loop trails are well marked. As the other trails are developed, they will also be marked. Make sure you stay on the mountain bike trails and keep off the horse trails and walking paths.

RIDE 76 · Newton Lake

AT A GLANCE

Length/configuration: 9-mile (4.5 each way) wide, dirt horse trail.

Aerobic difficulty: Easy

Technical difficulty: Easy to Moderate

Scenery: The trail winds through woods and fields along the left side of Newton Lake.

Special comments: Along the way, stop at the rest areas for some scenic views of the lake.

Newton Lake has chickens—not just any old chickens, but rare prairie chickens. You won't actually see them from the trail on the west side of the lake, but they are there on the east side. One way, the trail goes out a distance of four and a half miles, nine miles round-trip. On the return, you can follow the same route back or take one of several shortcut loops back to the trailhead. Half of the dirt horse trail passes through the woods, and the other half goes through grass fields. The trail is wide, easy to follow, and well maintained, so people of all abilities should be able to enjoy it. There are some big hills, and you'll encounter a few sharp curves. Also, you'll enjoy quite a few gravelly creek crossings. You may not see any chickens, but perhaps you'll spot a pair of bald eagles.

General location: About 20 miles southeast of Effingham

Elevation change: You'll pass in and out of hills, but any gain is insignificant.

Season: Summer is the best time to ride because it's drier. The trails may be closed when wet, especially in the winter and early spring, so check ahead at the address listed below.

Services: Water is available at the office. Food and lodging can be found in Newton. For bicycle service, go to Effingham.

Hazards: Some caution is needed going through the creek beds.

Rescue index: There is a phone at the office. You should see other trail users or boaters out on the lake.

Land status: Illinois Department of Conservation

RIDE 76 · Newton Lake

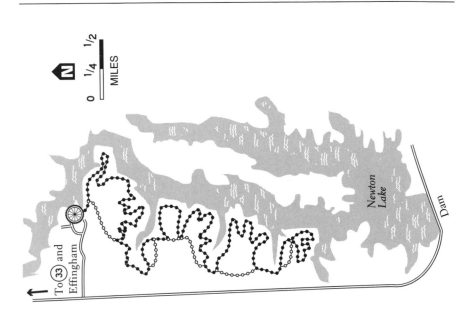

Maps: Newton Lake has a good map showing the trail and the various short-cut options. Write for it at the address below. The USGS 7.5 minute quad for this area is Latona.

Finding the trail: From Effingham, take State Highway 33 south about 20 miles. The signs will direct you to Newton Lake. Park at the North Access.

Source of additional information:

Newton Lake State Fish and Wildlife Area
RR 4, Box 178B
Newton, IL 62448
(618) 783-3478

Notes on the trail: From the North Access, you'll see the sign for the trailhead. The trail is marked, especially the points that show the trail shortcuts.

SHAWNEE NATIONAL FOREST

I confined my riding in Illinois to just one area, the Shawnee National Forest, for two reasons. First, the rest of the state was pretty well covered by Dave when he did his research for this book. Second, I love the Shawnee and the people who ride there.

Here are a few pertinent warnings. The area has lots of bluffs. Falling from them is hazardous, maybe fatal. The area also has lots of old homesteads, complete with rickety buildings, hidden wells, and rusting barbed wire. Also hazardous. Ride with someone, and watch where you're going. Watch closely.

Let's start off with some bad news.

Item one: The area is a hopelessly confusing web of interconnecting trails, fire roads, dead ends, drop-offs, private property, and public roads. Getting lost is guaranteed.

Item two: No place on earth is the term "trail" applied more loosely. Some of what you'll ride here is clearly a trail. Much of it is no more distinct than if a schoolkid had scratched the dirt with a stick while playing hooky one day.

Item three: Although a few buff trails exist, most of the terrain here is absurdly technical. Rocks pose the biggest challenge; you'll see them in your sleep at night after your ride. There are also lots of fallen trees, steep climbs, loose descents, and narrow slots to shoot through. You can be beaten to death trying to make three miles in an hour. If that type of riding thrills you, this is your home place.

Item four: As of this writing, the Shawnee Forest is without a forest plan. The history of what went wrong could be a book in itself. The net effect is that there is no legal riding in the Shawnee.

Now let's look at the good news in the same order.

Item one: Getting lost is guaranteed, but also guaranteed to be temporary. No matter how lost you become, you'll soon blunder across a public road or recognizable landmark. Consult your map—you did bring a map and a compass, didn't you?—and you'll be to terra cognito in no time. (To emphasize: of all the areas I've ridden, this is among the worst in which to be caught map-less.)

Item two: That some trails are indistinct is good; it means the considerable number of trail users are well dispersed. There are popular areas. There are also areas where you can ride all day, or for several days, and not see another soul on the trail. Obvious trails often result from overuse. Here, you can imagine you're one of the first to pass this way.

Item three: There are some less challenging trails in southern Illinois, but they lack the reward found in the Shawnee. Sure it's frustrating to slam into the earth 17 different ways before noon. But it's also intensely gratifying to clean something you thought you couldn't. Shawnee is the place to get better at technical riding.

Item four: Though it's true there's no legal riding in the Shawnee, the Shawnee Mountain Bike Association (SMBA) has signed a memorandum of understanding with the Forest Service saying they can ride in the forest. Most trails remain on National Forest property, but within the forest are private property, wilderness, and natural areas. These are off-limits, but that still leaves hundreds of miles of open trails. (Where the trails described here cross private property, permission has been secured from property owners.)

All these conditions breed a riding style best summed up by Jeff Jones, president of the Shawnee Mountain Bike Association. Jeff, fellow SMBA member Rick Humphreys, and I were sitting in the war room in Jeff's basement. This is where great strategies are concocted to save the Shawnee for bicyclists. "We're not mountain bikers," Jeff explained. "We're trail riders."

The difference is in the goals and the techniques necessary to achieve them. Mountain bikers look for the fastest way to cover good trails, but trail riders look for any way to clean rough trails.

"We're competitive," says Jones. "But the competition isn't for speed or distance. It's who can ride a tough section, or clear a big obstacle."

Armed with thumb shifters, torn T-shirts, and gloves from Tractor Supply Company, these diehards attack the terrain. They often win. Twenty-inch logs? No problem. Sixty feet of loose slab rock? No problem. Logs, rock, a 12% grade and an off-camber trail? Watch and learn.

Jeff, Rick, and the rest of the SMBA are your best source for information for riding in the Shawnee. They have detailed maps, an encyclopedic knowledge of the area ("Somebody moved that Model A fender deeper into the woods — better not use that as a landmark"), and will almost surely accept your invitation to ride along as you explore their woods. It was this encyclopedic knowledge and willingness to ride that saved me. Although I've ridden many of the trails in the Shawnee at one time or another, I didn't have the opportunity to do them all again while researching this book. Jeff and Rick and a few of their cohorts rescued me by providing detailed trail information.

Contact the SMBA (and the forest supervisor's office, if you wish) before riding here. The Shawnee is poised for big changes in access and trail inventory, so you're wise to confirm the details before you set out.

The first time I rode with these SMBA characters I was stunned. Stunned at their technical ability, their disdain for trick equipment, their ability to work with a Forest Service saddled with inertia. Five years later, they're still stunning.

RIDE 77 · Kinkaid Lake—Buttermilk Hill

AT A GLANCE

Length/configuration: A 30-mile (15 each way), dirt, single-track out-and-back.

Aerobic difficulty: Moderate

Technical difficulty: Moderate to challenging

Scenery: Forest surrounding Kinkaid Lake.

Special comments: Your stamina will be tested as you navigate through the rocky sections.

This roughly 15-mile one-way (30 miles total) out-and-back features some aggressive dirt single-track, but also overlooks beautiful Kinkaid Lake. The obstacle rich trail becomes easier to ride after you pass the initial challenge near Crisenberry Lake, allowing you the opportunity to glimpse the shoreline and boating on the lake. You'll ride along the slopes above the lake through a diverse section of timber. Expect the trail to become very rocky again just past Buttermilk Hill Beach and just before Hidden Cove. If you're quiet, perhaps you'll glimpse wild turkey and deer.

General location: Shawnee National Forest, 7.5 miles west of Murphysboro

Elevation change: The overall elevation gain amounts to around 100 feet. There are no really steep climbs. The steepest section is by the dam.

Season: Early spring and early fall are best because the temperatures are more temperate than other times of year.

Services: There is no water at the state trailhead (Crisenberry Dam), but the Highway 151 trailhead by Johnson Creek Recreation Area has water. Food and lodging are available in Murphysboro. For bicycle service, consider Phoenix Cycles in Carbondale.

Hazards: Aside from the slippery sections near the rocky portions, there are rattlesnakes and copperheads in this area, as well as poison ivy.

Rescue index: If you get into trouble, you can make your way down to the lake and flag down a boater.

Land status: Shawnee National Forest—Murphysboro Ranger District

Maps: You can get a map of the trail from Shawnee National Forest. Write to the address below. The USGS 7.5 minute quad for Lake Kinkaid is Oraville, and the IL 151 trailhead spills onto the Raddle quad.

RIDE 77 · Kinkaid Lake/Buttermilk Hill

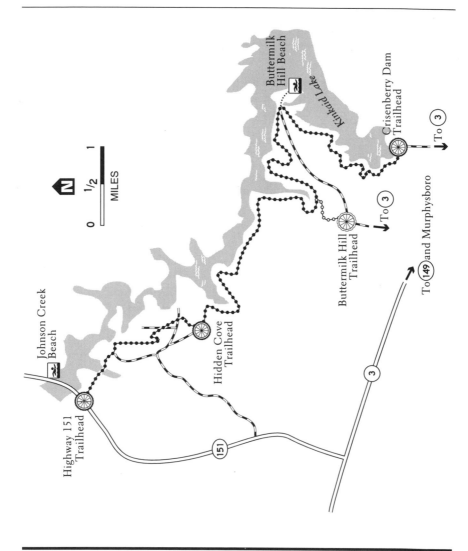

Finding the trail: To the Dam (State) trailhead: From IL 127 in Murphysboro, take IL 149 west for 7.3 miles to Spillway Road and turn right. (Note: Don't turn where you see a sign for Kinkaid Lake.) Go 1.7 miles to the parking area. To get to the trailhead, ride back to the parking area entrance and turn right. Go up the gravel road. The trail entrance will be on your left, immediately to the left of the top of the dam, marked by some wooden beams.

To the Buttermilk Hill trailhead: From IL 127 in Murphysboro, take IL 149

The technical single-track will attract the expert rider.

west for 8 miles. Turn right on IL 3 and go 1.5 miles to a sign for the Buttermilk Hill trailhead. Turn right and follow the signs to the parking area to your left. To get to the trail from the parking area, ride down the short grassy trail until you see the trail markers.

To the Highway 151 trailhead: From IL 127 in Murphysboro, take IL 149 west for 8 miles. Turn right on IL 3 and go 4.5 miles to IL 151. Turn right. Just before you get to Johnson Creek Road, about 5 miles, look carefully to your right for a sign for the Route 151 trailhead. For parking, keep heading down toward the Johnson Creek Recreation Area.

Sources of additional information:

U.S. Forest Service
Murphysboro Ranger District
2221 Walnut, P.O. Box 787
Murphysboro, IL 62966-0787
(618) 687-1731

Phoenix Cycles
300 South Illinois Avenue
Carbondale, IL 62901
(618) 549-3612

Notes on the trail: Although finding the trailhead off Spillway Road can be tricky, the trail itself is well marked by white diamonds. As you ride the trail, of course, don't feel obligated to ride the branch down to the Buttermilk Hill trailhead. Head toward the Hidden Cove trailhead if you wish.

RIDE 78 · Cedar Lake Trail

AT A GLANCE

Length/configuration: 15 miles of single-track: an 11-mile out-and-back and a 4-mile loop.

Aerobic difficulty: Moderate

Technical difficulty: Moderate, with some challenging sections.

Scenery: Forest surrounding Cedar Lake.

Special comments: You may need to get off and portage at the rocky areas north of Ponoma Road.

IL

You'll get a little workout riding the rolling hills on this trail. The 11-mile (total distance) out-and-back portion of this ride travels along the west side of Cedar Lake before making a 4-mile loop around Little Cedar Lake. (Your out-and-back and loop trail total is therefore 15 miles.) The fun on the loop portion begins right away with a series of moguls before the trail crosses over the rocky foundation separating the two lakes. Most of the trail is dirt single-track and easily passable, but there are some rocky stretches just north of Pomona Road requiring technical skills. Most of the trail won't require as many technical skills as this section, but you'll need energy for climbing the short hills. Don't worry—there's nothing too steep.

Most of the trail travels through the forest surrounding the lake, and several spots on the out-and-back section offer gorgeous views of the lake. Near Cove Hollow, you'll find a unique feature: several rock shelters where you can stop and rest. While not quite caves, these natural formations are large enough to enter. You won't need your spelunking gear.

General location: Shawnee National Forest, 8 miles south of Murphysboro

Elevation change: You'll experience about 100 feet of elevation change.

Season: The best riding is in the early spring and early fall. Ticks and heat can be a problem during the summer months, as can the poison ivy.

RIDE 78 · Cedar Lake Trail

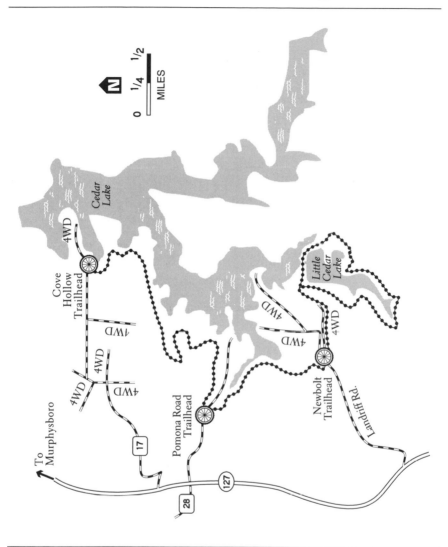

Services: Bring your own water. Food and lodging are available in Murphysboro. For bicycle service, visit Phoenix Cycles in Carbondale.

Hazards: Use a little caution on the rockier section of the trail. Rattlesnakes and copperheads can be found here. When I visited, I saw a dead copperhead in the middle of the trail.

Rescue index: The lake often has boaters and fishermen. There are also some residences in the area.

Look out at Little Cedar Lake from the trail.

Land status: Shawnee National Forest—Murphysboro Ranger District

Maps: Shawnee National Forest has a map with topographical markings of Cedar Lake. Write to the address below. The USGS 7.5 minute quads are Pomona and Cobden.

Finding the trail: To Newbolt trailhead: From the intersection of IL 149 and IL 127 in Murphysboro, go south on IL 127 about 20 miles to Landriff Road, which is at the dividing line between Jackson and Union Counties. Turn left on Landriff. The gravel road will end soon and turn to double-track. Because your vehicles may have difficulty traveling down the double-track, you might want to park on the side of the road and ride the mile or so to the trailhead marker.

Contact the Murphysboro Ranger District for directions to the Cove Hollow and Pomona Road trailheads.

Sources of additional information:

U.S. Forest Service
Murphysboro Ranger District
2221 Walnut, P.O. Box 787
Murphysboro, IL 62966-0787
(618) 687-1731

Phoenix Cycles
300 South Illinois Avenue
Carbondale, IL 62901
618 549-3612

Notes on the trail: Beginning at the Newbolt trailhead will give you the option of doing just the 4-mile loop around Little Cedar Lake or heading north on the out-and-back to Cove Hollow. To enter the loop trail, follow the narrow grass single-track from the trailhead marker. After you cross over to the east side of Little Cedar Lake, turn right and follow the trail around.

RIDE 79 · Pine Hills Ride

AT A GLANCE

Length/configuration: A 16-mile loop on gravel and some paved roads.

Aerobic difficulty: Moderate to challenging

Technical difficulty: Easy

Scenery: Except for the final 5 miles along the highway, you'll be in a heavily forested area that affords several scenic overlooks.

Special comments: At the Crooked Tree Observation Area, get off your bike and follow a short hiking trail down for a secluded view of the Missouri Ridge Line.

A re you looking for a nontechnical ride that challenges your stamina, yet affords some of the most spectacular views in Illinois? If so, this ride is for you. This 16-mile loop skirts the western border of the Clear Springs Wilderness Area in Shawnee National Forest. The first 11 miles of the loop are on gravel Forest Service roads, but to complete the loop, you'll travel the last 5 miles on a paved state highway.

As you travel down the heavily forested area around Forest Service Road 236, several scenic vistas await you. From the Crooked Tree Observation Area, you'll be able to see the Missouri Ridge Line in the distance. Other impressive views await you at Saddle Hill, Pine Ridge, and Old Trail Point. The gravel road is not technically challenging, but it will require a modest amount of exertion because of the 300-foot elevation gain. All this changes drastically, though, once you hit FS 345. You now leave the forest and head down a flat, graveled road

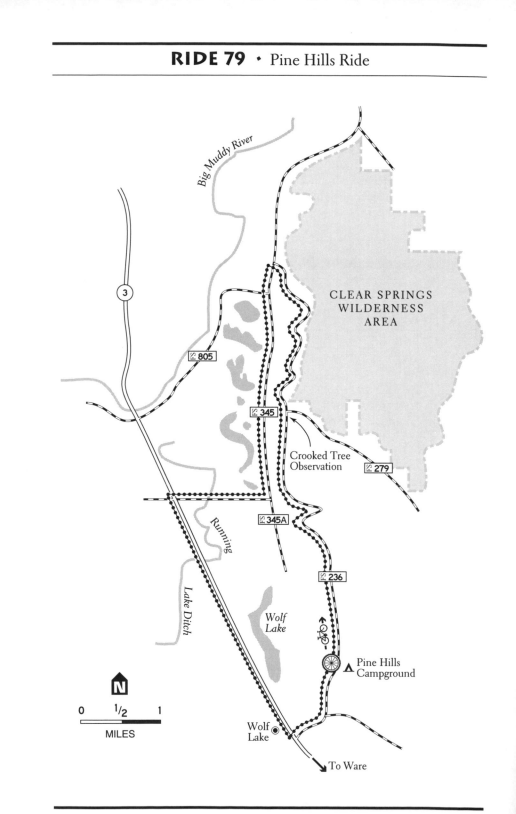

CLEAR SPRINGS
WILDERNESS
AREA

Big Muddy River

3

805

345

Crooked Tree
Observation

279

345A

Running

236

Lake Ditch

Wolf
Lake

Pine Hills
Campground

N

0   1/2   1
MILES

Wolf
Lake

To Ware

The serenity of Shawnee National Forest makes for a secluded ride just miles from the Missouri border.

along the wetlands. Winters Pond is an old borrow pit, an area where soil was "borrowed" to build up a nearby levee. Over time, water and plants filled in the pit, creating the wetlands.

General location: Shawnee National Forest, 21 miles northwest of the intersection of Interstate 57 and IL 146, near the town of Wolf Lake

Elevation change: The ride begins at 420 feet and gains 300 feet. The stretch down FS 345 is virtually flat.

Season: This ride is the southernmost ride in the book. A southern Illinois summer can be quite hot. Nevertheless, I like the summer green on this ride. Of course, autumn views at the vistas are quite remarkable, too.

Services: Primitive camping is available at the Pine Hills Campground. Food and lodging are available in Anna. For bicycle repair, try Phoenix Cycles in Carbondale.

Hazards: You'll find no obstacles to speak of here, but the traffic on IL 3 can be swift.

Rescue index: FS 236 and FS 345 have light traffic, and IL 3 has much more.

Land status: Shawnee National Forest

Maps: The USGS 7.5 minute quad is Wolf Lake.

Finding the trail: From I-57, take Exit 30, IL 146 for Anna/Vienna. Go right (west) on IL 146 for 15.5 miles. At IL 3 in Ware, turn right (north) for 4 miles.

When you get near the town of Wolf Lake, look for an unmarked road with the sign, "Trail of Tears State Forest—Union State Nursery." Turn right on that road, and shortly, you'll come to FS 236. Turn left and go to the Larue–Pine Hills Campground. You can begin your ride here.

Source of additional information:

Shawnee National Forest
901 South Commercial Street
Harrisburg, IL 62946
(618) 253-7114

Notes on the trail: From the LaRue–Pine Hills Campground, turn right, heading north on FS 236. After 7 miles, turn left on FS 345 (Pine Hills Road). Four and a half miles later, you'll hit IL 3. Turn left and go 3.5 miles to the road marked "Trail of Tears State Forest." Turn left again and go back to FS 236. Turn left and head to the campground.

Stay out of the wilderness area.

RIDE 80 · Camp Cadiz

AT A GLANCE

Length/configuration: 7-mile loop, most of it dirt road or double-track.

Aerobic difficulty: Moderate with a few steep climbs.

Technical difficulty: Easy, except for a creek crossing and 1 or 2 steep grades. If you're looking for a beginner's trail in the Shawnee, this is one of the few you'll find.

Scenery: Hardwoods, non-native pines, rock formations.

Special comments: Mundane by local standards, but fairly easy and not overrun with horses or hikers.

Camp Cadiz was used by the Civilian Conservation Corps (CCC) as a base camp back in the 1930s. Remnants (mostly fireplaces) of the old CCC buildings remain in the primitive campground, which is used today. CCC workers reclaimed much of the Shawnee by replanting trees and doing other chores. I remember my father relating the technique he used in planting trees

RIDE 80 · Camp Cadiz

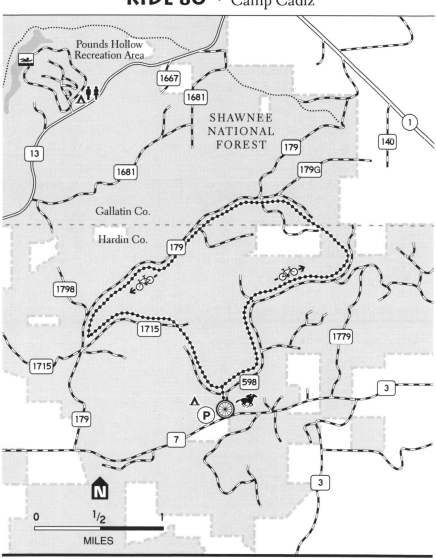

as a member of the "Cees," as he called them. While he spoke, his hands followed the motions they'd practiced 60 years earlier in northern Wisconsin.

Some people's idea of "multiple use" is that riders with different brands of bikes can share the trail. They're not crazy about dodging horses and hikers all day. For them, the Camp Cadiz trail is a good one. Unlike many of the other trails in the Shawnee, this one has few horseback riders, and hikers are fairly rare on most Shawnee trails.

General location: About 20 minutes south of Harrisburg

Elevation change: The few climbs clock in at about 330 feet.

Season: Year-round; mud is likely to be a problem in spring and again from Thanksgiving to May.

Services: Everything in Harrisburg; the nearest bike shops are in Paducah (KY), Evansville (IN), and Carbondale (IL).

Hazards: None

Rescue index: Ride with someone; other users tend to disperse widely and any given piece of trail may only see a person every few days or even every few weeks.

Land status: National Forest property; nicks the corner of private property at one point

Maps: Shawnee Mountain Bike Association

Finding the trail: Take IN 34 south from Harrisburg to Karber's Ridge Road (it's the next left after the gravel road to the left leading to Garden of the Gods Wilderness Area). Go east on Karber's Ridge Road for about 6 miles. Turn right on the county road; there's a sign for Camp Cadiz. In about 4 miles you'll be at the parking area and campground.

Sources of additional information:

Shawnee Mountain Bike Association
190 Battleford Road
Harrisburg, IL 62946
(618) 252-3577

Forest Supervisor's Office
50 Highway 145 South
Harrisburg, IL 62946
(800) 699-6637 or (618) 253-7114

There are also district offices in Vienna (phone (618) 658-2111), Elizabethtown (phone (618) 287-2201), Jonesboro (phone (618)833-8576) and Murphysboro (phone (618) 687-1731).

Notes on the trail: Go north and northeast on the gravel road. At about 1.5 miles, turn left at the cemetery and descend to the creek. Cross the creek, then continue on to FS 179; turn left. Continue on FS 179 to the River-to-River Trail. Turn left on the trail and follow it back to the start.

RIDE 81 · Williams Hill, Option 1

AT A GLANCE

Length/configuration: 7-mile out-and-back (3.5 miles each way); mostly double-track and dirt road.

Aerobic difficulty: Easy. This is another of the few beginner's trails in the Shawnee. (Camp Cadiz also qualifies.)

Technical difficulty: Easy, except for a few creek crossings.

Scenery: Hardwoods, non-native pines, rock formations.

Special comments: The ride along the creek is scenic, as are the views of the bluffs when the leaves are off the trees.

IL

The memorable aspect of this trail is Little Lusk Creek. The creek bed is rocky and gravelly and, in all but the driest times of the year, will have flowing water. There are multiple crossings of the creek, most of which are easy. A particularly wet period can occasionally result in pools of standing water at some crossings. The Shawnee Mountain Bike Association riders are conscientious about keeping drainage open, or when that's not practical, building alternate crossings.

The creek provides a riparian ecosystem that makes the character of this ride a little different from any other in the forest. It's an especially nice ride in summer, when shade and frequent stream crossings make for a cool ride.

General location: About 20 minutes south of Harrisburg

Elevation change: There's 300 feet of elevation change here, but it comes infrequently and gently.

Season: Year-round; mud is likely to be a problem in spring and again from Thanksgiving to May.

Services: Everything in Harrisburg; the nearest bike shops are in Paducah (Kentucky), Evansville (Indiana), and Carbondale (Illinois).

Hazards: Creek crossings can be slippery.

Rescue index: Ride with someone; other users tend to disperse widely and any given piece of trail may only see a person every few days or even every few weeks.

Land status: Mostly National Forest property; skirts private property in several spots and crosses private property once.

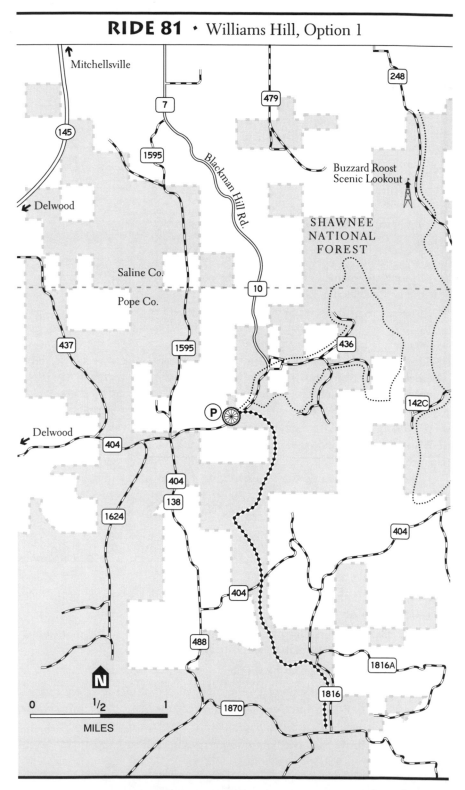

Maps: Shawnee Mountain Bike Association

Finding the trail: Take IL 34 south from Harrisburg to Blackman Hill Road; it's the first right after IL 34 and IL 145 split. Turn right (south) on Blackman Hill Road 4.5 miles. A Forest Service road comes in from the left, and there is limited parking there. (If you reach the T intersection, you've gone past it.)

Sources of additional information:

Shawnee Mountain Bike Association
190 Battleford Road
Harrisburg, IL 62946
(618) 252-3577

Forest Supervisor's Office
50 Highway 145 South
Harrisburg, IL 62946
(800) 699-6637 or (618) 253-7114

There are also district offices in Vienna, (phone (618) 658-2111); Elizabethtown, (phone (618) 287-2201); Jonesboro, (phone (618) 833-8576); and Murphysboro, (phone (618) 687-1731).

Notes on the trail: Follow to a clearing; turn right on the trail that comes off the corner of the clearing. Descend to the creek, then follow the creek to County Road 404 (a gravel road). Turn right. Cross the bridge, then take an immediate left onto the trail (the start of the trail looks like an old roadbed). At the T with the trail, turn right and immediately begin a rocky, technical descent. At the bottom, bear right at the Y. Follow the creek. At the next trail T, turn left. Follow the trail, which becomes an old road, to the end of the trail at Bethesda Church.

RIDE 82 · Williams Hill, Option 2

AT A GLANCE

IL

Length/configuration: 4.5-mile loop; mostly double-track with some pavement.

Aerobic difficulty: Moderate with several difficult climbs.

Technical difficulty: Moderate with some tough climbs and creek crossings.

Scenery: Hardwoods, non-native pines, rock formations.

Special comments: Expect extreme hills.

There will be times on this ride you'll question whether anyone could clean these hills. They are rutted, rocky, and steeper than any piece of earth should be. Though not hour-long grinders, they do seem to go on too long at times. There are three or four hills—maybe five, depending on your rating criteria—that are extremely steep. "Ahh," you're thinking, "steep up means ripping down." That would be true, except that the roughness of the descents prevents fast riding.

There are multiple crossings of Spring Valley Creek in the middle third of the ride. This creek tends to be shallower than Little Lusk (Williams Hill, Option 1) and is more often dry. The creek crossings pose little challenge, especially to any rider skilled enough to conquer these murderous hills.

General location: About 20 minutes south of Harrisburg

Elevation change: There are frequent, steep hills on this route, some of which exploit the full 300 feet of available elevation change.

Season: Year-round; mud will likely be a problem in spring and again from Thanksgiving to May.

Services: Everything in Harrisburg; the nearest bike shops are in Paducah (Kentucky), Evansville (Indiana), and Carbondale (Illinois).

Hazards: Sketchy descents

Rescue index: Ride with someone; other users tend to disperse widely and any given piece of trail may only see a person every few days or even every few weeks.

Land status: Mostly national forest property with 3 brief forays onto private property.

RIDE 82 • Williams Hill, Option 2

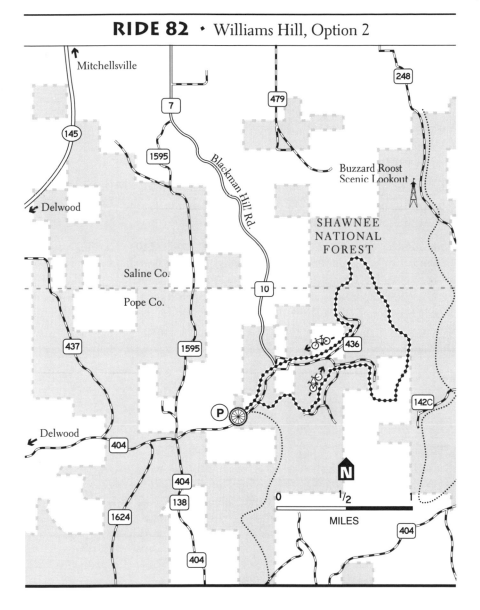

Maps: Shawnee Mountain Bike Association.

Finding the trail: Take IL 34 south from Harrisburg to Blackman Hill Road; it's the first right after IL 34 and IL 145 split. Turn right (south) on Blackman Hill Road 4.5 miles. A Forest Service road comes in from the left and there is limited parking there. (If you reach the **T** intersection, you've gone past it.)

Sources of additional information:

Shawnee Mountain Bike Association
190 Battleford Road
Harrisburg, IL 62946
(618) 252-3577

Forest Supervisor's Office
50 Highway 145 South
Harrisburg, IL 62946
(800) 699-6637 or (618) 253-7114

There are also district offices in Vienna, (phone (618) 658-2111); Elizabethtown, (phone (618) 287-2201); Jonesboro, (phone (618) 833-8576); and Murphysboro, (phone (618) 687-1731).

Notes on the trail: Start on the Forest Service road. At the clearing, turn left. In about 1 mile is another clearing; bear right. At the bottom of a long descent to Spring Valley Creek, turn left. Follow the creek until the trail begins to climb. When the trail intersects a Forest Service road near the top of the climb, turn left. Descend, then climb again. At the top of the rise, turn right onto the Forest Service road. Follow that road back to Blackman Hill Road. Turn left there and return to the start.

RIDE 83 · Williams Hill Option 3

AT A GLANCE

Length/configuration: 8-mile combination with a long out-and-back and a little loop; mostly double-track or dirt-road with some single-track.

Aerobic difficulty: Moderate, with a fire road at the start, but some climbing on the loop section.

Technical difficulty: Easy with some moderate sections. The ride starts as an easy fire road, narrows down to double-track, then becomes single-track for most of the loop section.

Scenery: Hardwoods, non-native pines, rock formations.

Special comments: This hits the highest point in southern Illinois, which is the second highest point in the state.

RIDE 83 · Williams Hill, Option 3

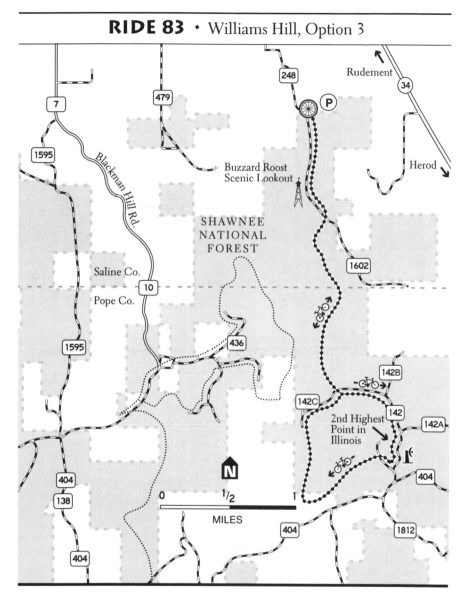

Jeff Jones, president of the Shawnee Mountain Bike Association and county engineer in this part of Illinois, says, "The most distinctive feature of this ride is climbing to the second-highest point in Illinois, which is the highest in southern Illinois, and highest in Illinois above mean ground plane." Then, with his typical candor, he adds, "I guess it's not a real thrill when you get there, but you can at least say you made it."

I agree the thrill doesn't compare to, for example, riding all day above the treeline in Summit County, Colorado. But there is a nice view from the top on a clear day. (It took three trips on this trail over the years for me to arrive on a

clear day.) Besides, the ride is a fun mix of trail types. There's some pleasantly technical single-track through the trees at the top and a return down the fire road to the start point.

General location: About 20 minutes south of Harrisburg

Elevation change: This one climbs quite a bit. Total gain is about 540 feet, although it mostly comes in manageable doses.

Season: Year-round; mud is likely to be a problem in spring and again from Thanksgiving to May. It's less of a problem here than on other trails in the Shawnee because you're not in bottomlands. Mud can make the fire road kind of gruesome, however.

Services: Everything in Harrisburg; the nearest bike shops are in Paducah (Kentucky), Evansville (Indiana), and Carbondale (Illinois).

Hazards: None

Rescue index: Ride with someone; other users tend to disperse widely and any given piece of trail may only see a person every few days or even every few weeks.

Land status: National Forest

Maps: Shawnee Mountain Bike Association

Finding the trail: Take IL 34 south from Harrisburg to Rudement. (IL 34 is actually running due east in the town of Rudement.) Go south on gravel Beech Hollow Road; it's the only cross street in Rudement. In less than 2 miles, the gravel ends. The trail goes from here on the old roadbed.

Sources of additional information:

Shawnee Mountain Bike Association
190 Battleford Road
Harrisburg, IL 62946
(618) 252-3577

Forest Supervisor's Office
50 Highway 145 South
Harrisburg, IL 62946
(800) 699-6637 or (618) 253-7114

There are also district offices in Vienna, (phone (618) 658-2111); Elizabethtown, (phone (618) 287-2201); Jonesboro, (phone (618) 833-8576); and Murphysboro, (phone (618) 687-1731).

Notes on the trail: Continue on the old roadbed from where you parked at the end of the gravel. At about 1 mile, go right at the Y. The old road becomes a trail. When you reach FS 142, turn left. Climb to the radio towers. At the next Forest Service road (FS 1420), turn right. You'll come to an open circle; the trail continues straight across. Soon you'll come to a clearing. The main (most obvious) trail goes right; you go left. At the bottom of the descent, turn right at the T. The trail becomes FS 142C. When it intersects FS 142, turn left and retrace your steps to the start.

RIDE 84 · Millstone, Option 1

AT A GLANCE

Length/configuration: 4-mile loop; single-track with some double-track and a little bit of dirt road.

Aerobic difficulty: Moderate, with some climbing throughout.

Technical difficulty: Moderate to challenging. There are 2 rocky, technical sections. One is at about the halfway point, the other about two-thirds of the way through.

Scenery: Hardwoods, non-native pines, and some especially notable rock formations.

Special comments: Very scenic, especially around Sand Cave. The rocky sections are extremely technical.

RIDE 84 · Millstone, Option 1

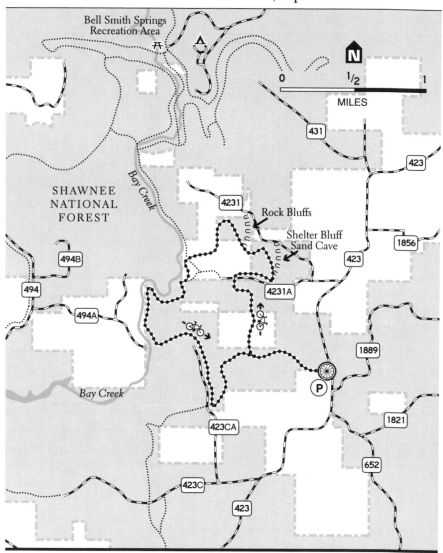

T here are two rocky, technical sections that distinguish this trail. One runs under the rock bluffs around the shelter bluff (a.k.a. Sand Cave) for about a half mile. The other is on FS 423CA coming out of Bay Creek. The former is the more technical of the two. The latter is less technical, but it's uphill. Some fun, eh?

Jeff Jones, president of the Shawnee Mountain Bike Association, says the challenge in these technical sections is to complete them without dabbing (putting down a foot). I think the challenge is to walk less this time than last time.

The most scenic feature of this ride is the Sand Cave. It's several hundred feet deep, and you can ride inside. Jeff describes it as a clamshell, and that's pretty accurate. The area around Sand Cave is noteworthy for its beauty.

General location: About 20 minutes south of Harrisburg

Elevation change: There's only about 240 feet of change in any one spot on the trail, but individual climbs can be challenging.

Season: Year-round; mud is likely to be a problem in spring and again from Thanksgiving to May.

Services: Everything in Harrisburg; the nearest bike shops are in Paducah (Kentucky), Evansville (Indiana), and Carbondale (Illinois).

Hazards: Technical, rocky sections.

Rescue index: Ride with someone; other users tend to disperse widely and any given piece of trail may only see a person every few days or even every few weeks.

Land status: Mostly National Forest property with some crossing of private property

Maps: Shawnee Mountain Bike Association

Finding the trail: Take IL 145 south from Harrisburg. When IL 145 turns south in Glendale, continue straight (west) on IL 147. In 0.25 mile, turn north on CR 423. In about 3 miles, you'll come to the River-to-River Trail. Park there on the shoulder.

Sources of additional information:

Shawnee Mountain Bike Association
190 Battleford Road
Harrisburg, IL 62946
(618) 252-3577

Forest Supervisor's Office
50 Highway 145 South
Harrisburg, IL 62946
(800) 699-6637 or (618) 253-7114

There are also district offices in Vienna, (phone (618) 658-2111); Elizabethtown, (phone (618) 287-2201); Jonesboro, (phone (618) 833-8576); and Murphysboro, (phone (618) 687-1731).

Notes on the trail: Go west on the River-to-River Trail. In 0.75 mile, turn right. Descend to the creek. Turn right onto CR 4231A, then left onto the trail to Sand Cave. The trail runs roughly northwest below the bluffs. Near the end of the bluffs, go left on the trail. Descend to Bay Creek. Go left to follow (do not cross) the creek to Maxwell Ford. Go left on the trail, which becomes FS 423CA. At the 4-way stop, turn left on the River-To-River Trail and return to the start.

RIDE 85 · Millstone, Option 2

AT A GLANCE

IL

Length/configuration: 12-mile loop; all types of trail and road.

Aerobic difficulty: Moderate with some challenging sections. One of those sections comes very near the beginning, several will have you pushing your bike, and at least one is a guaranteed hike-a-bike.

Technical difficulty: Moderate to challenging. There are some baby-head rocks scattered about. There's also some exposed ledge rock on the extreme upper end of Jackson Hollow, as well as ledge rock and boulders in the Jackson Falls area.

Scenery: Hardwoods, non-native pines, rock formations.

Special comments: There's a 0.75 mile-long railroad tunnel here (you ride over it, not in it); Jackson Falls is a rock climber's mecca. It's also a popular area for equestrians; watch for them at the falls and on the trails leading to it.

There are several unique features to this ride. One is the railroad tunnel near the beginning. You'll ride up and over the mouth of the tunnel; trains run every couple of hours, so you may well see one pass. You'll cross the dam for Bay Creek Lake Number 5. The name may be mundane, but the scenery is exceptional. Later in the ride you'll come to Jackson Falls. Here there's lots of exposed rocks and some boulders. Bring your chalk bag and climbing shoes, if you're so inclined. When there's been enough precipitation, the falls at Jackson Falls are beautiful. The executive summary for this ride is that although this ride has several easy sections, overall you work yourself silly, but the scenery makes it all worthwhile.

General location: About 20 minutes south of Harrisburg

Elevation change: There are spots with 350 feet of change, but it's the steepness, not the gain, that kills you.

Season: Year-round; mud can be a problem in spring and again from Thanksgiving to May.

Services: Everything in Harrisburg; the nearest bike shops are in Paducah (Kentucky), Evansville (Indiana), and Carbondale (Illinois).

Hazards: A fall from the tunnel entrance; also, watch for horseback riders in the Jackson Hollow area.

RIDE 85 · Millstone, Option 2

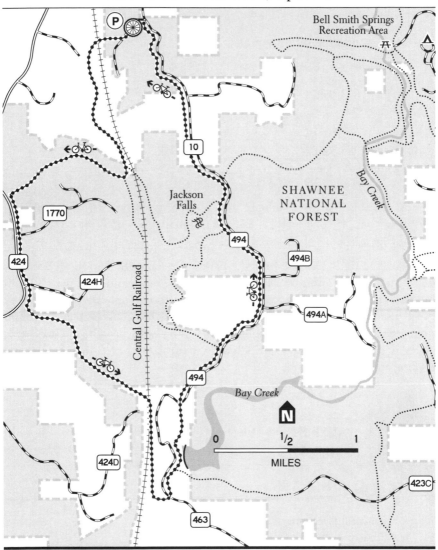

Rescue index: Ride with someone; other users tend to disperse widely and any given piece of trail may only see a person every few days or even every few weeks.

Land status: Mostly National Forest with some private property

Maps: Shawnee Mountain Bike Association

Finding the trail: IL 145 south from Harrisburg to Delwood; go west on the county road (the only one in town). In about 5 miles, at the **T**, turn right onto the gravel road. In about 4.5 miles (which is 1.75 miles past Olive Church), turn left onto CR 10/494. In 0.5 mile, turn right onto FS 426; there's room to park on the right.

Sources of additional information:

> Shawnee Mountain Bike Association
> 190 Battleford Road
> Harrisburg, IL 62946
> (618) 252-3577

> Forest Supervisor's Office
> 50 Highway 145 South
> Harrisburg, IL 62946
> (800) 699-6637 or (618) 253-7114

There are also district offices in Vienna, (phone (618) 658-2111); Elizabethtown, (phone (618) 287-2201); Jonesboro, (618) 833-8576); and Murphysboro, (phone (618) 687-1731).

Notes on the trail: Go west from the parking area on FS 426, which becomes double-track and crosses over the entrance to the railroad tunnel before heading south to Jackson Hollow. In about 1 mile, turn right onto the trail, climb to FS 424, and turn left. At the River-to-River trail, turn left. Descend, and go under the railroad tracks. Bear right (south) along Little Bay Creek. At FS 463, go left. Cross the dam at Bay Creek Lake. Go north to FS 494, then back to the parking area.

RIDE 86 · Palestine Church, Option 1

AT A GLANCE

Length/configuration: 5-mile combination—a little out-and-back with a big loop; dirt and gravel roads with some single- and double-track.

Aerobic difficulty: Moderate (due to 2 climbs)

Technical difficulty: Moderate; some loose rock, most of which comes in a short stretch on the descent to the creek, and a few creek crossings.

Scenery: Hardwoods, non-native pines, rock formations.

Special comments: Nice creek-bottom ride, especially in spring.

RIDE 86 · Palestine Church, Option 1

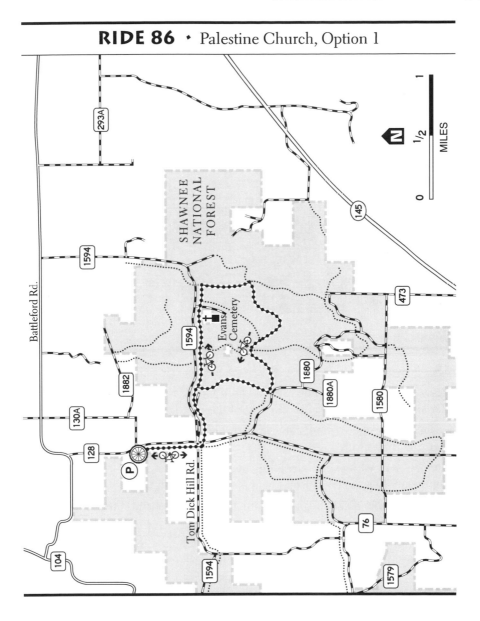

Palestine Church rides, in general, have less horse traffic than many other trails in the Shawnee. The other thing about this area is that there are no features that leap out at you. This trail, for example, offers some scenic riding adjacent to Battle Ford Creek, a short stretch of rock, a few roots, and a moderate climb up out of the creek area. It's a nice sampler of what mountain biking is all about and suitable for intermediate riders.

General location: About 20 minutes south of Harrisburg.

Even when it's cold enough for icicles to dangle from rock outcroppings, southern Illinois offers rideable weather.

Elevation change: The drop to Battle Ford Creek and the climb back out both offer about 150 feet of change; the rest of the ride is flat to slightly rolling.

Season: Year-round; mud can be a problem in spring and again from Thanksgiving to May

Services: Everything in Harrisburg; the nearest bike shops are in Paducah (Kentucky), Evansville (Indiana), and Carbondale (Illinois).

Hazards: Minimal, although there are creek crossings and some loose rock at the bottom of the first descent.

Rescue index: Ride with someone; other users tend to disperse widely and any given piece of trail may only see a person every few days or even every few weeks.

Land status: Some public roads, otherwise all National Forest.

Maps: Shawnee Mountain Bike Association

Finding the trail: Take IL 34/145 south from Harrisburg. When the roads split, go straight to remain on IL 145. In less than 1 mile, turn right (west) on Battleford Road. In 3.5 miles, Battleford Road curves left, then right. When it goes right, Palestine Church Road goes left. Follow Palestine Church road south 0.5 mile to the church; park there.

Sources of additional information:

Shawnee Mountain Bike Association
190 Battleford Road
Harrisburg, IL 62946
(618) 252-3577

Forest Supervisor's Office
50 Highway 145 South
Harrisburg, IL 62946
(800) 699-6637 or (618) 253-7114

There are also district offices in Vienna, (phone (618) 658-2111); Elizabethtown, (phone (618) 287-2201); Jonesboro, (phone (618) 833-8576); and Murphysboro, (phone (618) 687-1731).

Notes on the trail: Continue south on Palestine Church Road from the church for 0.5 mile, then left onto Evans Cemetery Road. Just before the wildlife clearing (about 0.25 mile past the cemetery), turn right onto the trail. At the bottom of the hill, turn right on the trail to follow the creek west (upstream). In less than 2 miles, turn right on the Forest Service road (it's the first right past the wildlife clearing). Climb back to Evans Cemetery Road, then retrace back to Palestine Church.

RIDE 87 · Palestine Church, Option 2

AT A GLANCE

Length/configuration: 7.5-mile loop; mostly dirt and gravel roads with some single-track.

Aerobic difficulty: Moderate to challenging. There are some tough climbs, at least one of which is a hike-a-bike.

Technical difficulty: Easy to moderate except for the ascents. The last 100 or so yards down to Bill Hill Hollow Road are rocky, steep, and challenging.

Scenery: Hardwoods, non-native pines, rock formations.

Special comments: Lots of variety on this loop, including a scenic overlook and a section of road along a wilderness area.

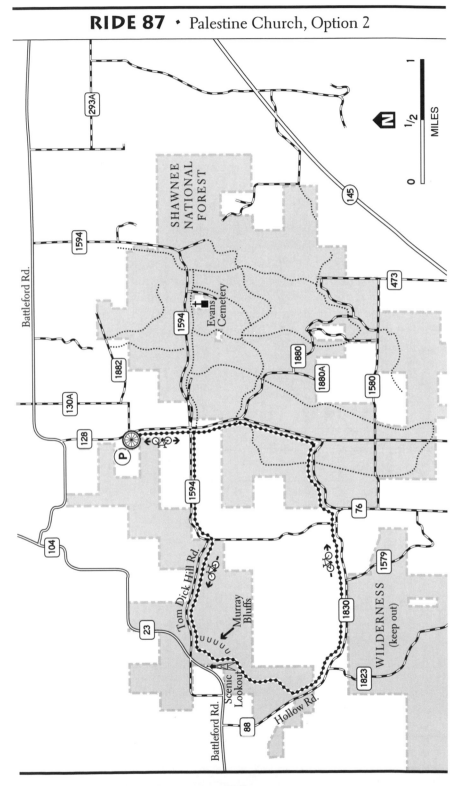

SHAWNEE NATIONAL FOREST

Evans Cemetery

Murray Bluffs

Scenic Lookout

WILDERNESS
(keep out)

Tom Dick Hill Rd.

Hollow Rd.

Battleford Rd.

Battleford Rd.

MILES

293A

1594

1882

130A

128

104

23

88

145

473

1880

1880A

1580

76

1830

1823

1579

1594

1594

Rock—from loose scree to massive slabs—defines the Shawnee National Forest.

There are a number of scenic spots along this ride. Two of the best come near the middle. First you'll encounter some rock bluffs where you turn off of a gravel road onto single-track. After that turn comes the hike-a-bike section; within a quarter-mile of that is a scenic lookout. Hop off your bike and look back to the north. Both the bluffs and the lookout are worth a photo.

Another nice feature of this ride is the stretch along Bill Hill Hollow Road. Even though you're on a public road, the scenery is great. Most of the road runs along a creek; there's a section of a few hundred yards where the road is in the creek bed. This leg is always moist and cool, a welcome relief if you're here in July or August.

The southern part of this ride, between Bill Hill Hollow and Tom Dick Hill Road, skirts a wilderness area. Be sure to stay on the trail and not stray into the wilderness where mountain biking is prohibited.

General location: About 20 minutes south of Harrisburg

Elevation change: There's a big drop on (gravel) Tom Dick Hill Road. The climb to Murray Bluff is too steep to ride, and the descent from Buzzard Roost to Bill Hill Hollow Road is steep. There's a great dirt road descent to Rocky Branch Creek, and a fairly demanding dirt road climb back up again.

Season: Year-round; mud can be a problem in spring and again from Thanksgiving to May.

Services: Everything in Harrisburg; the nearest bike shops are in Paducah (Kentucky), Evansville (Indiana), and Carbondale (Illinois).

Hazards: Descent off Buzzard's Roost Ridge is very technical; otherwise, nothing out of the ordinary.

Rescue index: Ride with someone; other users tend to disperse widely and any given piece of trail may only see a person every few days or even every few weeks.

Land status: Some public roads, otherwise all National Forest

Maps: Shawnee Mountain Bike Association

Finding the trail: Take IL 34/145 south from Harrisburg. When the roads split, go straight to remain on IL 145. In less than mile, turn right (west) on Battleford Road. In 3.5 miles, Battleford Road curves left, then right. When it goes right, Palestine Church Road goes left. Follow Palestine Church road south 0.5 mile to the church; park there.

Sources of additional information:

Shawnee Mountain Bike Association
190 Battleford Road
Harrisburg, IL 62946
(618) 252-3577

Forest Supervisor's Office
50 Highway 145 South
Harrisburg, IL 62946
(800) 699-6637 or (618) 253-7114

There are also district offices in Vienna, (phone (618) 658-2111); Elizabethtown, (phone (618) 287-2201); Jonesboro, (phone (618) 833-8576); and Murphysboro, (phone (618) 687-1731).

Notes on the trail: Continue south on Palestine Church Road for 0.5 mile, then right onto Davenport Road (Evans Cemetery Road goes left at this intersection). In about 1 mile, turn right onto Tom Dick Hill Road. At the bottom of the hill, turn left onto the trail. (If you get to Battleford Road, go back 100 yards.) Hike-a-bike up a steep section of about 100 feet; just beyond is a great overlook. Follow the trail, including a technical descent at the end, to Bill Hill Hollow Road. Turn left. This road will rejoin Tom Dick Hill Road. In less than 0.25 mile, the road goes right; you turn left onto the trail, which is also a Forest Service road. At the **T**, go left onto FS 1879, which becomes Palestine Church road and returns to the start point.

RIDE 88 · Palestine Church, Option 3

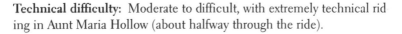

AT A GLANCE

Length/configuration: 9-mile combination; mostly dirt roads and double-track with some single-track.

Aerobic difficulty: Moderate to difficult. The route is laid out so that the climbs are less steep than the descents, but there are still some difficult sections.

Technical difficulty: Moderate to difficult, with extremely technical riding in Aunt Maria Hollow (about halfway through the ride).

Scenery: Hardwoods, non-native pines, rock formations.

Special comments: Extremely technical in Aunt Maria Hollow (south end of the loop section); this is the favorite ride of Rick Humphreys, a Shawnee Mountain Bike Association member who thrives on technical riding. In fact, Rule #1 of riding with the SMBA is: Don't follow Rick. He'll take you places where only he can go.

The part of the trail that runs along the creek is scenic. It's not as drop-dead gorgeous as other riparian areas in the Shawnee, but it ain't bad. The same could be said about the section running through Aunt Maria Hollow, especially the upper section where's there's some bluff rock.

General location: About 20 minutes south of Harrisburg

Elevation change: There are a few spots offering 200 feet of gain or loss.

Season: Year-round; mud can be a problem in spring and again from Thanksgiving to May.

Services: Everything in Harrisburg; the nearest bike shops are in Paducah (Kentucky), Evansville (Indiana), and Carbondale (Illinois).

Hazards: Technical sections, creek crossings, loose rock

Rescue index: Ride with someone; other users tend to disperse widely and any given piece of trail may only see a person every few days or even every few weeks.

Land status: Some public roads, otherwise all National Forest

Maps: Shawnee Mountain Bike Association

Finding the trail: Take IL 34/145 south from Harrisburg. When the roads split, go straight to remain on IL 145. In less than 1 mile, turn right (west) on

RIDE 88 · Palestine Church, Option 3

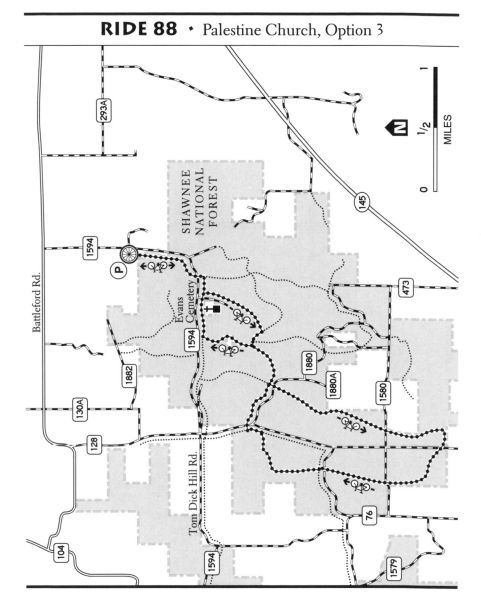

Battleford Road. Go west on Battleford Road 1.75 miles to Keneippe Road. Turn left. In 0.5 mile the road ends and the trail starts.

Sources of additional information:

Shawnee Mountain Bike Association
190 Battleford Road
Harrisburg, IL 62946
(618) 252-3577

Forest Supervisor's Office
50 Highway 145 South
Harrisburg, IL 62946
(800) 699-6637 or (618) 253-7114

There are also district offices in Vienna, (phone (618) 658-2111); Elizabethtown, (phone (618) 287-2201); Jonesboro, (phone (618) 833-8576); and Murphysboro, (phone (618) 687-1731).

Notes on the trail: Follow Keneippe Road/FS 1594. At the cemetery, bear left—not hard left, which is FS 1594G—but angle left to ride along the front of the cemetery. In about 300 yards, ride over the sandstone, then turn left onto single-track. There's a steep descent, then some up-and-down. At the bottom of the main hill, bear right; you're going west, or upstream. (Palestine Church options 1, 3, and 4 overlap here). At the wildlife clearing, turn left up the horse trail single-track (the short, steep ascent, not FS 1890A). At the fork, bear left. Take a short dogleg on Forest Service road. At the next trail intersection, turn right. Descend to the second Forest Service road, turn right, begin to climb. At the next Forest Service road, turn left and descend. Just after crossing Rocky Branch creek, turn right onto FS 1890. Turn left on the first Forest Service road that goes left, begin a steep, rocky climb. Turn right on the next Forest Service road, FS 1594/Evans Cemetery Road, and retrace your path to the start.

RIDE 89 · Palestine Church, Option 4

AT A GLANCE

IL

Length/configuration: 6.5-mile combination that is mostly loop with a little out-and-back; mostly single- and double-track with some dirt roads.

Aerobic difficulty: Moderate overall with some tough climbing coming out of Battle Ford Creek, which you'll do twice.

Technical difficulty: Moderate except for the rocky creek crossings and poor traction on the uphills.

Scenery: Hardwoods, non-native pines, rock formations.

Special comments: More good-time single-track than other trails in this area.

The descents down to Battle Ford Creek can be big fun, especially if taken at speed. One of those drops comes fairly early in the ride, the other comes after you leave FS 1880 and get onto the single-track.

The woods through which this trail runs are generally pristine. It's not hard to imagine you're an intrepid adventurer of two centuries ago following a game trail. Except that they didn't have bikes. Or guidebooks.

General location: About 20 minutes south of Harrisburg

Elevation change: Getting down to Battle Ford Creek and climbing back out again is good for about 200 feet of change. The rest of the ride has minimal elevation change.

Season: Year-round; mud can be a problem in spring and again from Thanksgiving to May.

Services: Everything in Harrisburg; the nearest bike shops are in Paducah (Kentucky), Evansville (Indiana), and Carbondale (Illinois).

Hazards: Technical sections in creek crossings and on the uphills, although they're less a hazard than a test of your abilities.

Rescue index: Ride with someone; other users tend to disperse widely and any given piece of trail may only see a person every few days or even every few weeks.

Land status: Some public roads, but mostly National Forest

Maps: Shawnee Mountain Bike Association

RIDE 89 · Palestine Church, Option 4

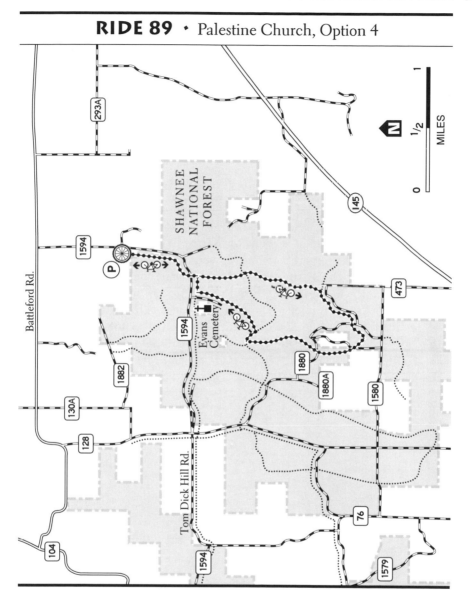

Finding the trail: Take IL 34/145 south from Harrisburg. When the roads split, go straight to remain on IL 145. In less than 1 mile, turn right (west) on Battleford Road. Go west on Battleford Road 1.75 miles to Keneippe Road. Turn left. In 0.5 mile the road ends and the trail starts.

Sources of additional information:

Shawnee Mountain Bike Association
190 Battleford Road
Harrisburg, IL 62946
(618) 252-3577

Forest Supervisor's Office
50 Highway 145 South
Harrisburg, IL 62946
(800) 699-6637 or (618) 253-7114

There are also district offices in Vienna, (phone (618) 658-2111); Elizabethtown, (phone (618) 287-2201); Jonesboro, (phone (618) 833-8576); and Murphysboro, (phone (618) 687-1731).

Notes on the trail: Continue south on Keneippe Road to Evans Cemetery Road. Turn sharp left onto FS 1594G, descend to Battleford Creek. Turn left to follow the creek. Cross a dry creek bed; in 150 yards, bear right and cross the main creek. At the top of the hill, turn right at the trail intersection. The trail becomes FS 1888A. Turn left at the next fire road, FS 1888, then right at the next fire road, FS 1580. In 200 yards, turn right onto FS 1880. In 0.25 mile, when the road goes sharp right; you turn sharp left onto the trail, which will cross FS 1880. Cross the main creek, then go left to ride alongside it. At the wildlife clearing, cross the main creek again on FS 1880. In 100 yards, turn right up a steep, rocky fire road. At FS 1594/Evans Cemetery Road, turn right and retrace your path back to the start.

RIDE 90 · War Bluff, Option 1

AT A GLANCE

Length/configuration: 9-mile loop; mostly double-track with some dirt and gravel roads and a little bit of single-track.

Aerobic difficulty: Moderate to challenging, depending on how fast you want to go. The hills here are less steep than many others in the Shawnee, but tend to be longer; some run nearly a mile without a break. The optional ascent to War Bluff, especially the last quarter-mile, is super-steep.

Technical difficulty: Moderate, since most of this is double-track or fire road. After descending from War Bluff, there's a creek crossing that can be messy, depending on how high the water is running.

Scenery: Hardwoods, non-native pines, rock formations. War Bluff itself provides an excellent vantage point, especially when looking back to the northeast toward High Knob.

Special comments: The view from War Bluff makes this ride worthwhile. War Bluff is also an archaeological site.

War Bluff doesn't sit right on the trail, so the last brutal grunt up to it is listed as an option. Think of it as a required option, oxymoronic as that may be. The view from War Bluff is this ride's raison d'être.

The top of War Bluff is an ancient Indian fort, evidenced by a crumbling rock wall along one side. Not much remains of that wall—this ain't Fort Sumter, after all—but a careful search will reveal a pattern of stones laid by human hands.

It's not hard to see why the Native Americans chose this spot for a fort. The commanding view offered excellent security, and the near-vertical climb kept all but the most aerobically fit intruders far below. Those that made it to the top were presumably too tired to fight.

General location: About 20 minutes south of Harrisburg

Elevation change: There are several climbs and drops of some 300 feet.

Season: Year-round; mud can be a problem in spring and again from Thanksgiving to May.

Services: Everything in Harrisburg; the nearest bike shops are in Paducah (Kentucky), Evansville (Indiana), and Carbondale (Illinois).

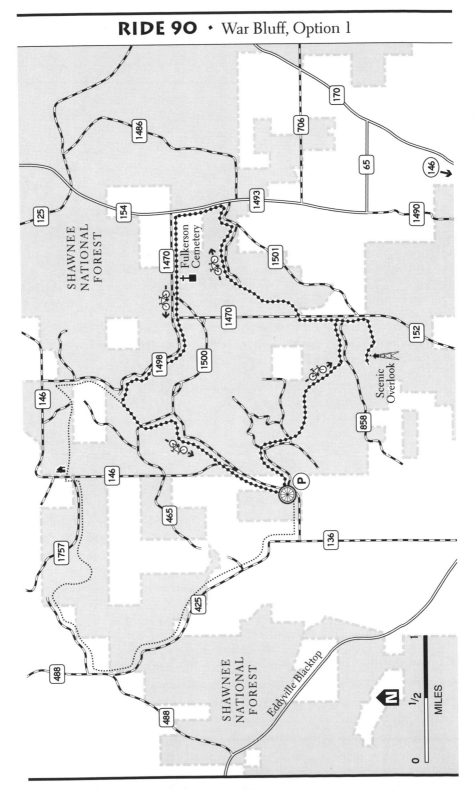

Hazards: Creek crossing can be challenging, depending on the season.

Rescue index: Ride with someone; other users tend to disperse widely and any given piece of trail may only see a person every few days or even every few weeks.

Land status: Nearly all National Forest with some stretches of public road

Maps: Shawnee Mountain Bike Association

Finding the trail: Take IL 34/145 south from Harrisburg. When IL 34 and IL 145 split, go straight to continue on IL 145. In the teeming metropolis of Eddyville (pop.145) turn left (east) on the Eddyville Blacktop Road. After about 5.5 miles, turn left onto Raum Road. In less than 1.5 miles, turn right onto FS 853. Park where FS 853 and CR 146/Raum Road split.

Sources of additional information:

Shawnee Mountain Bike Association
190 Battleford Road
Harrisburg, IL 62946
(618) 252-3577

Forest Supervisor's Office
50 Highway 145 South
Harrisburg, IL 62946
(800) 699-6637 or (618) 253-7114

There are also district offices in Vienna, (phone (618) 658-2111); Elizabethtown, (phone (618) 287-2201); Jonesboro, (phone (618) 833-8576); and Murphysboro, (phone (618) 687-1731).

Notes on the trail: Continue on FS 853. Left at the first fire road, FS 1862. In 100 yards, turn right onto the single-track. Descend to FS 1470; turn right. In 200 yards, turn right onto the trail and begin a tough climb to War Bluff. This trail becomes FS 858. From the intersection of FS 858 and FS 1470, you can go right to the lookout atop War Bluff, or turn left onto FS 1470. On FS 1470, take the first trail to the right. Cross the creek, then turn left at the T. Take the next trail to the right, which becomes FS 1501B. Turn left on FS 1493, then turn left onto FS 1470. In about 0.75 mile, FS 1470 veers left at the clearing; go straight onto FS 1498. This becomes single-track until it joins FS 1761B. When FS 1761B makes a hairpin right, go left onto single-track. When the trail meets FS 175S, turn left. Descend to FS 1500; turn right. Climb to CR 146 and return to the start.

RIDE 91 · War Bluff Option 2

AT A GLANCE

IL

Length/configuration: 10-mile loop; a mix of dirt roads, single- and double-track.

Aerobic difficulty: Challenging, with several long, steep climbs. The worst is coming up out of Rock House, the first 0.5 mile of which is extra-tough.

Technical difficulty: Moderate to challenging. The descent to the Rose Ford crossing of Lusk Creek is rough and demanding, made more so by the speed you'll gather. Rose Ford itself is a hike-a-bike section, due to deep water and the steepness of the far bank. And the climb to Rock House is sketchy as it runs across the fall line.

Scenery: Hardwoods, non-native pines, rock formations.

Special comments: Be prepared for the challenging technical, rocky climbs.

Jeff Jones, president of the Shawnee Mountain Bike Association emphasizes that "your encounters with Lusk Creek, both at Rose Ford and Rock House, are going to be memorable." That's the diplomatic way of saying you're in for a rough time. You'll likely be carrying your bike in both locations. At Rose Ford, it's the only way to get back out of the creek. At Rock House, it's the only way, according to Jeff, "to save from breaking your neck." Climbing up from Lusk Creek near Rock House will require most riders to get off and push at least part of the way.

Assuming you're not a masochist, what's the appeal of such a demanding ride? Lots of great scenery, the most inspiring of which is Rock House. Geological forces have created a room that's some 30 by 40 feet. It's located about 50 feet above Lusk Creek; the trail goes right past it.

Whatever evidence of Indians occupying Rock House has been obliterated by relic hunters and general human activity. Although no evidence remains, Jeff Jones is convinced the Native Americans used this spot. "It's simply too handy a feature for them to pass up."

General location: About 20 minutes south of Harrisburg

Elevation change: Both crossings of Lusk Creek have steep ups and downs. There are stretches elsewhere in the ride where the hills are less severe but still noteworthy.

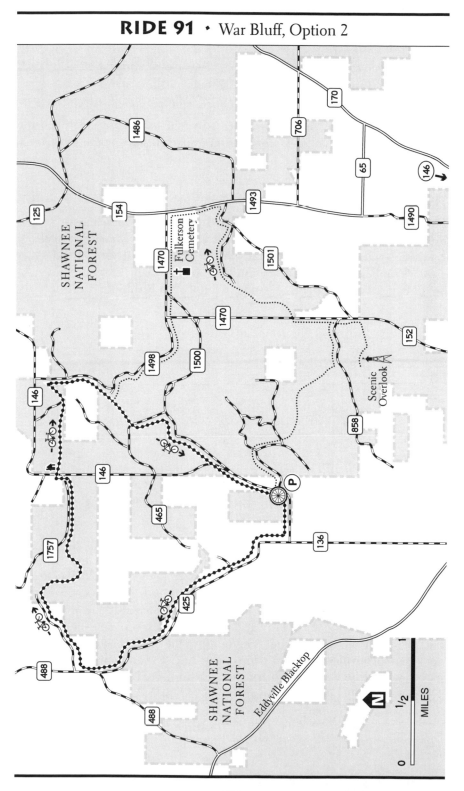

Season: Year-round; mud can be a problem in spring and again from Thanksgiving to May.

Services: Everything in Harrisburg; the nearest bike shops are in Paducah (Kentucky), Evansville (Indiana), and Carbondale (Illinois).

Hazards: Very rocky in spots; watch for bluffs and drop-offs.

Rescue index: Ride with someone; other users tend to disperse widely and any given piece of trail may only see a person every few days or even every few weeks.

Land status: About half public roads, half National Forest

Maps: Shawnee Mountain Bike Association

Finding the trail: Take IL 34/145 south from Harrisburg. When IL 34 and IL 145 split, go straight to continue on IL 145. In the teeming metropolis of Eddyville (pop. 145) turn left (east) on the Eddyville Blacktop Road. After about 5.5 miles, turn left onto Raum Road. In less than 1.5 miles, turn right onto FS 853. Park where FS 853 and CR 146/Raum Road split.

Sources of additional information:

Shawnee Mountain Bike Association
190 Battleford Road
Harrisburg, IL 62946
(618) 252-3577

Forest Supervisor's Office
50 Highway 145 South
Harrisburg, IL 62946
(800) 699-6637 or (618) 253-7114

There are also district offices in Vienna, (phone (618) 658-2111); Elizabethtown, (phone (618) 287-2201; Jonesboro, (phone (618) 833-8576); and Murphysboro, (phone (618) 687-1731).

Notes on the trail: Go back (west) on Raum Road to the T, then right onto the gravel road. Descend to Lusk Creek. Hike-a-bike across the creek and climb the opposite bank. Bear left along the creek, then turn right up the old road to join FS 488. In less than 0.25 mile, turn right onto a dirt road, which becomes single-track at an old homestead. Follow the bluff, then descend to the creek. Rock House is about two-thirds of the way down. This is a scenic descent; it's worth a stop to go in and look around. After crossing the creek, bear left, then right onto the trail. Climb to FS 1757; turn right. At CR 146/Raum Road, turn left for 200 yards, then right onto the single-track (turn just before the farmhouse). This becomes FS 1761C. Turn right on FS 1761B. When FS1761B makes a hairpin left, go right onto the trail. When the trail meets FS 175S, turn left onto FS 175S. Descend to FS 1500; turn right. Climb to CR 146 and return to the start.

RIDE 92 · Camp Ondessonk

AT A GLANCE

IL

Length/configuration: 9-mile loop; mostly single- or double-track with some dirt road.

Aerobic difficulty: Moderate, except for a segment along the East Branch of Cedar Creek between the first and second waterfalls, and the climb out of Gum Springs on FS 1810, which is almost a mile long.

Technical difficulty: Moderate, except for multiple creek crossings and several short, steep climbs. The worst of these come between the departure from FS 429 and Cedar Falls.

Scenery: Hardwoods, non-native pines, rock formations; the waterfalls are the scenic highlights of this trail.

Special comments: Perhaps the most scenic ride in the Shawnee, with waterfalls and lots of rock formations.

The scenery on this route is nothing short of stunning. That would be true even without Cedar Falls. In a way, it's a shame so much beauty is concentrated on one ride, rather than dispersed more evenly throughout the Shawnee. But hey, this is a course in geology, not democracy, so you'll just have to ooh and aah in between anaerobic gasps.

Because the falls are the highlight of this ride, it only makes sense the beauty is all the better when there's water flowing. Do this route a day or two after a moderate rain for maximum effect. Don't forget to bring your camera.

General location: About 20 minutes south of Harrisburg

Elevation change: Several short, steep climbs of 200 to 300 feet gain, with corresponding descents. Those come mostly before the middle of the ride. After that, the hills are kinder.

Season: Year-round; mud can be a problem in spring and again from Thanksgiving to May.

Services: Everything in Harrisburg; the nearest bike shops are in Paducah (Kentucky), Evansville (Indiana), and Carbondale (Illinois).

Hazards: A few sketchy creek crossings, some tall bluffs. The biggest hazard is other trail users, since many are attracted to this beautiful area. Be especially watchful for hikers near Cedar Falls and equestrians near Gum Springs.

RIDE 92 · Camp Ondessonk

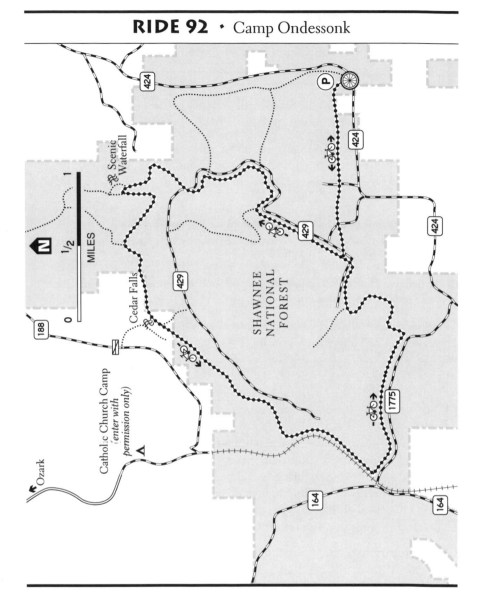

Rescue index: Ride with someone; other users tend to disperse widely and any given piece of trail may only see a person every few days or even every few weeks.

Land status: Virtually all National Forest.

Maps: Shawnee Mountain Bike Association

Finding the trail: Take IL 145 south from Harrisburg. When IL 145 turns south in Glendale, continue straight (west) on IL 147. In about 5 miles, turn right onto FS 424. This road twists and turns; at the second hard left past the lookout tower, there is parking and the trailhead. (Look for signs for the River-to-River Trail.)

Sources of additional information:

Shawnee Mountain Bike Association
190 Battleford Road
Harrisburg, IL 62946
(618) 252-3577

Forest Supervisor's Office
50 Highway 145 South
Harrisburg, IL 62946
(800) 699-6637 or (618) 253-7114

There are also district offices in Vienna, (phone (618) 658-2111); Elizabethtown, (phone (618) 287-2201); Jonesboro, (phone (618) 833-8576); and Murphysboro, (phone (618) 687-1731).

Notes on the trail: Go west from the parking lot and trailhead on the River-to-River Trail. Turn right on FS 429, then right again at the **T** to remain on FS 429. About 0.25 mile past Trail 32 where FS 429 goes hard left, turn right onto the trail. Descend to the creek and turn left. Bear left at the first **Y**, then take the next left. Climb up around rocks, then descend back to the creek. Left again at the creek. Follow the creek to the railroad grade. At the intersection with a Forest Service road,follow the road. You'll immediately cross the wooden bridge and begin climbing. Near the top, go straight. The Forest Service road turns right and goes to the lookout tower.) Pick up the River-to-River Trail and follow it back to the start.

RIDE 93 · High Knob, Option 1

AT A GLANCE

Length/configuration: 8-mile loop; lots of single-track with some dirt road and a paved road start.

Aerobic difficulty: Moderate on average, with a couple of short, steep climbs on the Beaver Trail just before the Pounds Hollow Dam. Climbing from the lake to FS 323 also has some steep sections.

Technical difficulty: Moderate to challenging with some extreme sections on the back side of the lake, where there are rocks, drops, and lots of low-speed, technical riding.

Scenery: Hardwoods, non-native pines, rock formations.

Special comments: Pounds Hollow Recreation Area offers good camping with showers and swimming. This loop has some very challenging technical, rocky sections.

The stretch along Pounds Hollow Lake defines this ride. There are few lakes in the Shawnee. (Okay, technically this isn't a lake, either. It's an impoundment. Let's not quibble.) So the lake is unique because it's a lake; it's also unique because it offers great scenery. It's tucked into the surrounding hills and hardwoods like a butterfly cupped in the hands of a child.

The High Knob area offers (seasonal) camping with swimming and showers at Pounds Hollow Recreation Area. There are several trails worth riding; the three described in this book are a representative but hardly inclusive list. And to cap it all off, there's great hiking at the Rim Rock Recreation Area and the nearby Garden of the Gods.

General location: About 20 minutes south of Harrisburg

Elevation change: There are several short, tough climbs. You'll have to have the lungs of a gazelle and the traction of a goat to ride them all. Maximum change is 330 feet, although most climbs provide less than that.

Season: Year-round; mud can be a problem in spring and again from Thanksgiving to May.

Services: Everything in Harrisburg; the nearest bike shops are in Paducah (Kentucky), Evansville (Indiana), and Carbondale (Illinois).

Hazards: Rocky sections; steep descent to dam. All areas around High Knob can have a lot of horse traffic.

RIDE 93 · High Knob, Option 1

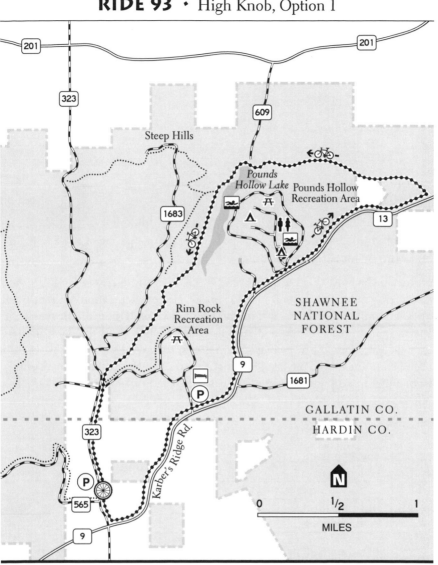

Rescue index: Ride with someone; other users tend to disperse widely and any given piece of trail may only see a person every few days or even every few weeks.

Land status: Mostly National Forest except for stretches of public road

Maps: Shawnee Mountain Bike Association

Finding the trail: Take IL 34 south from Harrisburg to Karber's Ridge Road (it's the next left after the gravel road to the left leading to Garden of the Gods

Wilderness Area). Go east on Karber's Ridge Road for about 7 miles to FS 323; turn north. Within 0.25 mile is a wide spot on the left for parking. Watch for signs; the River-to-River Trail crosses here.

Sources of additional information:

Shawnee Mountain Bike Association
190 Battleford Road
Harrisburg, IL 62946
(618) 252-3577

Forest Supervisor's Office
50 Highway 145 South
Harrisburg, IL 62946
(800) 699-6637 or (618) 253-7114

There are also district offices in Vienna, (phone (618) 658-2111); Elizabethtown, (phone (618) 287-2201); Jonesboro, (phone (618) 833-8576); and Murphysboro, (phone (618) 687-1731).

Notes on the trail: Go back on FS 323 to Karber's Ridge Road and turn left. About 1.25 miles past the entrance to Pounds Hollow Recreation Area, turn left onto the trail; watch closely, as the trail is not obvious. This is the Beaver Trail. Stay on this to reach the dam at Pounds Hollow Lake. Cross the dam, then go left to follow along the lake. This stretch is very rocky and technical. About 0.25 mile before the end of the lake, turn right up a steep, rocky, single-track climb. Remain on this trail, traveling generally southwest, until you meet FS 323; turn left to return to the start.

RIDE 94 · High Knob, Option 2

AT A GLANCE

Length/configuration: 6-mile out-and-back (3 miles each way); mix of single- and double-track with gravel and dirt roads.

Aerobic difficulty: Moderate, although the last 0.5 mile upon returning to High Knob is challenging.

Technical difficulty: Moderate; fewer rock ledges than High Knob, Option 3. Mostly typical fire road.

Scenery: Hardwoods, non-native pines, rock formations.

Special comments: Great scenery, including a stunning overlook and several exceptional rock formations.

IL

RIDE 94 · High Knob, Option 2

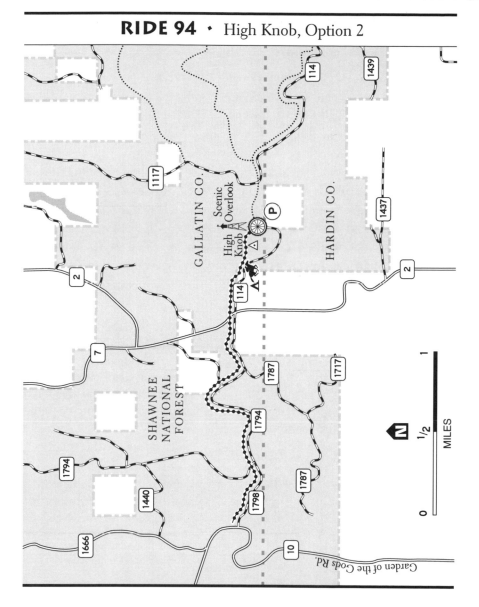

This route offers access to the more demanding trails north of here, although the next ride is a better bet for accessing that area. The views from this trail are exceptional. But the most memorable aspect is the climb back up to High Knob at the end. It would be a tough climb on fresh legs; when you're whipped, it's almost impossible.

You can avoid that unpleasantness by picking an alternate start point. Instead of turning around where FS 1798 meets Garden of the Gods Road, you could start there. Then your climb to High Knob comes in the middle instead of at the end.

So why do it this way? It offers more flexibility. From the start point I've described, you can do this ride and High Knob, Option 3, plus any of the ancillary trails that head north from either of these.

General location: About 20 minutes south of Harrisburg

Elevation change: There are several lesser climbs; the one you'll remember is the one back up to High Knob at the end.

Season: Year-round; mud can be a problem in spring and again from Thanksgiving to May.

Services: Everything in Harrisburg; the nearest bike shops are in Paducah (Kentucky), Evansville (Indiana), and Carbondale (Illinois).

Hazards: Generally technical; some rocky parts. There's an old horse camp just west of the start point; watch for equestrians.

Rescue index: Ride with someone; other users tend to disperse widely and any given piece of trail may only see a person every few days or even every few weeks.

Land status: National Forest

Maps: Shawnee Mountain Bike Association

Finding the trail: Take IL 34 south from Harrisburg to Karber's Ridge Road (it's the next left after the gravel road to the left leading to Garden of the Gods Wilderness Area). Go east on Karber's Ridge Road for about 5 miles to the hamlet of Karber's Ridge. Turn north onto the gravel county road (see the signs there for High Knob.) In less than 1.5 miles, turn right onto a gravel road. Go through the horse camp area. Park at the picnic area (watch for the flagstone gateposts). There are rest rooms here.

Sources of additional information:

Shawnee Mountain Bike Association
190 Battleford Road
Harrisburg, IL 62946
(618) 252-3577

Forest Supervisor's Office
50 Highway 145 South
Harrisburg, IL 62946
(800) 699-6637 or (618) 253-7114

There are also district offices in Vienna, (phone (618) 658-2111); Elizabethtown, (phone (618) 287-2201); Jonesboro, (phone (618) 833-8576); and Murphysboro, (phone (618) 687-1731).

Notes on the trail: From the west side of the parking area, descend the single-track to the gravel road at the horse camp. Turn right. Continue straight across the county road. Follow the signs for the River-to-River Trail. This route ends at the Garden of the Gods Road, where you can rest before returning the same way.

RIDE 95 · High Knob, Option 3

AT A GLANCE

Length/configuration: 7-mile out-and-back (3.5 miles each way); mostly degraded fire road.

Aerobic difficulty: Moderate; mostly rolling fire road with a few steeper sections.

Technical difficulty: Moderate, although some riders will struggle over the areas of ledge rock, which form steps. Only the best riders will be able to go both up and down these.

Scenery: Hardwoods, non-native pines, rock formations

Special comments: More prone to be muddy than some other trails in the Shawnee. This is an excellent jumping-off point for trails north of this area.

IL

There's nothing that jumps out at you from this ride. If you want to hone your trialsin abilities, here's the place to do it. There are a couple of stretches of rock steps. Each step is only 4–6 inches high, but a series of them will make up a ledge of 12–18 inches. And because this is an out-and-back, you get to ride them both ways, up and down.

Maybe you're not into trialsin. Okay. This trail's still fun to ride. But the best thing about is that it supplies a gateway to other trails north of this area. Any of the High Knob trails do that; this one does it best. Take any of the trails that lead north of this one and you'll be treated to some of the most wonderfully technical riding you've ever seen.

General location: About 20 minutes south of Harrisburg

Elevation change: Total elevation change on this ride is about 370 feet. The start point at High Knob is—surprise—the highest point. Most of the change comes fairly gently.

Season: Year-round; mud can be a problem in spring and again from Thanksgiving to May.

Services: Everything in Harrisburg; the nearest bike shops are in Paducah (Kentucky), Evansville (Indiana), and Carbondale (Illinois).

RIDE 95 · High Knob, Option 3

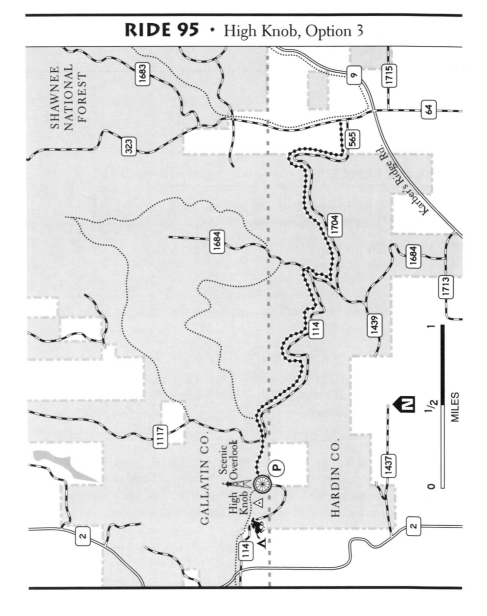

Hazards: Lots of horses. Watch for their tailpipe emissions; ride with your eyes open and mouth closed.

Rescue index: Ride with someone; other users tend to disperse widely and any given piece of trail may only see a person every few days or even every few weeks.

Land status: National Forest

Maps: Shawnee Mountain Bike Association

Finding the trail: Take IL 34 south from Harrisburg to Karber's Ridge Road (it's the next left after the gravel road to the left leading to Garden of the Gods Wilderness Area). Go east on Karber's Ridge Road for about 5 miles to the hamlet of Karber's Ridge. Turn north onto the road (you'll see signs there for High Knob). In less than 1.5 miles, turn right onto a gravel road. Go through the horse camp area. Park at the picnic area (watch for the flagstone gateposts). There are rest rooms here.

Sources of additional information:

Shawnee Mountain Bike Association
190 Battleford Road
Harrisburg, IL 62946
(618) 252-3577

Forest Supervisor's Office
50 Highway 145 South
Harrisburg, IL 62946
(800) 699-6637 or (618) 253-7114

There are also district offices in Vienna, (phone (618) 658-2111); Elizabethtown, (phone (618) 287-2201); Jonesboro, (phone (618) 833-8576); and Murphysboro, (phone (618) 687-1731).

Notes on the trail: Go east from the parking area. Simply follow the River-to-River Trail all the way to FS 323, from where you'll turn around and return the same way.

RIDE 96 · One Horse Gap

AT A GLANCE

Length/configuration: 13-mile loop; mostly dirt and gravel roads.

Aerobic difficulty: Moderate, with some tough climbing near One Horse Gap and again coming up from Grand Pierre Creek.

Technical difficulty: Moderate to challenging. There's sketchy section just before One Horse Gap, and baby head rocks as you descend from the Gap. The ascent from Grand Pierre is as technically challenging as it is aerobically demanding.

Scenery: Hardwoods, non-native pines, rock formations. If you don't squeeze through the Gap to the slickrock above, you're missing the best part this ride. One Horse Gap Lake ties with Grand Pierre Creek for a close second.

Special comments: Knock-out scenery that includes overlooks, a lake, and spectacular rock formations. This area hosts a huge equestrian rally the first week of August; don't ride here then.

IL

Every time I've ridden with Shawnee Mountain Bike Association members, they've taken me here. We also ride other trails, but One Horse Gap is the one they never miss and for good reason.

This trail has plenty of technical sections, mostly loose rock on sloping terrain. You're often traversing the fall line while you're riding mobile rock.

While the technical nature of the trail is an attraction, the real selling point is the scenery. Approaching the Gap, you're hugging the base of the bluffs, winding between spindly trees and massive rock walls. At the Gap, the trail twists through a labyrinth of boulders; as I'm riding I'm thinking, one horse if it's a *skinny* horse.

We always take some time to hike-a-bike through the Gap to the slickrock above. The views from there are spectacular, and the riding is incredible. There's a football field's worth of rolling, exposed rock. And traction—it's as if your tires are made of Silly Putty.

General location: About 20 minutes south of Harrisburg

Elevation change: Much of this ride is on gently rising fire road. There are a couple of sections of steep stuff, but they're fairly short.

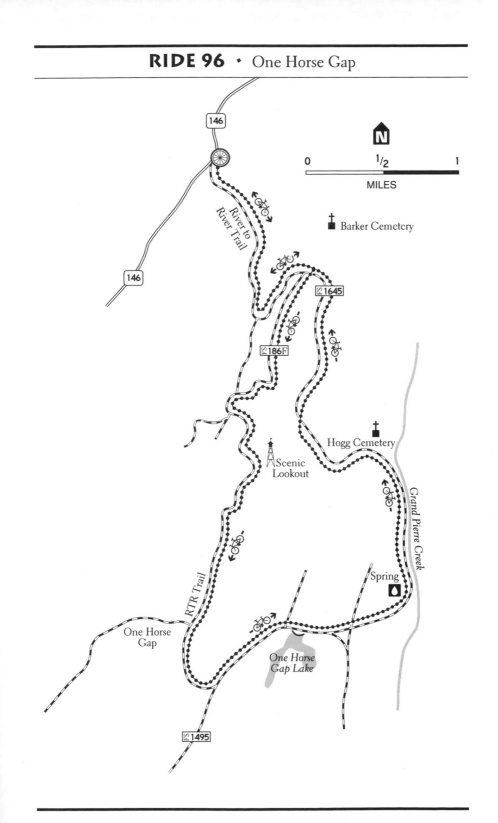

146

N

0   1/2   1
MILES

✝ Barker Cemetery

River to River Trail

1645

186F

✝ Hogg Cemetery

Scenic Lookout

Grand Pierre Creek

RTR Trail

Spring

One Horse Gap

One Horse Gap Lake

1495

This is One Horse Gap, which could just as well be called One Bike Gap.

Season: Year-round; mud can be a problem in spring and again from Thanksgiving to May.

Services: Everything in Harrisburg; the nearest bike shops are in Paducah (Kentucky), Evansville (Indiana), and Carbondale (Illinois).

Hazards: High bluffs; lots of horses (1,000+) the first week in August.

Rescue index: Ride with someone; other users tend to disperse widely and any given piece of trail may only see a person every few days or even every few weeks.

Land status: National Forest

Maps: Shawnee Mountain Bike Association

Finding the trail: Take IL 34 south from Harrisburg to Herod. Turn south on the gravel road in Herod. In 1.5 miles you'll come to a concrete slab ford where there's room to park on the near side.

Some Shawnee Mountain Bike Association riders take a break in the middle of the ride.

Sources of additional information:

Shawnee Mountain Bike Association
190 Battleford Road
Harrisburg, IL 62946
(618) 252-3577

Forest Supervisor's Office
50 Highway 145 South
Harrisburg, IL 62946
(800) 699-6637 or (618) 253-7114

There are also district offices in Vienna, (phone (618) 658-2111); Elizabethtown, (phone (618) 287-2201); Jonesboro, (phone (618) 833-8576); and Murphysboro, (phone (618) 687-1731).

Notes on the trail: Head east from the parking area (don't cross the road) on the River-to-River Trail. In 200 feet, cross the creek. Climb the switchbacks, following the RTR blazes. At the gravel road, turn left. Follow it to the end of the gravel, then right onto FS 186F. In less than 1 mile, turn right and return to the gravel road. Turn left. In 0.75 mile, turn left onto the RTR Trail. At One Horse Gap, you can turn right, go up through the cleft in the rock, and ride on the exposed rock above. If you don't want to do this (or after you've done this and it's time to continue on), go straight on the trail to intersect FS 1495. Turn left; in 0.75 mile you're at the lake. Turn right, descend, and cross the dam.

Continue to FS 458, turn right. In 200 feet, turn right onto the single-track. Descend to Grand Pierre Creek. Stay on this trail with the creek on your right and the hill on your left until you cross the creek. Then turn right and climb. Stay on the trail to FS 1645; turn left. When the route turns to gravel, retrace your path to the start.

RIDE 97 · Eagle Mountain

AT A GLANCE

Length/configuration: 14-mile out-and-back (7 miles each way); virtually all dirt road.

Aerobic difficulty: Most grades are moderate, so the aerobic demands are relative to the speed you maintain.

Technical difficulty: Easy to moderate, with isolated sections of ledge rock and a few short, steep sections. This is a fire road, but there are some ruts and roots.

Scenery: Hardwoods, non-native pines, rock formations.

Special comments: This is much less technical than other area trails, and is better for less experienced riders. You can also maintain a higher average speed.

For the most part, this ride stays on a ridge top. The result is some stunning views and, when the weather's right, the chance to actually ride above the clouds. Even without that effect, the sense of elevation is sharper here than any other place in the Shawnee.

Unlike many of the other trails in the Shawnee (notably those around High Knob), Eagle Mountain does not make a good springboard for further exploration. At least not as a mountain biker. This trail is a thread of legal riding pulled through a patchwork of restrictions. That's not to say there aren't options from Eagle Mountain; there are. Just be sure to consult a good map before you go traipsing off into a wilderness or natural area.

General location: About 20 minutes south of Harrisburg

Elevation change: Although the trail stays mostly on the ridge top, it's not flat. There are several rollers and few short, steep climbs.

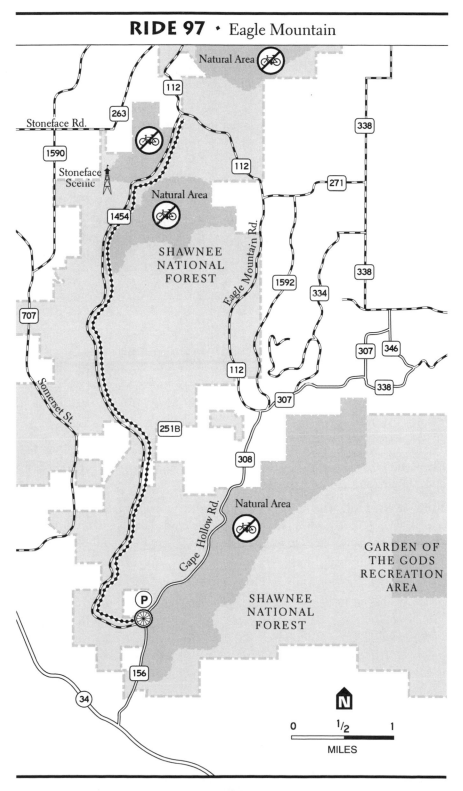

Natural Area

Stoneface Rd.

263

112

338

1590

112

Stoneface Scenic

271

1454

Natural Area

SHAWNEE NATIONAL FOREST

338

1592

334

707

307 346

112

338

Somerset St.

307

251B

308

Cape Hollow Rd.

Natural Area

GARDEN OF THE GODS RECREATION AREA

P

SHAWNEE NATIONAL FOREST

156

34

N

0   1/2   1

MILES

Season: Year-round; mud can be a problem in spring and again from Thanksgiving to May.

Services: Everything in Harrisburg; the nearest bike shops are in Paducah (Kentucky), Evansville (Indiana), and Carbondale (Illinois).

Hazards: None

Rescue index: Ride with someone; other users tend to disperse widely and any given piece of trail may only see a person every few days or even every few weeks.

Land status: National Forest

Maps: Shawnee Mountain Bike Association

Finding the trail: Follow IL 34 south from Harrisburg to Herod, where you'll turn north on the paved road. Go 1 mile to the Hitchin' Post trailhead, which will be on the left.

Sources of additional information:

Shawnee Mountain Bike Association
190 Battleford Road
Harrisburg, IL 62946
(618) 252-3577

Forest Supervisor's Office
50 Highway 145 South
Harrisburg, IL 62946
(800) 699-6637 or (618) 253-7114

There are also district offices in Vienna, (phone (618) 658-2111); Elizabethtown, (phone (618) 287-2201); Jonesboro, (phone (618) 833-8576); and Murphysboro, (phone (618) 687-1731).

Notes on the trail: The trail goes west from the parking lot. Stay on the main trail. At the T before Horton Hill, go left up the eroded double-track. Turn right at the T at the power line. In a 0.25 mile, turn left and ride to the terminus at Eagle Mountain Road.

GLOSSARY

This short list of terms does not contain all the words used by mountain bike enthusiasts when discussing their sport. But it should serve as an introduction to the lingo you'll hear on the trails.

ATB
: all-terrain bike; this, like "fat-tire bike," is another name for a mountain bike

ATV
: all-terrain vehicle; this usually refers to the loud, fume-spewing three- or four-wheeled motorized vehicles you will not enjoy meeting on the trail—except, of course, if you crash and have to hitch a ride out on one

blaze
: a mark on a tree made by chipping away a piece of the bark, usually done to designate a trail; such trails are sometimes described as "blazed"

blind corner
: a curve in the road or trail that conceals bikers, hikers, equestrians, and other traffic

blowdown
: see "windfall"

BLM
: Bureau of Land Management, an agency of the federal government

bollard
: a post (or series of posts) set vertically into the ground that allow pedestrians or cyclists to pass but keep vehicles from entering (wooden bollards are also commonly used to sign intersections)

braided
: a braided trail condition results when people attempt to travel around a wet area; networks of interlaced trails can result and are a maintenance headache for trail crews

buffed
: used to describe a very smooth trail

Carsonite sign
: a small, thin, and flexible fiberglass signpost used extensively by the Forest Service and BLM to mark roads and trails (often dark brown in color)

catching air	taking a jump in such a way that both wheels of the bike are off the ground at the same time
cattle guard	a grate of parallel steel bars or pipes set at ground level and suspended over a ditch; cows can't cross them (their little feet slip through the openings between the pipes), but pedestrians and vehicles can pass over cattle guards with little difficulty
clean	while this may describe what you and your bike won't be after following many trails, the term is most often used as a verb to denote the action of pedaling a tough section of trail successfully
combination	this type of route may combine two or more configurations; for example, a point-to-point route may integrate a scenic loop or an out-and-back spur midway through the ride; likewise, an out-and-back may have a loop at its farthest point (this configuration looks like a cherry with a stem attached; the stem is the out-and-back, the fruit is the terminus loop); or a loop route may have multiple out-and-back spurs and/or loops to the side; mileage for a combination route is for the total distance to complete the ride
cupped	a concave trail; higher on the sides than in the middle; often caused by motorcycles
dab	touching the ground with a foot or hand
deadfall	a tangled mass of fallen trees or branches
decomposed granite	an excellent, fine- to medium-grain, trail and road surface; typically used in native surface road and trail applications (not trucked in); results from the weathering of granite
diversion ditch	a usually narrow, shallow ditch dug across or around a trail; funneling the water in this manner keeps it from destroying the trail
double-track	the dual tracks made by a jeep or other vehicle, with grass, weeds, or rocks between; mountain bikers can ride in either of the tracks, but you will find that whichever one you choose, no matter how many times you change back and forth, the other track will appear to offer smoother travel
dugway	a steep, unpaved, switchbacked descent
endo	flipping end over end
feathering	using a light touch on the brake lever, hitting it lightly many times rather than very hard or locking the brake

four-wheel-drive	this refers to any vehicle with drive-wheel capability on all four wheels (a jeep, for instance, has four-wheel drive as compared with a two-wheel-drive passenger car), or to a rough road or trail that requires four-wheel-drive capability (or a one-wheel-drive mountain bike!) to negotiate it
game trail	the usually narrow trail made by deer, elk, or other game
gated	everyone knows what a gate is, and how many variations exist on this theme; well, if a trail is described as "gated" it simply has a gate across it; don't forget that the rule is if you find a gate closed, close it behind you; if you find one open, leave it that way
Giardia	shorthand for *Giardia lamblia*, and known as the "backpacker's bane" until we mountain bikers expropriated it; this is a waterborne parasite that begins its life cycle when swallowed, and one to four weeks later has its host (you) bloated, vomiting, shivering with chills, and living in the bathroom; the disease can be avoided by "treating" (purifying) the water you acquire along the trail (see "Hitting the Trail" in the Introduction)
gnarly	a term thankfully used less and less these days, it refers to tough trails
graded	refers to a dirt road that has been smoothed out by the use of a wide blade on earth-moving equipment; "blading" gets rid of the teeth-chattering, much-cursed washboards found on so many dirt roads after heavy vehicle use
hammer	to ride very hard
hammerhead	one who rides hard and fast
hardpack	a trail in which the dirt surface is packed down hard; such trails make for good and fast riding, and very painful landings; bikers most often use "hardpack" as both a noun and adjective, and "hard-packed" as an adjective only (the grammar lesson will help you when diagramming sentences in camp)
hike-a-bike	what you do when the road or trail becomes too steep or rough to remain in the saddle
jeep road, jeep trail	a rough road or trail passable only with four-wheel-drive capability (or a horse or mountain bike)
kamikaze	while this once referred primarily to those Japanese fliers who quaffed a glass of sake, then flew off as human bombs

in suicide missions against U.S. naval vessels, it has more recently been applied to the idiot mountain bikers who, far less honorably, scream down hiking trails, endangering the physical and mental safety of the walking, biking, and equestrian traffic they meet; deck guns were necessary to stop the Japanese kamikaze pilots, but a bike pump or walking staff in the spokes is sufficient for the current-day kamikazes who threaten to get us all kicked off the trails

loop   this route configuration is characterized by riding from the designated trailhead to a distant point, then returning to the trailhead via a different route (or simply continuing on the same in a circle route) without doubling back; you always move forward across new terrain but return to the starting point when finished; mileage is for the entire loop from the trailhead back to trailhead

multipurpose   a BLM designation of land that is open to many uses; mountain biking is allowed

off-camber   a trail that slopes in the opposite direction than one would prefer for safety's sake; for example, on a side-cut trail the slope is away from the hill—the inside of the trail is higher, so it helps you fall downhill if your balance isn't perfect

ORV/OHV   a motorized off-road vehicle (off-highway vehicle)

out-and-back   a ride where you will return on the same trail you pedaled out; while this might sound far more boring than a loop route, many trails look very different when pedaled in the opposite direction

pack stock   horses, mules, llamas, etc., carrying provisions along trails

point-to-point   a vehicle shuttle (or similar assistance) is required for this type of route, which is ridden from the designated trailhead to a distant location, or endpoint, where the route ends; total mileage is for the one-way trip from the trailhead to endpoint

portage   to carry your bike on your person

pummy   soil with high pumice content produced by volcanic activity in the Pacific Northwest and elsewhere; light in consistency and easily pedaled; trails with such soil often become thick with dust

quads   bikers use this term to refer both to the extensor muscle in the front of the thigh (which is separated into four parts) and to USGS maps; the expression "Nice quads!" refers always to the former, however, except in those instances when the speaker is an engineer

runoff   rainwater or snowmelt

scree   an accumulation of loose stones or rocky debris lying on a slope or at the base of a hill or cliff

side-cut trail   a trail cut on the side of a hill

signed   a "signed" trail has signs in place of blazes

single-track   a single, narrow path through grass or brush or over rocky terrain, often created by deer, elk, or backpackers; single-track riding is some of the best fun around

skid road   the path created when loggers drag trees through the forest with heavy equipment

slickrock   the rock-hard, compacted sandstone that is great to ride and even prettier to look at; you'll appreciate it even more if you think of it as a petrified sand dune or seabed (which it is), and if the rider before you hasn't left tire marks (from unnecessary skidding) or granola bar wrappers behind

snowmelt   runoff produced by the melting of snow

snowpack   unmelted snow accumulated over weeks or months of winter—or over years—in high-mountain terrain

spur   a road or trail that intersects the main trail you're following

squid   one who skids

stair-step climb a climb punctuated by a series of level or near-level sections

switchback   a zigzagging road or trail designed to assist in traversing steep terrain; mountain bikers should not skid through switchbacks

talus   the rocky debris at the base of a cliff, or a slope formed by an accumulation of this rocky debris

tank trap   a steep-sided ditch (or series of ditches) used to block access to a road or trail; often used in conjunction with high mounds of excavated material

technical   terrain that is difficult to ride due not to its grade (steepness) but to its obstacles—rocks, roots, logs, ledges, loose soil . . .

topo	short for topographical map, the kind that shows both linear distance and elevation gain and loss; "topo" is pronounced with both vowels long
trashed	a trail that has been destroyed (same term used no matter what has destroyed it . . . cattle, horses, or even mountain bikers riding when the ground was too wet)
trialsin	highly technical riding over natural and artificial obstacles at low speeds, with points assessed for putting down a foot, or "dab" (to complete a section without dabbing it is to "clean" it)
two-track	see "double-track"
two-wheel-drive	this refers to any vehicle with drive-wheel capability on only two wheels (a passenger car, for instance, has two-wheel drive); a two-wheel-drive road is a road or trail easily traveled by an ordinary car
waterbar	an earth, rock, or wooden structure that funnels water off trails to reduce erosion
washboarded	a road that is surfaced with many ridges spaced closely together, like the ripples on a washboard; these make for very rough riding, and even worse driving in a car or jeep
whoop-de-doo	closely spaced dips or undulations in a trail; these are often encountered in areas traveled heavily by ORVs
wilderness area	land that is officially set aside by the federal government to remain natural—pure, pristine, and untrammeled by any vehicle, including mountain bikes; though mountain bikes had not been born in 1964 (when the United States Congress passed the Wilderness Act, establishing the National Wilderness Preservation system), they are considered a "form of mechanical transport" and are thereby excluded; in short, stay out
windchill	a reference to the wind's cooling effect on exposed flesh; for example, if the temperature is 10 degrees Fahrenheit and the wind is blowing at 20 miles per hour, the windchill (that is, the actual temperature to which your skin reacts) is minus 32 degrees; if you are riding in wet conditions things are even worse, for the windchill would then be minus 74 degrees!
windfall	anything (trees, limbs, brush, fellow bikers . . .) blown down by the wind

INDEX